D0163274

CHILDHOOD SEXUAL ABUSE

A Reference Handbook

Other Titles in ABC-CLIO's
CONTEMPORARY WORLD ISSUES
Series

Books in the Contemporary World Issues series address vital issues in today's society such as genetic engineering, pollution, and biodiversity. Written by professional writers, scholars, and nonacademic experts, these books are authoritative, clearly written, up-to-date, and objective. They provide a good starting point for research by high school and college students, scholars, and general readers as well as by legislators, businesspeople, activists, and others.

Each book, carefully organized and easy to use, contains an overview of the subject, a detailed chronology, biographical sketches, facts and data and/or documents and other primary-source material, a directory of organizations and agencies, annotated lists of print and nonprint resources, and an index.

Readers of books in the Contemporary World Issues series will find the information they need in order to have a better understanding of the social, political, environmental, and economic issues facing the world today.

CHILDHOOD SEXUAL ABUSE

A Reference Handbook,
Second Edition

Karen L. Kinnear

CONTEMPORARY WORLD ISSUES

A B C ● C L I O

Santa Barbara, California
Denver, Colorado
Oxford, England

Copyright © 2007 by ABC-CLIO, Inc.

All rights reserved. No part of this publication may be reproduced,
stored in a retrieval system, or transmitted, in any form or by any
means, electronic, mechanical, photocopying, recording, or otherwise,
except for the inclusion of brief quotations in a review, without prior
permission in writing from the publisher.

Library of Congress Cataloging-in-Publication Data

Kinnear, Karen L.
  Childhood sexual abuse : a reference handbook / Karen L. Kinnear.
     p. cm. — (Contemporary world issues)
  Includes bibliographical references and index.
  ISBN-10: 1-85109-905-0 (hard copy : alk. paper)
  ISBN-10: 1-85109-906-9 (e-book)
  ISBN-13: 978-1-85109-905-4 (hard copy : alk. paper)
  ISBN-13: 978-1-85109-906-1 (e-book)
  1. Child sexual abuse. 2. Child sexual abuse—Prevention.
  3. Sexually abused children. I. Title.

  HV6570.K55 2007
  362.76--dc22

                                  2006035241

ISBN-13: 978-1-85109-905-4   (ebook) 978-1-85109-906-1
ISBN-10: 1-85109-905-0   (ebook) 1-85109-906-9

11 10 09 08 07   10 9 8 7 6 5 4 3 2 1

ABC-CLIO, Inc.
130 Cremona Drive, P.O. Box 1911
Santa Barbara, California 93116-1911

This book is also available on the World Wide Web as an ebook.
Visit www.abc-clio.com for details.

This book is printed on acid-free paper ∞
Manufactured in the United States of America

To Stephen and Kathleen,
with the hope that your generation will see
reduced numbers of children who are
sexually abused.

Contents

Preface

The purpose of this book is to provide a survey of the available literature and other resources on the topic of childhood sexual abuse and to direct readers to sources for further research. The literature and resources available provide insight into the causes, treatment, and prevention of childhood sexual abuse. Tremendous growth in knowledge and research has occurred in this field in recent years, and this book provides a resource for students, writers, and researchers as well as professionals in the field.

Thoughts and attitudes toward childhood sexual abuse have changed over the years. Earlier, many people believed that if children were sexually abused, they had brought the abuse on themselves by somehow seducing the adult, and that they were not harmed by this contact. Over time, however, the attitude that children were responsible for any sexual abuse they experienced changed to the realization that the adults involved were responsible, not the children. The extent and seriousness of the effects of sexual abuse have also been recognized and studied, from earlier attitudes that little damage was done to a child who was fondled or otherwise abused to the current understanding that the effects of this abuse can be manifested in many ways and can indeed be serious. This book reviews current knowledge and resources in order to help the reader understand the issues involved in this important and timely topic.

This book, like other books in the Contemporary World Issues series, provides a balanced survey of the resources available and a guide to further research on the topic of childhood sexual abuse. Chapter 1 reviews the literature concerning types of sexual abuse, causes, effects, indicators of childhood sexual abuse, intervention and treatment, the legal system, and prevention. Chapter 2 examines the major problems, controversies, and solutions in the field, including identifying abuse, various perpetrators, treatment issues, repression and false memories, and community notification laws. Chapter 3 offers a worldwide perspective, examining international laws and conventions, incidence and prevalence, worldwide issues, child trafficking, ritual abuse, and treatment. Chapter 4 provides a chronology of the significant events relevant to issues surrounding childhood sexual abuse. Chapter 5 offers biographical sketches of individuals who have played or are currently playing key roles in the area of childhood sexual abuse. Chapter 6 provides statistical information on the prevalence and incidence of child sexual abuse, as well as state statutes defining sexual abuse of children, summaries of U.S. laws and international conventions, and summaries of a sample of U.S. Supreme Court and Court of Appeals cases. Chapter 7 provides a directory of private and public organizations, associations, and governmental agencies involved in treating children who have been sexually abused, as well as those that treat offenders. In Chapter 8, books, handbooks, manuals, periodicals, and videos are annotated; the literature varies from popular accounts to primary research and provides a wide perspective on this problem.

1

Background and History

Society's views toward and definitions of child sexual abuse have changed over the years. Sexual relations between adults and children were not always considered abusive and against the law. In early Christian history, women were considered the property of first the father and then the husband, and had no rights of their own; female children also were considered property and had no rights. In fact, both the Bible and Talmud encouraged men to have sexual relations with young girls; they were allowed to do so through socially sanctioned marriage, concubinage, and slavery. The Talmud indicates that a "female of 'three years and one day' could be betrothed by sexual intercourse with her father's permission. Intercourse with one younger was not a crime but invalid" (Rush 1980, 17).

Over time, attitudes have changed. In the United States and many other countries, children are no longer seen as possessions, adult sexual relations with children are generally considered wrong, and laws exist to protect children from sexual relations with adults.

Child Sexual Abuse Defined

While specific definitions of child sexual abuse may vary considerably, certain elements exist in almost every definition: exploitation of the child; use of coercion, gentle though it may be; and some level of gratification gained by the adult.

1

Fraser defines child sexual abuse as "the exploitation of a child for the sexual gratification of an adult" (Fraser 1981, 58). Baker and Duncan suggest that "[a] child (anyone under 16 years) is sexually abused when another person, who is sexually mature, involves the child in any activity which the other person expects to lead to their sexual arousal" (Baker and Duncan 1985, 458). The Children's Bureau of the U.S. Department of Health and Human Services, in their 2003 report on child maltreatment, defines sexual abuse as the "involvement of the child in sexual activity to provide sexual gratification or financial benefit to the perpetrator, including contacts for sexual purposes, molestation, statutory rape, prostitution, pornography, exposure, incest, or other sexually exploitative activities" (U.S. Department of Health and Human Services, Administration for Children, Youth and Families 2005, 107).

Sexual abuse also can be defined situationally—that is, by the situation or circumstances in which it occurs. For example, in some families or cultures, it is acceptable, even expected, that family members kiss on the mouth or have a great deal of physical contact. In other families and cultures, such behavior would be considered inappropriate.

Definitions of sexual abuse often are broken down further into contact and noncontact abuse. Contact abuse can include any activity from kissing to oral sex to intercourse. Noncontact sexual abuse includes such activities as exhibitionism and sexual talk intended to arouse the adult. Sexually abusive behavior can range from an adult walking around naked in front of children to sexual intercourse. According to Jon Conte, it may include exhibitionism, voyeurism, kissing, fondling, fellatio, cunnilingus, vaginal or anal intercourse, or child pornography (Conte 1986). Suzanne Sgroi suggests that abusive behavior can include nudity, the adult disrobing in front of a child, exposing his or her genitals to the child, covertly watching the child undress or bathe, kissing the child in an intimate way, fondling the child inappropriately, masturbating while a child watches, masturbating the child, masturbating each other, fellatio, cunnilingus, penetrating the anus or vagina with a finger or other object, penetrating the anus with a penis, or actual sexual intercourse (Sgroi 1988).

Legally, child sexual abuse is defined in the Child Abuse Prevention and Treatment Act (see Chapter 6) as:

> the employment, use, persuasion, inducement, enticement, or coercion of a child to engage in, or assist any

other person to engage in, any sexually explicit conduct or the rape, molestation, prostitution, or other
form of sexual exploitation of children, or incest with a
child. (Child Abuse Prevention and Treatment Act, as
Amended, June 25, 2003)

Legal definitions can be either civil or criminal. Civil statutes consider sexual abuse a practice from which a child should be protected; through these laws, designated professionals must report
child sexual abuse, and the child protection agencies must investigate these reports. Certain sexual acts are prohibited by criminal
statutes; they specify what sexual acts are considered criminal and
the penalties for breaking these laws. The penalties differ depending on the age of the child, the level of force used, the relationship
between the child and the offender, and the type of sexual act.

Characteristics of Child Sexual Abuse

Child sexual abuse is characterized by several conditions, which
may determine whether or not an incident is considered sexual
abuse. One condition is lack of consent. Children do not consent
to sexual abuse because they usually are not able to understand
fully what is being proposed to them, and they are not in a position to refuse any sexual contact with appropriate power. Children are not capable of consenting to sexual activities with an
adult; just because the child participates in this abuse does not
mean that the child has consented. Another condition is exploitation. Children are manipulated or coerced into sexual behavior by
adults who are stronger, more resourceful, and more knowledge-
able. They may buy the child gifts, persuade the child that all fathers teach their daughters about sex, threaten the child with
punishment or with the death of the other parent ("if your mother
ever finds out, she'll probably die of a heart attack"), or provide
attention to the child in other ways.

Ambivalence is also a characteristic in child sexual abuse.
Children often feel ambivalent about what is happening to them;
they do not like or understand the sexual part of the experience,
but they may enjoy the attention they are receiving, as well as any
rewards or special privileges they may receive because of the
abuse. Some children may be confused because some of the physical sensations they experience are enjoyable; these sensations
make them feel good. However, they know that the behavior is

wrong, and although they want the abuse to stop, they do not want to stop receiving the gifts, privileges, or attention they gain by remaining silent.

Force is another factor or characteristic of child sexual abuse that is always present, even if it is not physical. Usually definitions contain an element of power or force: that "it is forced, tricked, or coerced sexual behavior between a young person and an older person" (Conte 1986, 2). Many ways exist, both physical and psychological, to force the child into a sexual relationship. These may include threatening to withhold attention or special favors, killing an animal in front of the child and telling her that the same fate awaits her if she does not cooperate, threatening to abuse other siblings in the family, or suggesting that the family will be broken up if the child tells anyone. A related factor is secrecy; the abuser must somehow convince the child that he or she should not tell anyone else about the abuse. Ways to keep the child silent include threats, force, bribery, and intimidation.

Dr. Roland Summit has identified the "sexual abuse accommodation syndrome," a means of characterizing the responses of girls who are sexually abused by adults, often by their father or another close male relative. The syndrome has five characteristics: (1) secrecy; (2) helplessness; (3) entrapment and accommodation; (4) delayed unconvincing disclosure; and (5) retraction. Summit believes that children feel helpless in abusive situations because the abuser has sworn them to secrecy by threatening them with harm, telling them that no one will believe them, or in some other way coercing them into secrecy. Once the sexual abuse has occurred, the child feels trapped and either continues to maintain the secret or decides to disclose it to the other parent or another trusted adult. If the disclosure is not believed or causes too much stress for the child to handle, the child may retract the disclosure (Summit 1983; Conte 2002). Some controversy continues to exist concerning the validity of Summit's syndrome.

Who Is Abused?

The general perception is that girls are more likely to be abused sexually than boys, and the statistics generally support that perception. Most studies show that the overall prevalence of sexual abuse of girls is higher than that of boys. For example, Bolen and

Scannapieco found that the prevalence of boys who were sexually abused was 13 percent, while the prevalence of girls being abused was 30 to 40 percent (Bolen and Scannapieco 1999). While girls generally are sexually abused more frequently than boys, there are certain exceptions. For example, research on the sexual abuse allegations against the Catholic Church indicates that boys are abused far more frequently than girls; some surveys put the percentage of boys abused by Catholic priests at 81 percent (Terry and Tallon 2004). Furthermore, most researchers will agree that child sexual abuse is significantly under-reported. Males are generally less likely to report sexual abuse (see Chapter 6).

A study of sexual abuse rates among Caucasians, African Americans, and Hispanic Americans generally showed no significant differences between the groups, except in the area of recognizing and reporting child sexual abuse: Caucasian Americans were less likely than African Americans and Hispanic Americans to recognize and report such abuse (Lowe et al. 2005).

Perpetrators

We often believe that children's safety is threatened more by strangers than by people known to the children. At home and in school, parents and teachers emphasize to children that they should not talk to strangers or accept candy or rides. The image of dirty old men in trench coats ready to flash or snatch children is common. However, the truth is that children who are sexually abused are most likely to be abused by someone they know and trust, including parents, siblings, teachers, day-care operators, priests, or coaches. Sexual abusers come from all walks of life, all races, and all socioeconomic levels. Furthermore, adults are not the only abusers. Adolescents and teenagers, including brothers and sisters, are also capable of abusing children.

In an attempt to identify abusers, Conte found that there are no unique characteristics that separate abusers from nonabusers. The ages, psychological characteristics, demographic information, and histories of men who have sexually abused children vary considerably. Studies using the MMPI (Minnesota Multi-Phasic Inventory) to determine the identifying characteristics of abusers have not been able to develop a profile of abusers that is distinct from that of nonabusers. Most of these studies have examined incarcerated sexual offenders, rather than studying abusers who are still out in the community (those who are not stereotyped as dirty old men) (Conte 1986).

Although determining consistent identifying characteristics has proven difficult, Conte has suggested six clinical characteristics that are helpful in providing a framework for understanding abusers: denial, sexual arousal, sexual fantasy, social skills, cognitive distortions, and other psychological and social problems (Conte 1985). Many perpetrators deny that they are abusing anyone or deny that what they are doing is sexual abuse. Most perpetrators also are sexually aroused by children. Sexual fantasies have been suggested as a behavior characteristic of abusers; although its significance remains unclear, many researchers believe that the role of sexual fantasy should be considered. Abusers also may have problems relating to other adults, individually and in group social situations. They may find that it is easier to interact with children. Cognitive distortions help abusers rationalize their behavior and include statements such as: "The child didn't physically resist, therefore she must have wanted it," and "Having sex with my daughter helped teach her about sex in a safe way." Adult abusers believe that these statements are true and are thus able to continue the abusive behavior even though they are hurting the children and risking severe punishment if discovered. Finally, many abusers display other psychological and social characteristics, including drug and alcohol abuse, depression, poor self-image, and feelings of inadequacy. Most adults who sexually abuse children are not likely to admit this behavior. Serious consequences, both legal and social, face anyone who is convicted of child sexual abuse, and thus such denial is easily understandable.

Nicholas Groth, a psychologist who has worked with inmates in a state prison system, developed a system for classifying child abusers into one of two broad categories: regressed or fixated. Regressed abusers are adult men who live fairly normal, ordinary lives; they had girlfriends as teenagers and have wives and children as adults. At some point in their lives, however, often in their thirties, they develop a sexual interest in children, primarily young girls. Fixated abusers, on the other hand, develop an interest in children while still young, usually in their teens, and continue to be interested in children; they may never be sexually interested in someone their own age (Groth 1978). John Crewdson developed a third category of abuser: the crossover abuser, who is usually a father whose primary sexual interest is in children (Crewdson 1988).

Lanning (2001) examined sexual offenders by focusing on their motivation; he hypothesized that they can be placed on a continuum from preferential offenders to situational offenders. Preferential abusers appear to be more intelligent and have more deviant sexual needs and desires; this category includes pedophiles. Situational child molesters do not tend to have any of the compulsive sexual preferences that the preferential offenders have. They are more likely to abuse depending on the situation in which they find themselves; for example, if they work in a daycare setting they may sexually abuse children, but they do not normally seek out children for abusive activities.

Sgroi found that child sexual offenders apparently are not motivated primarily by sexual desire; as Burgess and Groth also discovered, offenders tend to abuse children sexually to serve nonsexual needs, primarily the need to feel powerful and in control (Sgroi 1982).

Pedophiles are one subcategory of abuser, and generally they are considered the most dangerous and least likely to be rehabilitated. Pedophilia is defined in this way:

A. Over a period of at least 6 months, the person experiences recurrent, intense, sexually arousing fantasies, sexual urges, or behaviors involving sexual activity with a prepubescent child or children (generally age 13 years or younger).
B. The person has acted on these sexual urges, or the sexual urges or fantasies cause marked distress or interpersonal difficulty.
C. The person is at least age 16 years and at least 5 years older than the child or children in Criterion A. (APA 2000, 571–572)

Pedophiles often explain their behavior as helping the child understand the processes and pleasures of sexual activity. They generally believe that the child also derives pleasure from the activity. They also may explain away their behavior by claiming that the child was sexually provocative and lured them into the activity. Estimates of the numbers of pedophiles are difficult to make and may vary considerably because pedophiles rarely seek help; their behavior and activities are discovered when someone else reports them. Most diagnosed pedophiles are men.

Parents/Step-Parents

In most cases of incest, fathers are the perpetrators; daughters are usually the victims. Instances of mother-son, father-son, and mother-daughter incest also occur, although father-daughter incest is by far the most commonly reported. Because of the changing nature of the U.S. family, with more second marriages and blended families, several researchers have started comparing rates of incest committed by biological fathers with that of stepfathers. Russell interviewed a random sample of more than 900 adult women in San Francisco, and found that 17 percent, approximately one in six, had been sexually abused by a stepfather, while 2 percent, or approximately one in forty, had been sexually abused by their biological father. When Russell studied the seriousness of the abuse, she found that 47 percent of the stepfathers, compared with 26 percent of the biological fathers, committed "very serious sexual abuse" with their children (Russell 1984). Other studies agree with Russell's finding that children are more often sexually abused by stepfathers than by biological fathers (Herman 1981; Gordon and Creighton 1988).

In a study on the perception that children are more likely to be abused by a stepfather than a biological father, Claxton-Oldfield and Whitt (2003) found that less than half (45 percent) of the 186 university students questioned believed that children are at higher risk of sexual abuse by stepfathers. A study in the United Kingdom of biological fathers, stepfathers, and father substitutes supported this finding; stepfathers are more likely than biological fathers to abuse a child sexually, although biological fathers are more likely to engage in sexual intercourse with a child (Gordon and Creighton 1988).

Fathers may sexually abuse one child, or all of their children, for a variety of reasons. They may be promiscuous, indiscriminant about whom they engage in sexual activities; they may have an intense desire for children (pedophilia), and their children are the most available children around; or they may choose a daughter for sexual activities because their wives are not satisfying to them and they do not want to "destroy" the family by having sexual relations outside of the family. They use their position of authority to control their daughters and obtain sexual pleasure from them.

Getting help is often difficult for many incest victims, although when other siblings are threatened, the victim may decide to reveal the abuse. Research indicates that when a daughter believes that a younger sister is threatened with similar abuse, she is more likely to report the abuse (see, for example, Gordon 1988).

Finkelhor suggests reasons why parents are more likely than other offenders to be reported as perpetrators of child sexual abuse.

> One is that they are conspicuous, create concern, and are thus likely to be pursued by those who know about them until they become official statistics. Another is that, although many families try to contain knowledge about parent-child incest, the dynamics are so volatile and the potential for conflict so great that parent-child incest is more difficult to hush up permanently than other kinds of children's sexual abuse. Therefore, although the motivation for silence may be greater, it is less likely to be achieved. (Finkelhor 1979, 140)

Most people are more likely to perceive closeness between a father and daughter as sexual abuse than a similar relationship between a mother and son. If a daughter naps or sleeps in the same bed as her father, many people may see that as wrong, but, as Kempe and Kempe suggest, a "mother who allows her boy to sleep in her bed may be thought to 'infantilize' him but not to be acting on unconscious incestuous impulses" (Kempe and Kempe 1984, 69).

Fathers who sexually abuse their daughters generally have no compassion for their victim and do not recognize that any consequences exist for their behavior. Many offenders may be horrified at their own behavior, but not enough to stop the abuse. Many incestuous fathers have a deep and constant need for unconditional love and attention. In some cases, they see incest, like rape, as an act of power and control (Forward and Buck 1978).

Contrary to the beliefs of some researchers and others, mothers in the home of an incestuous father-daughter relationship may not always know about the incest. If they are aware of it, they may not always be consciously allowing the father to molest the daughter. Many mothers may be giving up their personal power, letting their husbands dominate and control them; the mothers become the silent partners in the incest. Men in these situations are looking for power and control, as well as unconditional love, and they can find it most easily when they can lead the mother into denying that anything is wrong, which allows the father to molest the daughter.

In cases of mother-son incest, the father is often absent from the home. The mother relies on her son to be "the man of the house," to take care of things the way a man would. The son may love his mother but hate the fact that she is forcing him into his father's role. Forward and Buck believe that "because there is often no element of force involved, the boy almost invariably comes away with crushing guilt feelings, for he believes he must accept his share of the blame without the mitigating excuse of having been violated" (ibid., 74).

Cases of mother-son incest are often difficult to uncover because many boys are not sure they have been abused. Even though they may feel exploited and used, societal attitudes vary considerably depending on whether the person is male or female. There is not such a great stigma placed on boys who have sex as on girls who have sex. Often, boys and the friends of boys who have sex with an adult female claim that they are lucky because they have had the opportunity to have sex with an experienced female. Also, mothers may be able to get away with more fondling and touching of their sons' genitals and other parts of their bodies because of motherly responsibilities such as bathing and dressing (Crewdson 1988).

Mic Hunter found similar attitudes:

> Many of my clients were told by friends or family when they talked about a woman being sexual with them when they were boys that they ought to feel happy, because they were lucky to have the opportunity to be sexual at such a young age. In addition to being told that they were fortunate to have had the opportunity to be sexual by the perpetrator(s) of the sexual abuse, friends, or family, these men also got this message from the media. (Hunter 1990, 36)

Researchers have found other negative impacts that mother-son incest has on sons. Nasjleti believes that boys "often fear that having sex with the mother is indicative of their having a mental illness. Because mothers are viewed as nonsexual beings in this culture, incapable of sexually abusing their own children, boys molested by their mothers often assume responsibility for their own molestation" (Nasjleti 1980, 273).

Kempe and Kempe believe that the number of incest cases may continue to rise, in large part because of changes in the structure of the family: more divorces, more blended families, an increase in acceptance of sexuality in general, and a "more tolerant view of sexual acts between nonrelated household members who come from divorced or previously separated homes. This is particularly true of brother-sister incest between stepchildren who are living as a family but are not related" (Kempe and Kempe 1984, 48).

In most cases of child sexual abuse committed by a family member, physical force or violence is rarely used, primarily because the child has a trusting and dependent relationship with the abuser. Because the abuser has control and dominance over the child, he or she is often able to coerce the child into sexual activities without resorting to violence. However, some studies indicate that more violence may be used to persuade the child to participate than most experts originally have thought. Burgess and her colleagues studied forty-four cases of attempted and completed sexual abuse by a family member and found that 39 percent of the offenders pressured the child to participate in the sexual activity, while 61 percent threatened harm or used physical force. In those cases in which force was threatened or used, the offending parent resorted to intimidation to gain power over the child (Burgess, Holmstrom, and McCausland 1977).

Siblings

Most researchers agree that sibling abuse is probably more common than statistics indicate, in part because both offender and victim may be embarrassed and ashamed of their behavior and unwilling or unable to confide in anyone. Sibling abuse has often been ignored in the past, because much of the abusive behavior is considered normal (for example, children fight, wrestle, and play doctor with each other). Parents do not spend all of their time with their children, and therefore they cannot always be aware of what their children are doing. Siblings have plenty of time to play with each other, and they also have time to abuse each other. Professionals are currently becoming more aware of sibling abuse and the consequences of this abuse for the victims.

Children do not often report sexual abuse to their parents or other trusted adults, and that also holds true for cases of sibling abuse, for many of the same reasons. The victims initially may not be aware that the behavior is abusive; if an older sibling is the abuser, he or she may use the power and authority of the "older brother or sister" to keep the younger child quiet; victims may be threatened with retaliation, either physical or emotional, if they tell; victims may feel that they are responsible for the abuse or for not resisting the abuse when it first began; or the family environment may not encourage revelation of the abuse.

While sexual abuse of siblings may stop because the perpetrator loses interest before parents or other authority figures become aware of it, some research indicates that sibling abuse can continue into adulthood. There are instances of brother-sister abuse that occurs even after the children have grown and moved away from home. For example, one girl assumed that her brother's sexual abuse of her would stop when he went away to college; however, when she visited him in his dormitory room, he tried to force her to have sex with him. Another woman who had been sexually abused by her older brother was amazed when her brother tried to rape her even though she was married and had several children (Wiehe 1990).

When treating victims of sibling incest, professionals must be aware of how these cases can divide parents, who must choose between two children. Whom do they support, the victim or the perpetrator? This issue is often difficult for parents. Marianne Celano, in a meeting sponsored in conjunction with the Sixth National Symposium on Child Sexual Abuse, describes this dilemma:

> Parents of victims of sibling incest have to divide their concern between two children, and they sometimes have to make a choice to remove one child. Many parents alternate between sympathy for the victim and sympathy for the offender, whom they may perceive as immature, emotionally unstable or victimized him- or herself. I have had a case in which a child was victimized by her older brother and the entire extended family rallied behind the older brother and protected him by sending him out of state to elude criminal prosecution. The victim was furious and blamed herself for the abuse. (Lloyd 1990b, 5)

Other speakers at this meeting emphasized the importance of involving the justice system and of holding perpetrators accountable for their actions; they believe that to be the best way to prevent the perpetrator from abusing again and becoming part of the adult criminal justice system.

Multidisciplinary teams must be involved to help parents and children survive and heal from the experience. Professionals often find working with families in which sibling abuse has occurred a challenge because of the issues involved; for instance, breaking up families is difficult, as is trying to reunite them in a healthful manner. Many families find it extremely difficult to continue as a family unit. The sexual abuse may raise all sorts of feelings, such as resentment, anger, and confusion, and it often creates a lack of trust among family members.

Other Family Members

Other family members, including uncles, aunts, and grandparents, also are capable of abusing children in their families. The characteristics of cases of grandfather-granddaughter incest are usually quite similar to those of father-daughter incest. The young girls feel responsible for the incest, and grandfathers molest their granddaughters for many of the same reasons, and share many of the same characteristics, as other abusers.

Causes

Many theories exist that attempt to explain the causes of childhood sexual abuse. Some theories focus on the family or the offender. Theories focusing on the family perspective suggest that family dynamics are to blame for the abuse. For example, fathers may blame the mothers for abandoning them and believe that they themselves are not at fault, but rather that the family situation caused it. On the other hand, some professionals who suggest the offender as the primary cause of the abuse work in institutions that house offenders; they may fail to examine the role of families in the victimization, or its impact on the family (Faller 1993).

Other professionals who focus on the offender use different theories to explain child sexual abuse. For example, biological theories look for organic explanations, such as physiological factors like hormone levels (see Berlin 1983; Marshall and Barbaree 1990; Marques et al. 2000). Psychodynamic theories examine unresolved problems that occurred during various stages of the perpetrator's development (see Holmes and Holmes 2002; Schwartz 1995). Behavioral theories focus on deviant sexual behavior as a learned condition (see Laws and Marshall 1990). Attachment theories examine how humans need to establish strong bonds with others, and how when emotional stress or loss occurs, they act out and abuse children (see Marshall 1989; Seidman et al. 1994; Mulloy and Marshall 1999; Ward et al. 1995; Marshall and Marshall 2002). Integrated models or theories attempt to examine all of the reasons why individuals sexually abuse children, believing that there is not one cause for such behavior.

Finkelhor suggests that four conditions must be met for sexual abuse to occur: (1) factors relating to the offender's motivation to abuse a child sexually; (2) factors leading the offender to overcome internal inhibitions to sexual abuse; (3) factors leading the offender to overcome external inhibitions; and (4) factors leading the offender to believe that the child will provide little resistance to the abuse (Finkelhor 1986).

Faller suggests another model, in which some causal factors—such as being sexually aroused by children and a propensity to act on that arousal—are prerequisites for the occurrence of sexual abuse. Contributing factors can come from the family system, the culture, and the offender's current life situation, personality, or previous experiences (Faller 1993).

Effects

Children are affected in many ways by sexual abuse. The type and severity of the effects often depend on a variety of factors, including the age of the child when the abuse first occurred; how long the abuse lasted; the developmental status of the child; the relationship of the abuser to the child; whether force was used to ensure the child's participation, and the degree of force used; the degree of shame or guilt experienced by the child; and the reaction of the child's parent(s) and other professionals if and when the child reveals the abuse or it is discovered by another person. Children who have been sexually abused may display negative behaviors and attitudes, but studies have not clarified whether those behaviors existed before the sexual abuse occurred or were the effects of the abuse or the intervention process.

Hollenberg and Ragan believe that it is difficult to generalize the effects of sexual abuse on children:

Just as no single profile of child sexual abuse exists, there is no definitive description of the impact of sexual abuse on child victims. The effects of child sexual abuse are characterized by great variation and range from short-term effects to those that endure throughout adulthood. Many of the symptoms associated with child sexual abuse victimization—such as low self-esteem, anxiety, hostility, depression, hyperactivity, and psychosomatic disturbances—are common to a range of other problems as well. (Hollenberg and Ragan 1991, 179)

Finkelhor divides the effects of child sexual abuse into four main categories: traumatic sexualization, stigmatization, betrayal, and powerlessness. Traumatic sexualization results from inappropriate sexual contacts and relationships; the effects that victims may experience include avoidance of sex, disgust with anything sexual, a consuming interest in sex, or problems with sexual identity. Stigmatization results as children realize that sexual abuse is socially and morally unacceptable behavior and believe that they are responsible for the abuse or feel guilty because they have been abused; as a result, children may withdraw from friends and family members. Betrayal results when children realize that the adult they had trusted has hurt them; children may have a difficult time trusting other adults after they have been abused. Feelings of powerlessness can occur when children realize that they cannot stop the abuse or they may occur at a later time, if and when they reveal the abuse, when the intervention process begins, and they are overwhelmed by all that is happening to them (Finkelhor 1984).

Several studies examine the duration of abuse as a factor. In a study of women who were sexually abused as children, Russell found that 73 percent of those women whose abuse lasted for more than five years considered the experience extremely or considerably traumatic, compared with 62 percent whose abuse lasted from one week to five years, and 46 percent who were abused only once (Russell 1986). On the other hand, Finkelhor found no relationship between the seriousness of the effects and the duration of the abuse (Finkelhor 1979). In still other studies, such as one conducted by Christine Courtois, researchers have found that those people who have been sexually abused for the longest duration feel the least amount of trauma from the experience (Courtois 1979).

Following sexual abuse, a child's self-image often develops largely from that abuse experience; many children believe that they are dirty or bad and end up with low self-esteem. Children may learn to numb the feelings associated with the abuse experience, hoping to feel better about life and in the process increase levels of self-esteem. This coping strategy may help the child to dim the experience but does nothing to enhance feelings of self.

A sexually abused child typically loses trust in adults and other people in authority who are supposed to be nurturing and protective. Abusers, especially family members, often use shame or fear to keep the child from reporting the abuse to anyone who might be able to help. "This is our little secret," "Don't tell your mother, it would kill her," "You don't want anyone else to know what you are doing," and other similar comments are frequently made by abusers to ensure silence and obedience from the child. Abused children may feel a great deal of fear within this relationship, with a powerful adult making the rules. The child may be so frightened and ashamed about what is happening that he or she may be too embarrassed to reveal the abuse to anyone. Silence is thus ensured. When the abuser offers comfort after the abuse, perhaps by providing special privileges or gifts, confusion is normal, and the child may feel guilty for what is happening.

Sexually abused children may suppress their own needs and wants, believing that they are secondary to the needs of the adult. Or they may believe that they do not deserve anything, that their main purpose in life now is to please the adult and fulfill the adult's needs. The basic need of all children to feel safe, secure, loved, and protected by their parents is not fulfilled for abused children. Therefore they try to please everyone else, without realizing that they are important and have their own needs and desires that should be fulfilled.

Children normally become socialized and learn about sex with their peer group. They grow up together. However, sexually abused children learn about sex and their sexuality from an adult; it is defined by the adult, with adult terms and expectations. Confusion about sexuality and relationships occurs because the child sees relationships defined on the basis of sex—that is, the relationship does not exist without sex (Breslin 1990).

The effects of sexual abuse may be long lasting and devastating to victims, even as adults. For example, Dr. Richard

Berendzen, former president of the American University in Washington, D.C., was physically and sexually abused by his mother. He studied and worked hard, however, and believed that he had overcome the effects of the abuse—until he went home for his father's funeral and relived some of the experience. He began telephoning day-care centers, pretending to have a child needing day care, and asked several questions about sexual abuse; the calls were traced to his office, and he was forced to resign as president of the university. He sought treatment at the Sexual Disorders Clinic at Johns Hopkins Hospital in Baltimore and finally was able to understand what had happened to him and to do what he believed he needed to become a survivor (Berendzen and Palmer 1993). His experience clearly demonstrates that people who are sexually abused as children may suffer from long-lasting effects even when they think they are fine and have outgrown the experience.

As suggested earlier, the effects of sexual abuse for boys may be different in some ways than it is for girls. For example, Mike Lew observes:

> Since men "are not supposed to be victims," abuse (and particularly sexual abuse) becomes a process of demasculinization (or emasculation). If men aren't to be victims (the equation reads), then victims aren't men. The victimized male wonders and worries about what the abuse has turned him into. Believing that he is no longer an adequate man, he may see himself as a child, a woman, gay, or less than human: an irreparably damaged freak. (Lew 1988, 41)

Consequently, a man who has been sexually abused as a child may feel a need to prove to himself that he is a man, searching for wealth, recognition, and power.

Some adults who have been sexually abused as children seek help for some of their problems. Often these problems may be related to the sexual abuse, although they are not aware of the connection. They may have entered therapy to get help with depression, eating disorders, substance abuse, or other problems, not realizing that their early experiences of sexual abuse could be at the source of those problems. Several problem areas for sexual abuse victims are discussed below.

Post-Traumatic Stress Syndrome

The *Diagnostic and Statistical Manual of Mental Disorders* provides the following definition of post-traumatic stress disorder:

> The essential feature of Post Traumatic Stress Syndrome is the development of characteristic symptoms following exposure to an extreme traumatic stressor involving direct personal experience of an event that involves actual or threatened death or serious injury, or other threat to one's physical integrity . . . (Criterion A1). The person's response to the event must involve intense fear, helplessness, or horror (or in children, the response must involve disorganized or agitated behavior (Criterion A2). The characteristic symptoms resulting from the exposure . . . include persistent reexperiencing of the traumatic event (Criterion B), persistent avoidance of stimuli associated with the trauma and numbing of general responsiveness (Criterion C), and persistent symptoms of increased arousal (Criterion D). The full symptom picture must be present for more than 1 month (Criterion E), and the disturbance must cause clinically significant distress or impairment in social, occupational, or other important areas of functioning (Criterion F). (APA 2000, 463)

People who have been sexually abused as children may push aside the memory of the event; however, at some point they may relive the event, and often experience intense emotional distress as a result. The feelings experienced are similar to those felt by Vietnam War veterans; both have complied with what others expected of them, and both were informed by others that what they were doing was right.

Sexual Disorders

Adults who have been sexually abused as children may exhibit sexual acting out or promiscuous behavior. They may be trying to overcome feelings of powerlessness that they experienced as children, or they may be confused over the boundaries of behavior that define affection, sex, and abuse. Jon Briere and Karin Meiselman, in separate studies, examined a control group and a group who had been sexually abused as children; they found that adults sexually abused as children were more likely than the control group to experience sexual problems as adults (Briere 1984; Meiselman 1978).

Eating Disorders

Wiehe found that several respondents in his study on sibling abuse suffered from eating disorders, including bulimia and anorexia (Wiehe 1990). Many victims of sexual abuse are concerned about their physical appearance. Some may lose weight, while others may gain weight to ensure that no one is attracted to them. In another study, Wonderlich et al. examined data on twenty sexually abused girls and twenty nonabused girls between the ages of ten and fifteen years. They found that those who had been sexually abused were more likely to be dissatisfied with their weight and exhibited higher levels of purging and dieting behaviors (Wonderlich et al. 2000).

Substance Abuse

Many studies have established a link between sexual abuse and alcohol or drug problems in later life. In Wiehe's study on sibling abuse, he found that 25 percent of respondents admitted having a substance abuse problem with either alcohol or drugs (Wiehe 1990). In studying female drug abusers at a community treatment center, Jean Benward and Judianne Densen-Gerber interviewed 118 patients and found that 44 percent had been sexually abused as children: 45 percent of the abuse experiences occurred when the child was nine years old or younger; 73 percent of the incidents occurred before the child reached her thirteenth birthday. Based on their results, Benward and Densen-Gerber speculated that those girls who submitted to the sexual encounter without putting up a fight were more likely to exhibit psychological problems, including substance abuse (Benward and Densen-Gerber 1975).

Singer, Petchers, and Hussey found that adolescents who had been sexually abused as children had significantly different patterns of drug use and abuse. These patterns included the regular use of cocaine and stimulants, frequent drinking and drug use, and being high on drugs more often than those who had not been sexually abused. Their findings suggest that people who have been sexually abused as children may use mood-altering substances to help them deal with their emotional difficulties and help in their interpersonal relationships (Singer et al. 1989).

Depression

Adults who were sexually abused as children may also exhibit more serious bouts of depression than other people. Briere and Runtz, in studying a nonclinical sample of 278 university women, found that 15 percent had been sexually abused before the age of fifteen, and that those women exhibited more depressive symptoms than women who had not been sexually abused (Briere and Runtz 1988).

In Wiehe's study of sibling abuse, he found that 26 percent of his respondents had been hospitalized for depression and 33 percent had attempted suicide (Wiehe 1990). Other studies have also found rates for depression and attempted suicide higher for those people who were sexually abused as children than for those who were not. DeYoung found that 68 percent of the women she studied who had been sexually abused as children had attempted suicide, and half of those had tried more than once (DeYoung 1982). Another study examined seventy-four individuals, including forty-eight women, admitted to a general hospital after attempting suicide. The researchers found that 35 percent of the respondents had experienced severe sexual abuse as children (Ystgaard et al. 2004).

Indicators of Childhood Sexual Abuse

Most professionals differentiate between physical indicators and psychosocial indicators of child sexual abuse. Physical indicators usually are determined by a medical professional. In the past several years, medical professionals have gained increased experience in recognizing the signs of child sexual abuse. However, in a discussion of medical indicators, the reader should keep in mind that, in most cases of child sexual abuse, no medical evidence of the abuse exists. When physical indicators are present, the ones that most likely indicate sexual abuse are pregnancy and venereal disease. Other indicators include semen in the vagina of a child, a torn hymen, vaginal injury, an injury to the penis or scrotum, labial adhesions, vulvovaginitis, chronic urinary tract infections, anal bruising, or pharyngeal gonorrhea as a result of oral sex.

Sexual-psychosocial indicators include statements from children about sexual matters that a child of that age would not likely know of, sexually explicit drawings or comments, sexual aggression when playing with other children, suggestions of sex with adults, and in some cases, masturbation. Children often experiment with masturbation as they are growing, but if children masturbate many times each day, cannot stop, or insert various objects into their vagina or anus, these may be signs that they have been sexually abused.

Some nonsexual psychosocial indicators of sexual abuse include sleep disturbances, bedwetting, regressive behavior, fear of certain people, fear of being left alone, cruelty to animals, eating disturbances, depression, or social withdrawal. These symptoms also may be indicators of other problems in the family, so professionals must be extremely careful when diagnosing sexual abuse based solely on any of these nonphysical indicators.

Intervention/Treatment

One of the major concerns about the ways in which authorities intervene in cases of child sexual abuse is the damage that may be done to the child in the process of trying to help. Accused parents may try to blame the child or may focus on how the allegation has destroyed the family. Social and legal responses may pull the child from the home, or frighten the child with medical examinations, court appearances, and endless interviews with strangers who want to know in detail exactly what happened to the child. MacFarlane believes that

> [a]lthough society reacts with predictable horror at what is done to children by sex offenders, it apparently does not share a similar concern for what subsequently may happen to children in the hands of our intervention system. Whether a child has been sexually assaulted by a stranger, an acquaintance, or a family member, when the incident is disclosed, the family is usually experiencing extreme crisis as it works through feelings of anger, fear, shock, and confusion. During this vulnerable period, the criminal justice, health, and social service systems may

descend upon a child and family with such a devastating impact that recipients are left with the feeling that the "cure" is far worse than the original problem. Many authorities agree that the emotional damage resulting from the intervention of "helping agents" in our society may equal, or far exceed, the harm caused by the abusive incident. (MacFarlane 1978, 81)

Many things can happen to a child and the child's family when sexual abuse is believed to have occurred, especially if the offender is a family member. The child may be removed from the home; the perpetrator may be arrested and jailed; the child may be placed in foster care; the family's economic security may be in jeopardy if the father is the offender and he is jailed; the child may feel guilty and responsible for breaking up the family; and the family members may feel embarrassed and ridiculed by former friends and neighbors.

Faller suggests several practices that may reduce the trauma to the child of the initial investigation. These include minimizing the number of interviews of the child, using a skilled and sensitive interviewer to minimize the negative effects of the interview; allowing a support person to be present with the child; and conducting the interview in a safe and comforting environment. The trauma to the child of the medical exam can be mitigated by getting the child's permission for the exam and by using a sensitive health professional (Faller 1993).

Reporting

Reporting child sexual abuse to the authorities can be frightening, both to the child and to the family, and it can threaten the emotional and financial security of the family if a parent is the abuser. There are many reasons for reporting abuse, as well as for not reporting abuse.

Reasons for reporting include the following:

- The child may feel relieved that someone else knows about the abuse and reassured by contact with the authorities.
- The abuse will stop.
- The offender will not abuse other children.
- Most cases do not go to trial; they are settled out of

court, so the family often does not have to worry about the child's having to testify in court.
- Children's sense of justice and right can be affirmed.
- Crime victim compensation, which is financial assistance provided to victims of crime, is available only to those people who report the crime to law enforcement agencies.

The many reasons that people may have for not reporting sexual abuse include the following:

- Family members believe that they can confront the abuser themselves and stop the abuse.
- Family members may be afraid that the offender will be sent to jail, threatening the financial security of the family.
- The police cannot be trusted.
- Family members may be afraid that they are accusing the wrong person.
- The family will be embarrassed and possibly threatened by other family members, friends, neighbors, and society.
- The child may have to go through too much trauma.
- Family members do not want to "ruin the lives" or reputation of another family (if the abuse has been committed by a nonfamily member).

Investigation

Child Protection Services (CPS) personnel are the local authorities in the investigation of child sexual abuse. Both federal and state legislation mandates that the CPS protect children and investigate cases of sexual abuse when the sexual abuse is perpetrated by a family member. When the offender is not in a caretaking role, law enforcement personnel often are responsible for investigating the case, although CPS may also be involved.

Most states mandate that health care, mental health, and education professionals report all suspected cases of child sexual abuse; others, such as day-care providers or church officials, may be required to report in some states. Once CPS receives a report, they are required to investigate the allegations within a specified period of time, usually between twenty-four hours and five days, depending on the state. Many states require that law enforcement personnel participate in the investigation with CPS personnel when sexual abuse is alleged, primarily to gather evidence in the event that offenders are prosecuted.

Treatment

A variety of treatment options exists for children who have been sexually abused, as well as for their families. Treatment programs for child sexual abuse typically offer a variety of services that may include art and play therapy, marital counseling, psychological testing, individual and group therapy, parenting classes, substance abuse programs, court advocacy, and life skills courses. Multidisciplinary teams are often used to help develop comprehensive case management and treatment plans, as well as to review progress in each case.

Treatment goals in cases of child sexual abuse usually include reducing the crisis atmosphere that the family is experiencing; helping the family to cope with the situation; helping family members to control rage, hurt, and other emotions; helping family members to accept the existence of the abuse so that they can enter and profit from treatment; and reducing the family's isolation from society.

Interviewing the Child

Several issues arise when interviewing a child thought to have been sexually abused, including where the interview should occur, when it should occur, who should be present, how information will be recorded, and how many interviews may be required. Experts generally agree that the interview should take place in a location that the child believes is safe.

In most states, the CPS worker conducts the interview; in some states law enforcement personnel are also present, while in other states law enforcement personnel spend their time interviewing the alleged offender. Interviews may be videotaped, or audiotaped, or the interviewer may simply take notes on what is said. Child Advocacy Centers (CACs), child-oriented facilities specifically organized to centralize the investigation of child sexual abuse, are located in many cities. Usually housed in old homes or other homelike buildings to encourage the child to feel safe, CACs attempt to provide a comfortable, safe environment in which CPS personnel and other professionals can interview the child and provide a variety of services to the child and family.

Medical Examinations

Medical examination of a child may be performed for a number of reasons. The exam can reassure the child and parents that the child is healthy and will not be permanently harmed physically by the abuse. As physicians see more cases of child sexual abuse they are able to recognize the physical signs, if any exist, and are therefore becoming more reliable in their diagnoses of sexual abuse. Also, children who have been forced to have sexual intercourse with an adult may be at high risk for any number of sexually transmitted diseases, including AIDS, and the sooner such conditions are diagnosed the sooner treatment can begin.

Social and Law Enforcement Services

Social service agencies can play an important role in treating the child and the family in sexual abuse cases. Often children are not the only ones in need of support. If the abuse has been perpetrated by a family member, either the child or the family member is generally removed from the home. If one parent is charged with sexual abuse, that parent may be jailed if the rest of the family decide to prosecute, or the parent may have left the home. In either case, the family may now be in need of some type of financial support or other help until the situation is resolved. Emergency housing may be needed to remove the child and other family members from the home, and they may also need food or medical assistance. Social service agencies can help families find the needed shelter, financial support, and other types of help.

Law enforcement agencies are required to ensure that the victim is safe from further abuse and that the offender is prevented from harming others. They are also involved if family members decide to press charges against the offender. Law enforcement personnel may also participate in multidisciplinary teams to help in case management.

Some studies indicate that police officers in many areas may need additional training in the handling of child sexual abuse cases. In a survey of 250 police academies, Daly found that officers received generalized training but were for the most part not fully prepared to deal with child sexual abuse cases (Daly 2004).

The Legal System

The use of the legal system to protect children and prosecute offenders presents several complex issues. Many experts believe that children are often more traumatized by the court proceedings than by the sexual abuse. Court proceedings can be long and drawn out and quite frightening for a young child. Being on the witness stand and enduring questions of a very personal nature are hard for anyone, but especially a child. Some experts believe that children are better off not being involved in criminal proceedings—that is, that charges not be pressed—while other experts believe that, in the long run, the child benefits by the experience. Statistics show that most cases do not go to trial (see Chapter 6).

State statutes have improved over the years, with most now specifically defining prohibited acts involving sexual abuse of children. For example, many laws prohibiting incest used to require evidence of sexual intercourse in order to obtain a conviction. Today, many of the laws define incest broadly and do not always require such evidence.

State juvenile or family courts usually specify the procedures necessary to place a child in emergency custody, to remove an alleged abuser from the home, to authorize the placement of the child in protective services or with other substitute caretakers, and to terminate parental rights. All states have reporting laws, and approximately one-half of them require that reports be made directly to a child protective services office; the other half specify that either a child protective services office or law enforcement agency receives the reports.

Many communities recognize the importance of minimizing the trauma a child receives when involved in the legal process. These communities have looked for innovative ways to minimize the trauma, by coordinating multidisciplinary teams and services to minimize repeated interviews; by coordinating civil and criminal court proceedings; and by initiating policies, procedures, and projects to set up pretrial diversion programs for first-time offenders who show remorse and desire treatment. A diversion program focuses on the positive development and self-image of youth by diverting them from the criminal justice process and teaching them how to be responsible adults.

Children as Witnesses

When children are required to testify in court, prosecutors must play an active role in preparing the children for the trial. Even though some jurisdictions have created special units to prosecute sex crimes and crimes against children, most prosecutors are not comfortable with child witnesses; they are not familiar with children's needs, and they are not trained in dealing with children (National Center on Child Abuse and Neglect 1991). In most instances, child sexual abuse cases do not come to trial; they are resolved by plea bargains, often because prosecutors do not want to risk losing a case based on the testimony of a child and would rather attempt a plea bargain.

More than half of the states presume that children are competent to testify in court proceedings. Based on the 1990 Federal Victims of Child Abuse Act, competency hearings in federal courts can be held only after a written motion and demonstration of compelling need. Young children are generally capable of testifying in court, depending on their own developmental status, stress level, language ability, and socioeconomic factors. While some attorneys and other experts believe that children are highly suggestible, most research indicates that this is not the case when they are asked to remember something of critical importance in their lives. Some defense attorneys may suggest that children have been coached or brainwashed into suggesting that they have been abused; other defense attorneys may suggest that the children believe the abuse really happened when in fact it did not.

Another concern for those in the legal profession is recantation of allegations by child witnesses. Some children may become so frightened by the intensity and length of the legal process, or may be under such great pressure from family members, that they may recant their charges to relieve the stress they feel.

In criminal cases of sexual abuse of children, basic conflicts exist between the rights of the accused and the rights and needs of the child. For example, in adult criminal cases, the accused has the right to face the accuser, to confront and cross-examine witnesses, and to receive a public trial. When children are involved, the issue of face-to-face confrontation is especially critical. Many experts believe that requiring a child to face the sexually abusing adult in court is too traumatic for many children to handle. The adult, a person of authority in the child's life, may intimidate the child enough to make the child unwilling or unable to testify. Therefore, many courts have allowed children to have their testimony videotaped, so that they do not have to face their abuser. In 1990, the U.S. Supreme Court ruled in *Maryland v. Craig* (1990) that a Maryland law allowing children to testify via a closed-circuit television outside of the courtroom, with only the prosecutor and defense attorney present, did not violate the defendant's right of confronting the accuser.

The reliability of children as witnesses has also been questioned. Can they accurately remember what happened to them? Do they remember details? Often the child's testimony may provide the only evidence of sexual abuse—most abusers do not abuse children in front of witnesses, and often there is no physical evidence of the abuse. Some experts believe that children often have a difficult time distinguishing fact from fantasy; others believe that children are unlikely to disclose facts about sexual abuse if they have not been sexually abused, and that they rarely lie about abuse.

Several studies have also shown that children are highly resistant to accepting misinformation about events that concern their personal safety and well-being. Goodman and her colleagues found that children as young as four years old were able to provide accurate accounts of events as long as those events had some significance to them. The children rarely recalled wrong information and resisted accepting misinformation as fact. Children were more likely to leave out information than to provide incorrect information (Goodman et al. 1990). In another study, Goodman and her colleagues examined children's memories of stressful events. They hypothesized that while, over time, children would retain less and less information about an event, those children who were highly stressed would retain more information than the less stressed children, and they would resist attempts at misinformation. They found that children who were most stressed were the most resistant to misinformation and recalled more details than less stressed children. While the amount of information the children recalled decreased after one year, the amount of incorrect information did not increase during the same period (Goodman et al. 1991).

Because of the increasing number of child sexual abuse reports, more and more children are being required to testify in court proceedings against their abusers. The ability of jurors to assess the reliability of children's allegations of child sexual abuse is critical in determining the guilt or innocence of the alleged abuser.

After reviewing three studies on the effects on children of testifying in cases of sexual abuse, Debra Whitcomb and her colleagues found inconclusive evidence of harm or benefit:

> Based on the results of these studies, it cannot be stated conclusively that testifying is either harmful or beneficial to sexually abused children. . . . Virtually all of the children improved emotionally, regardless of their experience in court. At worst, testifying may impede the improvement process for some children . . . at best, it may enhance their recovery. . . . Only a small number of children appeared to suffer long-term trauma from the experience of testifying. (Whitcomb et al. 1994, 5)

Use of Expert Witnesses

In recent years, both the prosecution and defense have made increased use of expert witnesses in court proceedings. Many researchers believe that this trend is disturbing, including Debra Whitcomb, who cites four reasons:

1. Child sexual abuse is a relatively new and inexact field of study. Much remains unknown, and there are many areas of controversy.
2. The majority of behavioral scientists who testify as experts in these cases are not certified as forensic specialists in their respective disciplines (which include psychiatry, psychology, social work counseling, and, to a lesser extent, pediatrics). They may have little knowledge of the very circumscribed role expert testimony should play in most criminal cases.
3. A small number of behavioral scientists have become, in effect, professional experts who "ride circuit" around the country to testify in well-financed cases. This practice is

      detrimental both to the legal profession and to the
      mental health professions.
4. The absence of consensus among behavioral scientists
    about many of the issues surrounding child sexual abuse
    and children's testimony . . . paves the way for "battles of
    the experts" which tend to obscure, rather than clarify,
    the fact-finding process. (Whitcomb 1992, 111)

The presence of expert witnesses can have a serious impact on the level of stress the child experiences. For example, opposing experts may be called upon to conduct a psychological or physical examination of the child, adding to the child's confusion and stress. The majority of courts do agree on one subject—that prosecution witnesses almost universally are not allowed to express any direct opinions about the credibility of specific children as witnesses. However, many defense attorneys will suggest that children's testimony is not reliable because of improper questioning techniques, that children are unable to distinguish between fantasy and reality, and that children are unable to distinguish between truth and lies.

Child Advocate Programs

Community-based victim assistance and advocacy programs can be found throughout the United States. These programs offer a variety of services, such as referrals for counseling services; notification of court dates, investigation status, and case dispositions; provision of relevant information; accompaniment of the child and family to court proceedings; assistance with transportation and family support; and emotional support.

In juvenile court hearings, child victims of abuse have a guardian ad litem (GAL) appointed by the court to represent their best interests. The Child Abuse Prevention and Treatment Act of 1974, as amended, requires that a GAL be appointed in states that want to receive federal funds. Guardians ad litem usually play a larger role than child victim advocates. States vary in what they allow the GALs to do: their roles may include attending all depositions, hearings, and trial proceedings; recommending to the court measures to ensure the child's welfare; possessing all reports, evaluations, and records to advocate effectively for the child; and coordinating resource delivery and special services that the child may require.

Prevention

While many professionals believe that prevention is an important part of reducing the incidence of child sexual abuse, effective means of prevention are still being sought. Teaching children that they have a right to control access to their bodies, how to distinguish "good" from "bad" touches, not to keep secrets about bad touches, how to say no to someone, and that it is important to tell someone about the abuse are critical in protecting children, but the effectiveness of this approach is still undetermined. Children who are sexually abused are often placed in situations in which they are afraid of the abuser, are threatened with harm, fear breaking up the family, have no one to trust, or may indeed tell the other parent but find him or her unconvinced. Many children are embarrassed and therefore unable to tell anyone. Although teaching children to tell someone about abuse may not be the most effective way of preventing future sexual abuse, until professionals are able to determine what makes a person sexually abuse a child and how to find and help that person before abuse occurs, it may be the most effective means of reducing the number of children sexually abused.

Prevention efforts have grown in popularity since the late 1970s. Activities can be grouped into four main categories: (1) public awareness; (2) provision of materials to parents to teach their children about sexual abuse; (3) education for professionals; and (4) prevention education programs for all children. Several national organizations—such as the National Center of Child Abuse and Neglect, the American Medical Association, the National Education Association, the National Committee to Prevent Child Abuse, and the Committee for Children—have developed sexual abuse prevention resources for parents, to help them in talking with their children about sexual abuse. In 1985, the U.S. Department of Health and Human Services developed the Model Child Care Standards Act—Guidance to States to Prevent Child Abuse in Day Care Facilities, to help develop ways of screening day-care workers. The National Committee for the Prevention of Child Abuse encourages the development of quality sexual abuse prevention programs by publishing guidelines for local projects to use in creating such programs.

Parental Education Programs

Many people believe that providing prevention education for parents is the most effective means of reaching the children. Parents can reinforce information contained in educational materials better than any other group. However, many parents have a difficult time talking with their children about sex and may also have trouble talking about sexual abuse. Finkelhor studied 521 parents of children between the ages of six and fourteen in the Boston metropolitan area. He found that only 29 percent of the parents discussed sexual abuse with their children; when those discussions did occur, only 22 percent mentioned the possibility of abuse by a family member, and only 65 percent discussed the possibility of someone asking the child to take off his or her clothes. Most parental discussions with children occurred when the child was approximately nine years old; many studies have shown that at least one-third of all child sexual abuse occurs before the child reaches age nine, and therefore these parental discussions may have occurred too late to prevent abuse (Finkelhor 1982). Also, if either parent is the one abusing the child, then he or she is not likely to agree to teach the child about sexual abuse.

Prevention Programs for Professionals

Teachers, pediatricians, day-care workers, clergy, police, and other professionals who come into frequent contact with children must be trained in ways to identify the sexually abused child, as well as in ways to prevent abuse. Finkelhor and Araji have recommended several objectives for setting up professional training programs:

1. Professionals must be able to communicate, in ways that children can understand, any information about the nature and dynamics of sexual abuse.
2. They must be taught to identify children who have been or are being sexually abused, or who are at high risk of being abused.
3. They must be able to question a child about the possibility of abuse with sensitivity and understanding.
4. They must know how to react when a child divulges sexual abuse, without showing alarm or panic, and without blaming the child.

5. They must be able to refer children and their families to proper resources for treatment and support.
6. They must be able to talk with the child about the basic concepts of preventing sexual abuse. (Finkelhor and Araji 1983)

Prevention Programs for Children

Most prevention programs are focused on teaching children about sexual abuse and what to do if someone attempts to abuse. Most of these programs take into account the age and cultural background of the child, as well as the economic status of the child's family, when designing and presenting programs.

Conte believes that all prevention programs aimed at children should include the following ideas:

- Children own their bodies and nobody has the right to share them.
- There is a difference between good touches and bad touches.
- Secrets about touching or other forms of abuse should never be kept.
- Children should trust their own feelings about something being right or wrong.
- Children should be taught how to say no.
- Children should be encouraged to tell someone if they are being abused. (Conte 1986)

Gillham takes a slightly different perspective in looking at prevention programs. He categorizes prevention activities into three groups: primary, secondary, and tertiary. Primary prevention activities include increasing the awareness among all groups having contact with children of child molesters and their characteristics; recognizing that boys are at risk almost as much as girls; teaching children how to deal with strangers; teaching children about the privacy of their bodies; establishing legal policies that catch serious molesters and repeat offenders and keep them behind bars; and teaching children about all types of abuse. Secondary prevention activities include creating an atmosphere in which children feel safe to report abuse; encouraging parents, teachers, and other caretakers to act when they suspect that a child has been sexually abused; encouraging and training teachers to be aware of the signs of sexual abuse; recognizing that children rarely lie about something as serious as sexual abuse; being particularly aware of children at high risk for sexual abuse; and, if the offender lives in the same home as the child, removing the offender from the home. Tertiary prevention requires the provision of supportive responses to the disclosure that a child has been sexually abused; minimizing the impact of the interview and treatment process; convincing children that they are not to blame for the abuse; and offering counseling services to adults who were abused as children (Gillham 1991).

Other Types of Child Sexual Abuse

Child Exploitation and Prostitution

Child prostitution exists in most countries, from Southeast Asia to the United States. It may be more open and accepted in some developing countries, but wherever children are seen as desirable sexual objects, sexual exploitation of children can be found. In Western countries, the majority of child prostitutes are runaways; in Latin America, they are street children. The need for children to earn a living is often cited as the most common reason why children become prostitutes—either the children themselves decide to become prostitutes, or their families sell them into prostitution (Moorehead 1990). Chapter 3 explores this topic in more detail.

In the United States in 1988, the National Incidence Studies estimated that 450,000 children left home and stayed away for at least one night; another 27,000 children were thrown out of their homes. Many of those children end up on the streets, trying to survive as best they can, often through activities such as pornography, sexual exploitation, and drugs (Faller 1993). According to the National Center for Missing and Exploited Children,

> [s]exual victimization of these homeless children occurs in every state. Outreach workers in New York City estimate that children as young as eight years old are forced to prostitute themselves for money, affection, and drugs. Some children are held in virtual bondage. They have multiple sex partners on a daily basis and are bought and sold by exploiters. Many contract diseases such as

tuberculosis (TB), hepatitis-B, gonorrhea, syphilis, chlamydia, and human immunodeficiency virus (HIV)/acquired immune deficiency syndrome (AIDS). They often are malnourished and practice poor hygiene, leaving them vulnerable to disease. (National Center for Missing and Exploited Children 2002, vii)

Some organizations, such as the Rene Guyon Society and the North American Man/Boy Love Association (NAMBLA), believe that most child exploitation and sexual abuse laws should be removed from the statutes. Members advocate sex with children, arguing that children are fully capable of entering into loving relationships with adults, and that it is only our Victorian upbringing that prohibits us from realizing that there is nothing wrong with sex between a child and an adult.

Cults and Ritual Abuse

Allegations of children being sexually abused in cults and in ritual abuse have grown in recent years. Ritual abuse may include malicious acts of physical, sexual, and psychological abuse; group acts of religious worship involving abuse; and terrorizing people psychologically in order to force them to participate in certain activities. It may include animal or human sacrifice. Satanism is not always involved.

Lloyd believes that no clear, consistent definition of ritual abuse exists. The news media and professionals in the field of child sexual abuse may apply the term to situations that include any bizarre acts of either physical, sexual, or psychological abuse of children; abuse acts involving children during religious worship or displays of demonic powers; and psychological intimidation of children to force them to believe in demonic powers. Lloyd defines ritual child abuse as "the intentional physical abuse, sexual abuse, or psychological abuse of a child by a person responsible for the child's welfare, when such abuse is repeated and/or stylized and is typified by such other acts as cruelty to animals or threats of harm to the child, other persons, and animals" (Lloyd 1990a, 2). Ritual abuse is defined by Susan Kelley as "repetitive and systematic sexual, physical, and psychological abuse of children by adults as part of cult or satanic worship" (Kelley 1988, 228).

The study of Satanism is still relatively new, especially as it relates to child sexual abuse; few studies have been conducted, and most professionals in the field have limited knowledge about satanic cults and ritual abuse. Satanic cults are said to program their followers using techniques that are known only to the high priests and priestesses. According to most professionals in the field of cults and mind control, no one has yet found a practicing satanic cult that murders babies or animals. Katchen and Sakheim found that "[m]any Satanists believe therefore that a relationship exists between incest, magic, idolatry, sacrifice, and the consumption of blood. . . . It is thereby assumed that forbidden incestuous relationships, the consumption of blood, the human sacrifice all prove the power to do magic" (Katchen and Sakheim 1992, 25).

Kenneth Lanning, the FBI's expert on ritual abuse, found that

> [f]or at least eight years, American law enforcement has been aggressively investigating the allegations of victims of ritual abuse. There is little or no evidence for the portion of their allegations that deals with large-scale baby breeding, human sacrifice and organized satanic conspiracies. Now it is up to mental health professionals, not law enforcement, to explain why victims are alleging things that don't seem to be true. Mental health professionals must begin to accept the possibility that some of what these victims are alleging just didn't happen and that this area desperately needs study and research by rational, objective social scientists. (Lanning 1991, 172)

Crewdson examined satanic child abuse and found that, in most cases, real physical evidence has rarely been found, although some investigations have turned up suggestions of some type of ritual abuse:

> In Richmond, Virginia, one person was convicted in a sexual abuse case where police recovered candles and other ritualistic paraphernalia. In El Paso, Texas, across the Rio Grande from Mexico, a young prosecutor named Deborah Kanof won a conviction of a thirty-five-year-old mother who had been charged with abusing eight children at the East Valley YWCA. Some of the victims in that case said they had been taken from the "Y" to a nearby house, where they were made to have sex with the teacher while men dressed in masks and werewolf

costumes looked on. The woman got life in prison plus 311 years, the longest sentence for child sexual abuse in Texas history. (Crewdson 1988, 125)

Finkelhor and his colleagues, in their study of children sexually abused in day-care settings, found that children who were ritually abused appeared to suffer the most serious psychological impairments (Finkelhor et al. 1988).

Lanning suggests several possible explanations for why people think that they have been victims of ritual, or satanic, abuse. One explanation is pathological distortion:

> The allegations in question may be errors in processing reality influenced by underlying mental disorders such as dissociate disorders, borderline or histrionic personality disorders, or psychosis. These distortions may be manifested in false accounts of victimization in order to gain psychological benefits such as attention and sympathy. . . . Although not always pathological, many "victims" may develop pseudomemories of their victimization and eventually come to believe the events actually occurred. (Lanning 1992, 24)

Another possible explanation is traumatic memory—that is, events may become confused or distorted as a result of severe trauma. Victims may dissociate from the events by forcing their minds to go somewhere else, in order to avoid the experience and the memory of the abusive experience. Lanning considers repressed memory:

> It may be that we should anticipate that individuals severely abused as very young children by multiple offenders with fear as the primary controlling tactic will repress the memory. This repressed memory of their victimization may be distorted and embellished when later recalled. Perhaps a horror-filled yet inaccurate account of victimization is not only not a counterindication of abuse, but is in fact a corroborative indicator of extreme physical, psychological, and/or sexual abuse. (ibid., 25)

Lanning includes normal childhood fears and fantasy; misperceptions, confusion, and trickery; overzealous intervenors; urban legends; or a combination of many factors as other possible explanations.

Child Pornography and Sex Rings

Child pornography and sex rings are another form of child sexual abuse. Many pedophiles enjoy looking at photographs of naked children and use those photographs to excite their own sexual desires. Child sex rings are also used by pedophiles to share and exchange children for the explicit purpose of having sexual intercourse with these children.

One effective way of catching pedophiles is through the sale and exchange of child pornography. Many pedophiles enjoy taking pictures of their young victims. Crewdson found that:

> [h]omemade pornography not only feeds the pedophile's fantasies, it becomes a permanent record of the children he has known. The victims themselves may not stay young forever, but in the pedophile's album the eight-year-old remains forever eight. Not only do pictures of smiling children validate his behavior; such photographs also have a more practical application. In attempting to break down the resistance of a prospective victim, the pedophile can produce documentary evidence that children have sex with adults. (Crewdson 1988, 101)

Child pornography may also be used to review and select children for sexual intercourse. Offenders may leave pictures of children in various erotic poses where other children can see them, in the hope that these other children may think that the behavior is acceptable and be encouraged to try similar activities. A father may show child pornography to his own child in order to "prove" to the child that there is nothing wrong with what he wants to do with the child.

Some pedophiles who have trouble finding young children to molest will search for or create their own child sex rings. Lanning defines child sex rings as "one or more offenders simultaneously involved sexually with several child victims" (Lanning 1992, 9). Child sex rings are not necessarily commercial and do not always imply group sex. Offenders usually interact sexually with one child at a time. Characteristics of child sex rings include multiple victims and multiple offenders, and the children involved are usually adolescent boys, rather than girls, who are more likely to be sexually abused within the family.

Burgess divides child sex rings into three categories: solo, transition, and syndicated. Offenders keep their activities and any photographs they have secret in the solo rings, which always involve one offender and multiple victims. Offenders share their children, experiences, and photographs with other offenders in transition rings. Syndicated rings operate under a well-defined structure that recruits children, offers sexual services, produces pornography, and has an extensive list of customers (Burgess 1984).

Lanning divides child sex rings into two types: historical child sex rings and multidimensional child sex rings. Historical child sex rings have the following characteristics in common: offenders are male; most offenders are true pedophiles; at least two-thirds of the children involved are boys; sexual motivation is the only reason the offenders participate; offenders collect child pornography and child erotica; and offenders usually control the children through the use of seduction. Initially, offenders usually control boys through the "use of bonding, competition, and peer pressure" (Lanning 1992, 14). In order to bond boys together, the offenders can either use an existing organization, such as the Scouts or a sports team, or can create their own organization, such as a computer club or cult. Later, when attempting to keep a boy in the ring when he wants to leave, or when trying to get rid of a boy, the offenders may resort to blackmail, threats of violence, or actual violence. The boys rarely think of themselves as victims and therefore do not reveal the sexual abuse to anyone outside of the ring. Many of the boys involved are the more vulnerable boys in society; they are searching for attention and love, and they believe that belonging to a sex ring is one way of receiving that attention (ibid.).

Multidimensional child sex rings have the following characteristics in common: multiple offenders and multiple victims, the use of fear to control the victims, and involvement of some type of bizarre or ritualistic activity. In these rings, approximately half of the victims are girls; the offenders may not be true pedophiles, because they may not have sex as their primary motive; authorities investigating these groups have not found photographs of the victims, child pornography, or sexual paraphernalia; and the offenders control the children by frightening them and creating traumatic memories. Types of bizarre or ritualistic activities include "ceremonies, chanting, robes and costumes, drugs, use of urine and feces, animal sacrifice, torture, abduction, mutilation, murder, and even cannibalism and vampirism" (ibid., 18).

In investigating cases of child sexual abuse and child exploitation, Lanning believes that

[l]aw enforcement officers must stop looking at child sexual abuse and exploitation through a keyhole—focusing on one act, by one offender, against one victim, on one day. Law enforcement must "kick the door open" and take the big picture—focusing on proactive techniques, offender typologies, patterns of behavior, multiple acts, multiple victims, and child pornography. This is absolutely essential in the investigation of child sex rings. (ibid., 31)

In general, investigators must document any indicators of sexual abuse that they find; document both victim and offender patterns of behavior; identify adult witnesses and suspects; collect any medical evidence; search for other victims; obtain search warrants early in the process so that evidence is not destroyed; collect all physical evidence; search for all corroborative evidence, including child pornography and child erotica; monitor events with body tape recorders or video recorders, if possible, without involving or endangering the child; use surveillance techniques in monitoring the suspects; and be creative in prosecuting offenders. It is important that the investigators understand the seduction process when looking into sex rings; young boys may be hesitant to admit to being involved in sex rings because of the fear of being thought homosexual and the embarrassment of being caught in such activities (Lanning 1992).

The growth and popularity of the Internet over the past ten to fifteen years has also facilitated and encouraged the activities of pedophiles by making photographs available quite easily. Computerized bulletin boards are another tool currently available to pedophiles for finding others with similar interests, and often for finding young people, primarily young boys, to meet. See Chapter 2 for a discussion of the problems and issues of child pornography.

References

APA (American Psychiatric Association). 2000. *Diagnostic and Statistical Manual of Mental Disorders*. 4th ed. Washington, DC: American Psychiatric Association.

Baker, Anthony W., and Sylvia P. Duncan. 1985. "Child Sexual Abuse: A Study of Prevalence in Great Britain." *Child Abuse and Neglect* 9, no. 4: 457–467.

Benward, Jean, and Judianne Densen-Gerber. 1975. "Incest as a Causative Factor in Antisocial Behavior: An Explanatory Study." *Contemporary Drug Problems* 4: 323–340.

Berendzen, Richard, and Laura Palmer. 1993. *Come Here: A Man Overcomes the Tragic Aftermath of Childhood Sexual Abuse.* New York: Villard.

Berlin, F. S. 1983. "Sex Offenders: A Biomedical Perspective and a Status Report on Biomedical Treatment." Pp. 83–123 in *The Sexual Aggressor: Current Perspectives on Treatment,* edited by J. G. Greer. New York: Van Nostrand Reinhold.

Bolen, R. M., and M. Scannapieco. 1999. "Prevalence of Child Sexual Abuse: A Corrective Metanalysis." *Social Service Review* 73, no. 3: 281–313.

Breslin, Eleanor E. 1990. "Introduction." In *Therapy for Sexually Abused Children and Their Siblings: Group Therapists' Guide,* edited by Joanne Szybalski and Susan Setziol. San Jose, CA: Giarretto Institute.

Briere, Jon. 1984. "The Effects of Childhood Sexual Abuse on Later Psychological Functions: Defining a Post-Sexual Abuse Syndrome." Paper presented at the third National Conference on Sexual Victimization of Children, Children's Hospital National Medical Center, Washington, D.C. (April).

Briere, Jon, and Marsha Runtz. 1988. "Symptomatology associated with Prior Sexual Abuse in a Non-Clinical Sample." *Child Abuse and Neglect* 12: 51–59.

Burgess, Ann W. 1984. *Child Pornography and Sex Rings.* Lexington, MA: Lexington.

Burgess, Ann W., Lynda Lytle Holmstrom, and Maureen P. McCausland. 1977. "Child Sexual Abuse by a Family Member: Decisions Following Disclosure." *Victimology: An International Journal* 2, no. 2: 236–250.

Child Abuse Prevention and Treatment Act, as Amended. June 25, 2003. Washington, DC: US Department of Health and Human Services.

Claxton-Oldfield, Stephen, and Lisa Whitt. 2003. "Child Abuse in Stepfather Families: Do People Think It Occurs More Often Than It Does in Biological Father Families?" *Journal of Divorce and Remarriage* 40: 17–33.

Conte, Jon R. 1985. "Clinical Dimensions of Adult Sexual Abuse of Children." *Behavioral Sciences and the Law* 3: 341–354.

Conte, Jon R. 1986. *A Look at Child Sexual Abuse.* Chicago: National Committee for Prevention of Child Abuse.

Conte, Jon R., ed. 2002. *Critical Issues in Child Sexual Abuse: Historical, Legal and Psychological Perspectives.* Thousand Oaks, CA: Sage.

Courtois, Christine. 1979. "The Incest Experience and Its Aftermath." *Victimology: An International Journal* 4: 337–347.

Crewdson, John. 1988. *By Silence Betrayed: Sexual Abuse of Children in America*. Boston: Little, Brown.

Daly, Lawrence J. 2004. "Police Officers Do Not Receive Adequate Training to Prepare Them to Handle Child Sexual Abuse Investigations." Northfield, MN: Institute for Psychological Therapies. Available at: http://www.ipt-forensics.com/journal/issues04.htm (accessed September 28, 2006).

DeYoung, Mary. 1982. *The Sexual Victimization of Children*. Jefferson, NC: McFarland.

Faller, Kathleen Coulborn. 1993. *Child Sexual Abuse: Intervention and Treatment Issues*. Washington, DC: National Center on Child Abuse and Neglect.

Finkelhor, David. 1979. *Sexually Victimized Children*. New York: Free Press.

Finkelhor, David. 1982. "Child Sexual Abuse in a Sample of Boston Families." Unpublished paper. Durham, NH: University of New Hampshire Family Violence Research Program.

Finkelhor, David. 1984. *Child Sexual Abuse: New Theory and Research*. New York: Free Press.

Finkelhor, David. 1986. *A Sourcebook on Child Sexual Abuse*. Newbury Park, CA: Sage.

Finkelhor, David, and Sharon Araji. 1983. "The Prevention of Child Sexual Abuse: A Review of Current Approaches." Unpublished paper prepared for the National Center on Prevention and Control of Rape.

Finkelhor, David, Linda Williams, and Nanci Burns. 1988. *Sexual Abuse in Day Care: A National Study*. Durham, NH: University of New Hampshire Family Laboratory.

Forward, Susan, and Craig Buck. 1978. *Betrayal of Innocence: Incest and Its Devastation*. New York: Penguin.

Fraser, B. G. 1981. "Sexual Child Abuse: The Legislation and the Law in the United States." In *Sexually Abused Children and Their Families*, edited by Patricia Beezley Mrazek and C. Henry Kempe. New York: Pergamon.

Gillham, Bill. 1991. *The Facts about Child Sexual Abuse*. London: Cassell Educational.

Goodman, Gail S., J. E. Hirschman, D. Hepps, and L. Rudy. 1991. "Children's Memory for Stressful Events." *Merrill-Palmer Quarterly* 37: 109–158.

Goodman, Gail S., L. Rudy, B. L. Bottoms, and C. Aman. 1990. "Children's Concerns and Memory: Issues of Ecological Validity in the Study of Children's Eyewitness Testimony." In *Knowing and Remembering in Young Children,* edited by R. Fivush and J. Hudson. New York: Cambridge University Press.

Gordon, Linda. 1988. *Heroes of Their Own Lives: The Politics and History of Family Violence, Boston 1880–1960.* New York: Viking.

Gordon, M., and S. J. Creighton. 1988. "Natal and Non-Natal Fathers as Sexual Abusers in the United Kingdom: A Comparative Analysis." *Journal of Marriage and the Family* 50, no. 1: 99–105.

Groth, Nicholas A. 1978. "Guidelines for Assessment and Management of the Offender." In *Sexual Assault of Children and Adolescents,* edited by Ann Burgess et al. Lexington, MA: Lexington.

Herman, Judith L. 1981. *Father-Daughter Incest.* Cambridge, MA: Harvard University Press.

Hollenberg, Elizabeth, and Cynthia Ragan. 1991. *Child Sexual Abuse: Selected Projects.* Washington, DC: National Center on Child Abuse and Neglect.

Holmes, S. T., and R. M. Holmes. 2002. *Sex Crimes: Pattern and Behavior.* Thousand Oaks, CA: Sage.

Hunter, Mic. 1990. *Abused Boys: The Neglected Victims of Sexual Abuse.* New York: Columbine.

Katchen, Martin H., and David K. Sakheim. 1992. "Satanic Beliefs and Practices." In *Out of Darkness: Exploring Satanism and Ritual Abuse,* edited by David K. Sakheim and Susan E. Devine. New York: Lexington.

Kelley, Susan J. 1988. "Ritualistic Abuse of Children: Dynamics and Impact." *Cultic Studies Journal* 5: 228–236.

Kempe, Ruth S., and C. Henry Kempe. 1984. *The Common Secret: Sexual Abuse of Children and Adolescents.* New York: W. H. Freeman.

Lanning, Kenneth V. 1991. "Ritual Abuse: A Law Enforcement View or Perspective." *Child Abuse and Neglect* 15: 171–173.

Lanning, Kenneth V. 1992. *Child Sex Rings: A Behavioral Analysis.* Arlington, VA: National Center for Missing and Exploited Children.

Lanning, Kenneth V. 2001. *Child Molesters: A Behavioral Analysis.* Arlington, VA: National Center for Missing and Exploited Children.

Laws, D. R., and W. L. Marshall. 1990. "A Conditioning Theory of the Etiology and Maintenance of Deviant Sexual Preference and Behavior." Pp. 257–275 in *Handbook of Sexual Assault: Issues, Theories, and Treatment of the Offender,* edited by W. L. Marshall. New York: Plenum.

Lew, Mike. 1988. *Victims No Longer: Men Recovering from Incest and Other Sexual Child Abuse.* New York: Harper and Row.

Lloyd, David. 1990a. *Ritual Sexual Abuse: Understanding the Controversies.* Huntsville, AL: National Resource Center on Child Sexual Abuse.

Lloyd, David. 1990b. *Sibling Incest: Proceedings of a Think Tank.* Huntsville, AL: National Children's Advocacy Center.

Lowe, Walter, Thomas Pavkov, Casanova Gisele, and Joseph Wetchler. 2005. "Do American Ethnic Cultures Differ in Their Definitions of Child Sexual Abuse?" *American Journal of Family Therapy* 33, no. 2: 147–166.

MacFarlane, Kee. 1978. "Sexual Abuse of Children." In *The Victimization of Women,* edited by J. Chapman and M. Gates. Beverly Hills, CA: Sage.

Marques, J. K., C. Nelson, J. M. Alarcon, and D. M. Day. 2000. "Prevention Relapse in Sex Offenders: What We Learned from SOTEP's Experimental Treatment Program." Pp. 321–340 in *Remaking Relapse Prevention with Sex Offenders,* edited by D. R. Laws. Thousand Oaks, CA: Sage.

Marshall, L. E., and W. L. Marshall. 2002. "The Role of Attachment in Sexual Offending: An Examination of Preoccupied-attachment-style Offending Behavior." Pp. 1–7 in *The Sex Offender: Current Treatment Modalities and Systems Issues,* edited by Barbara Schwartz. Kingston, NJ: Civic Research Institute.

Marshall, W. L. 1989. "Intimacy, Loneliness and Sexual Offenders." *Behavior Research Therapy* 27: 491–503.

Marshall, W. L., and H. E. Barbaree. 1990. "An Integrated Theory of the Etiology of Sexual Offending." Pp. 257–275 in *Handbook of Sexual Assault: Issues, Theories, and Treatment of the Offender,* edited by W. L. Marshall. New York: Plenum.

Meiselman, Karin. 1978. *Incest: A Psychological Study of Causes and Effects with Treatment Recommendations.* San Francisco: Jossey-Bass.

Moorehead, Caroline, ed. 1990. *Betrayal: A Report on Violence toward Children in Today's World.* New York: Doubleday.

Mulloy R., and W. L. Marshall. 1999. "Social Functioning." Pp. 93–110 in *Cognitive Behavioral Treatment of Sexual Offenders,* edited by W. L. Marshall, D. Anderson, and Y. Fernandez. Chichester, West Sussex (England): John Wiley and Sons.

Nasjleti, M. 1980. "Suffering in Silence: The Male Incest Victim." *Child Welfare* 49: 269–275.

National Center on Child Abuse and Neglect (NCCAN). 1991. *Symposium on Judicial Needs Relating to Child Sexual Abuse.* Washington, DC: U.S. Department of Health and Human Services.

National Center for Missing and Exploited Children. 2002. *Female Juvenile Prostitution: Problem and Response.* Arlington, VA: National Center on Missing and Exploited Children.

Rush, Florence. 1980. *The Best Kept Secret: Sexual Abuse of Children.* New York: McGraw-Hill.

Russell, Diana E. 1984. "The Prevalence and Seriousness of Incestuous Abuse: Stepfathers vs. Biological Fathers." *Child Abuse and Neglect* 8: 15–22.

Russell, Diana E. 1986. *The Secret Trauma: Incest in the Lives of Girls and Women.* New York: Basic.

Schwartz, B., ed. 1995. *The Sex Offender: Corrections, Treatment and Legal Practice.* Kingston, NY: Civic Research Institute.

Seidman, B. T., W. L. Marshall, S. M. Hudson, and P. J. Robertson. 1994. "An Examination of Intimacy and Loneliness in Sex Offenders." *Journal of Interpersonal Violence* 9: 518–534.

Sgroi, Suzanne. 1982. *Handbook of Clinical Interventions in Child Sexual Abuse.* Lexington, MA: Lexington.

Sgroi, Suzanne. 1988. *Vulnerable Populations: Evaluation and Treatment of Sexually Abused Children and Adult Survivors.* Lexington, MA: Lexington.

Singer, M., M. Petchers, and D. Hussey. 1989. "The Relationship between Sexual Abuse and Substance Abuse among Psychiatrically Hospitalized Adolescents." *Child Abuse and Neglect* 13: 319–325.

Summit, Roland. 1983. "Child Sexual Abuse Accommodation Syndrome." *Child Abuse and Neglect* 7: 177–193.

Terry, Karen J., and Jennifer Tallon. 2004. *The Nature and Scope of the Problem of Sexual Abuse of Minors by Catholic Priests and Deacons in the United States.* New York: John Jay College of Criminal Justice.

U.S. Department of Health and Human Services, Administration for Children, Youth and Families. 2005. *Child Maltreatment 2003.* Washington, DC: U.S. Department of Health and Human Services.

Ward, T., K. Louden, S. M. Hudson, and W. L. Marshall. 1995. "A Descriptive Model of the Offence Chain for Child Molesters." *Journal of Interpersonal Violence* 10, no. 4: 452–472.

Whitcomb, Debra. 1992. *When the Victim Is a Child.* 2d ed. Washington, DC: National Institute of Justice.

Whitcomb, Debra, Gail S. Goodman, Desmond K. Runyan, and Shirley Hoak. 1994. "The Emotional Effects of Testifying on Sexually Abused Children." National Institute of Justice Research in Brief. U.S. Department of Justice (April).

Wiehe, Vernon N. 1990. *Sibling Abuse: Hidden Physical, Emotional, and Sexual Trauma.* Lexington, MA: Lexington.

Wonderlich, S. A., R. D. Crosby, J. E. Mitchell, and J. A. Roberts. 2000. "Relationship of Childhood Sexual Abuse and Eating Disturbance in Children." *Journal of the American Academy of Child and Adolescent Psychiatry* 39, no. 10: 1277–1283.

Ystgaard, Mette, Ingebjorg Hestetun, Mitchell Loeb, and Lars Mehlum. 2004. "Is There a Specific Relationship between Childhood Sexual and Physical Abuse and Repeated Suicidal Behavior?" *Child Abuse and Neglect* 28, no. 8: 863–875.

2

Problems, Controversies, and Solutions

This chapter will explore some of the major problems, issues, and controversies concerning child sexual abuse. Identifying children who have been sexually abused and the related difficulties in accurately estimating incidence and prevalence will be examined. The various types of perpetrators are examined, including teachers, coaches, and female offenders, as well as the question of whether homosexuals (especially male homosexuals) are more likely to abuse children sexually. Treatment options are explored, including the use of anatomically detailed dolls and issues with interviewing the mother when the father is the alleged abuser. Recidivism rates are discussed, and specifically the issue of whether child sexual abusers can be rehabilitated or "cured," and the use of chemical castration to control sexual urges. The controversies over the use of community notification laws are reviewed. Issues surrounding the various prevention programs are examined. Current controversies regarding repressed and false memories, as well as sexual abuse committed by Catholic clergy, are discussed.

Identifying Abuse

Many difficulties exist in accurately determining the number of children who have been sexually abused. For one thing, there are questions of children's credibility—that is, whether or not they can be believed when they claim to have been sexually abused. The validity of repressed memory is still being questioned. Researchers are not able to determine the number of children who are sexually abused because of the many reasons children have for not telling.

Estimates of Incidence and Prevalence of Sexual Abuse

Estimates of the number of children who are sexually abused are difficult to make. If the abuse is reported to the authorities, Child Protective Services usually becomes involved, and the numbers are reported. Most researchers agree, however, that more children are sexually abused than the number reported; the question is, how many more.

Numbers from the U.S. Department of Health and Human Services, Administration for Children, Youth and Families, indicate that the number of substantiated cases of child sexual abuse has fallen for the past several years, dropping 40 percent from 1992 to 2000. Researchers and other professionals in the field differ on the reasons for this decline. Finkelhor and Jones put forth six suggested reasons. One possible reason is that Child Protective Services (CPS) may have been adopting more conservative standards of identifying and counting the number of cases of child sexual abuse. Cases that involved allegations of abuse from children whose parents were divorced or in the process of getting a divorce, and cases involving allegations that appeared difficult to prove, were not being counted as official cases of abuse.

Second, CPS may not have been counting cases that did not involve a primary caregiver, since those cases are not within CPS jurisdiction. Because of increasing caseloads in many states, some state agencies have narrowed their focus and responsibilities. This may have eliminated a number of cases that otherwise would have been counted in the statistics. States have been required by law to treat cases of child sexual abuse by caretakers; in the past they also may have treated children who were abused by someone other than a caretaker, but because of shrinking budgets and increased caseloads, they may have narrowed their focus to caretakers only.

Third, there may have been changes to the data collection and classification methods. For example, some states went from classifying cases as substantiated, indicated, or unsubstantiated to classifying them as either substantiated or unsubstantiated.

Fourth, professionals have become hesitant to report such cases because of the negative publicity in the news media. There has been an increasing focus on false allegations, and an increased number of lawsuits being filed against those who have made reports of abuse.

Fifth, the 1980s brought an increased focus on child sexual abuse. As a result, older children as well as adults who had been sexually abused as children started reporting the abuse to the authorities. Therefore, reports of sexual abuse in the 1980s and 1990s included past as well as more recent cases of abuse.

Sixth, the decline could be real—that is, child sexual abuse is truly on the decline. Finkelhor and Jones find support for this hypothesis: (1) there has been a decline in the number of self-reports of sexual abuse; (2) other indicators of crime, sexual behavior, and family problems also show a drop in numbers over the same period; (3) child sexual abuse has seen increased focus since the early 1980s, with increased intervention and prevention activities; and (4) increased numbers of abusers have been incarcerated. They suggest that additional studies need to be conducted to examine this decline. Data-tracking systems should be improved, and evaluations of prevention efforts should be undertaken (Finkelhor and Jones 2004).

Children's Credibility

Many children who are sexually abused have no physical complaints or indications that they have been abused sexually, unless actual sexual intercourse or other penetration has occurred. Children who know their assailants generally experience less genital trauma than those who are abused by strangers, because "such trauma might arouse suspicion that abuse is occurring" (Hammerschlag 2002). Because there are frequently no physical symptoms associated with child sexual abuse and no physical evidence, one of the most important indicators of abuse is the child's account of the incident.

Several researchers agree that children are more susceptible than adults to providing the answers they think the interviewer wants, to conforming to expectations, and to responding to leading questions. While researchers disagree considerably on the extent of suggestibility and whether it actually leads to false allegations of sexual abuse, they generally agree that children are suggestible to such a significant degree that professionals in the field should be concerned (Ceci and Friedman 2000). The problem may be most severe when children are asked leading questions and are exposed to the use of other techniques that may suggest answers to them, an issue examined during and after the Mc-Martin trial and other trials of alleged sexual abuse of children in daycare settings.

Investigators have found that when a child is asked to tell the investigator what happened, in their own words, the child's information is generally more accurate than when the child is asked to respond to yes or no questions, or when asked leading questions. Unfortunately, the information provided by the child may not be very detailed. By asking questions to elicit additional information, the investigator risks encouraging the child to respond by providing information that the child thinks the investigator wants to hear. Researchers suggest that investigators should avoid asking suggestive questions, at least until they are convinced that the child can provide no additional information without help.

Perpetrators

Issues surrounding perpetrators of sexual abuse include the following: Are homosexuals more likely to be abusers, especially those in the priesthood, than heterosexuals? Can a sex offender be cured? Have community registration laws made children safer? Other issues include the crisis over priests in the Catholic Church sexually abusing children and the continuing revelations of teachers sexually abusing their students.

Homosexuals

Are homosexuals more likely to abuse children than are heterosexuals? In Shakeshaft and Cohan's (1995) study of sexual abuse of children committed by educators, 24 percent of the male educators targeted male students, and all of them described themselves as heterosexual. Earlier studies have found no relationship between homosexuality and male child sexual abuse. For example, Freund and his colleagues (1984) found no differences between the response of male homosexuals to pictures of male children and that of male heterosexuals to pictures of female children. Jenny et al. (1994) examined the medical records of 352 cases of child sexual abuse and found no indication that homosexuals were more likely to abuse children sexually than were heterosexuals; in only two cases was the molester a gay or lesbian adult.

After reviewing the scientific literature on this topic, Groth and Gary wrote:

> Are homosexual adults in general sexually attracted to children and are preadolescent children at greater risk of molestation from homosexual adults than from heterosexual adults? There is no reason to believe so. The research to date all points to there being no significant relationship between a homosexual lifestyle and child molestation. There appears to be practically no reportage of sexual molestation of girls by lesbian adults, and the adult male who sexually molests young boys is not likely to be homosexual. (Groth and Gary 1982, 147)

In 1998, McConaghy reviewed the literature on this topic and found no support for the theory that homosexuals are more likely to abuse children sexually than heterosexuals (McConaghy 1998).

Teachers

From teachers in local school districts around the country who have sexual relations with students and make the local news when they are caught, to Mary Kay Letourneau (see Chapter 5), who made national news after having a sexual relationship with one of her students, increasing numbers of reports of sexual abuse of students by teachers are in the headlines. Teachers are considered caregivers and "persons in a position of trust" and are held to a high standard of behavior around children. Just like the public's reaction to news of priests and other clergy sexually abusing children, society does not expect teachers to break that sacred trust.

There have been no national prevalence or incidence studies that focused on sexual abuse of children by teachers. Some studies have examined this topic as part of a larger prevalence or incidence study, or on a regional basis. For example, Cameron and his colleagues studied the sexual attitudes and experiences of 4,340 adults. One question concerned sexual advances made toward the individual by various caretakers, and 4.1 percent of the respondents reported a physical sexual experience with a teacher

(Cameron et al. 1986). In a survey of 1989 high school graduates in North Carolina, Wishnietsky studied the extent of sexual abuse by teachers. He found that 17.5 percent of the graduates reported that they had experienced sexual touching by a teacher, and 13.5 percent reported having had sexual intercourse with a teacher (Wishnietsky 1991).

Stein and her colleagues analyzed data gathered from a sexual abuse survey published in *Seventeen* magazine. The response to the survey included approximately 4,200 girls in grades 2 through 12 who reported that they had experienced sexual harassment or abuse during the school year. Of those, 3.7 percent said that a teacher, administrator, counselor, or other staff member was the abuser (Stein et al. 1993).

Shakeshaft examined data gathered for the American Association of University Women in 2000; respondents included students in 8th through 11th grade who were asked about their experiences of sexual harassment or abuse. An analysis of the data indicated that 9.6 percent of all respondents reported contact or noncontact sexual misconduct that was unwanted; 8.7 percent reported only noncontact sexual misconduct; and 6.7 percent reported contact misconduct (Shakeshaft 2003).

In terms of numbers of male and female teachers who sexually abuse students, studies indicate a wide disparity between male and female perpetrators: Hendrie (1998) examined newspaper articles reporting on sexual abuse of students by teachers and found that 20 percent were female teachers and 80 percent male teachers (in 244 cases over a six-month period). Gallagher (2000) reported 4 percent female and 96 percent male in his study. Jennings and Tharp (2003) found that 12.7 percent of perpetrators were female and 87.3 percent were male in a study of 606 teachers in Texas who were disciplined for sexual misconduct.

In addition to the concern over teachers having sexual contact with students, some observers believe that once a teacher is found to have had sexual contact with a student, male teachers appear to receive a more severe penalty than female teachers. In 2005 a twenty-five-year-old female schoolteacher in Florida, Debra Lefave, was charged and pleaded guilty to two counts of lewd and lascivious battery for having had sexual relations with a fourteen-year-old student. Lefave avoided a prison sentence with her plea and will serve three years of house arrest and seven years on probation. Several other examples can be found of female teachers who have also received light sentences. Pamela Diehl-Moore pleaded guilty in 2000 to sexual assault (for having had a sexual relationship with a thirteen-year-old male student) as part of a plea agreement to avoid a three-year prison sentence. Tiffany Copley, a former teacher, received a one-to-fifteen-year prison sentence, with all but six months suspended, for having had sexual relations with two fifteen-year-old boys. LeFave's and Moore's plea agreements, as well as other well-publicized cases of child sexual abuse committed by teachers, have led to discussions of whether female offenders are considered less of a threat to reoffend and as a result receive lighter sentences when convicted. Research is just beginning to examine this topic.

Not every state has a specific law prohibiting sexual relations between teachers and students. Those states that do not have specific laws often rely on statutory rape laws to prosecute offenders.

Another issue relating to teachers who sexually abuse children is the lack of a national register of teachers who have been found guilty or convicted of the sexual abuse of students. Not unlike the hierarchy in the Catholic Church, which often would move a priest who was accused of sexual abuse of children to another parish, school officials may protect a teacher who has been accused of sexually abusing children by allowing the teacher to resign when accused of sexual abuse (this is successful only when charges are not brought against the teacher). Those advocating for a national system of notification and registration of teachers convicted of child sexual abuse argue that such a system would protect children.

Female Offenders

Women committed only 3.5 percent of all sexual assaults or rapes committed by a single perpetrator in 2003, according to the U.S. Bureau of Justice Statistics, which is consistent with the rate since 1996. As a result of the small number of women who sexually abuse children, few studies have been conducted on the characteristics of female offenders. In a 1991 comparative study of men and women who sexually abuse children, Allen examined seventy-five male and sixty-five female perpetrators in the Midwest. Results indicated that charges were lodged against male and female offenders in almost equal numbers (55 percent of the men and 52 percent of the women). Surprisingly, this study found that female offenders were more likely to receive jail sentences than male offenders (30 percent of the women, versus 25 percent of the men) (Allen 1991).

Denov (2003) believes that the number of female sex offenders is higher than statistics indicate. She examined previous research and advances the theory that women are seen as generally incapable of aggressive behavior, that they are seen as nurturing, protective of others, caring, and nonsexual. The general societal perception is that a woman could not sexually abuse a child. Other researchers have found similar results. For example, one study surveyed 180 female and 180 male undergraduates on their perceptions of the effects of sexual abuse on the child. The undergraduates generally viewed sexual abuse of a male by a female as less representative of this type of abuse than the sexual abuse of a female by a male, and they viewed the effects of the abuse as less harmful to males than to females (Broussard et al. 1991).

Coaches

A special relationship often exists between sports coaches and their players. Players look up to coaches for guidance and trust their advice, and advice is often given concerning the larger issues of life, not just sports. Some coaches have taken advantage of their position of trust and have sexually abused children in their care. For example, in 2002, a volunteer basketball coach in Brooklyn, New York, pleaded guilty to sexually abusing a twelve-year-old girl during practice at the YMCA. Prior to that, he had been convicted of sexually abusing several girls and had received a sixty-day jail term (Katz 2002). In 2003, a soccer coach was found guilty of the sexual abuse of six boys while they were traveling on soccer team trips in New York (Gibbons and Campbell 2003).

Some individuals and organizations have called for a national registry of coaches, like the one proposed for teachers, to help protect children. Others have called for more stringent screening of coaches, but no uniform solution has been adopted. Some sports organizations screen the individuals who apply for coaching and other staff positions; in some organizations the screening is mandatory, while in others it is voluntary.

Juvenile Sex Offenders

The number of juveniles involved in sexual offenses against other juveniles and children is growing in the United States. While at one time this behavior was attributed to a "boys will be boys" attitude, law enforcement officials are now treating this behavior more seriously. Researchers began to discover that many adult sexual offenders they studied had begun their abusive behavior while they were juveniles (Righthand and Welch 2001).

Professionals have distinguished two types of juvenile sex offenders: those that abuse peers or adults, and others that target children (ibid.). Each group has distinctive characteristics, according to several researchers. Juvenile sex offenders who abuse their peers or adults tend to prefer to assault females. They are more likely to commit the sexual offense in conjunction with other criminal activity; are more likely to have a history of criminal behavior, including nonsexual offenses; and are more likely to display other delinquent-type behavior, higher levels of aggressive and violent behavior, and to employ a weapon in committing the assault. Juvenile sex offenders who tend to abuse younger children victimize girls at a slightly higher rate than boys. Almost half of the offenders assault at least one male. Almost half are siblings or relatives of the abused child; they tend to have low self-esteem, are frequently depressed, and often lack social skills (Richardson et al. 1997; Monto et al. 1998; Kaufman et al. 1996).

Treatment

Issues concerning treatment include the best treatment methods, effects of the treatment on the child and family, the effectiveness of anatomically detailed dolls, problems interviewing the mother when the father or other male relative is the abuser, confronting the abuser, recidivism rates, and treatment options such as chemical or physical castration.

In research for the National Center on Child Abuse and Neglect, Berliner and Conte studied the effects of disclosures and intervention on children who have been sexually abused. They found that these children did not associate the process of intervention with any negative feelings or impacts. The idea that removing a child from the home after sexual abuse has occurred causes more stress than the abuse itself was not supported in their findings. Berliner and Conte did discover, however, that children were less anxious when their parents and the professionals they were interacting with were honest about what was happening and what would happen to them; children who were shielded from that knowledge were more anxious. Children were also capable of understanding the need for intervention, yet the level of the children's anxiety increased as the number of professionals with whom they were required to interact rose. The researchers concluded that professionals working with sexually abused children must consider each child individually, not rely on parents for accurate reports of the child's anxiety levels. They also found that the experience of testifying in court is not necessarily traumatic to the child (Berliner and Conte 1990).

In assessing the sexually abused child and determining the appropriate treatment, Sgroi considers ten important issues that may have an impact on the decision to provide services and treatment to the child: the "damaged goods" syndrome, guilt, fear, depression, low self-esteem and poor social skills, repressed anger and hostility, inability to trust, blurred role boundaries and role confusion, pseudomaturity, and self-mastery and control (Sgroi 1998).

In studying current treatment approaches and programs, Hollenberg and Ragan found that

> [c]urrent research indicates that significant gaps exist in available treatment services in cases of child sexual abuse. Perhaps because child sexual abuse has been regarded primarily as the child's problem, most of the available treatment programs limit their focus to the child victim following an incident of sexual abuse. It is increasingly apparent, however, that sexual abuse is part of a cluster of serious intergenerational family problems that need to be addressed through family-oriented treatment. This is most apparent in regard to the importance of maternal support, which several studies have found to be a vital resource for the sexually abused child's recovery. Thus, mental health services that target a range of familial problems and help nonoffending parents support their sexually abused children may contribute positively to the children's recovery. (Hollenberg and Ragan 1991, 184–185)

The Use of Anatomically Detailed Dolls

Anatomically detailed dolls, formerly known as anatomically correct dolls, are usually cloth dolls with certain body features (fingers, mouths, penises, vaginal openings, anal openings, and pubic hair) that allow children to demonstrate any sexual activities in which they were involved. They were introduced in the late 1970s and became popular in the 1990s, being used in preparing for many of the day-care sexual abuse trials.

The use of anatomically detailed dolls is one means of assessing the extent and nature of the alleged sexual abuse. Some professionals are adamant about the reliability and validity of using these dolls, while other experts believe that their use does not yield reliable results. Proponents believe that the dolls help the child recall details of the sexual abuse and provide a means of expressing what happened to them by allowing them to show the abuse rather than trying to verbalize the experience. On the other hand, some professionals argue that the dolls may suggest possibilities to children that lead to false allegations of sexual abuse, may encourage sexual exploration without actually validating previous abuse, may encourage children to fantasize about events, and may be too suggestive for young children to understand.

In a study comparing abused and nonabused children and their actions in playing with anatomically detailed dolls, Jampole and Weber found that those children who were sexually abused were more likely than the nonabused children to involve the dolls in sexual activities: only two nonabused children out of ten engaged the dolls in sexual play (Jampole and Weber 1987). In another study, Glaser and Collins found that children used the dolls in 78 percent of their play activities, and only two out of the eighty-six nonabused children incorporated sexual activities in their play with the dolls (Glaser and Collins 1989). Other studies have shown similar results. Some report that none of their nonabused children involved the dolls in any type of sexual activity (Sivan et al. 1988; August and Foreman 1988). While these studies indicate that only children who have been sexually abused are likely to have the dolls engage in sexual activities, some studies do indicate that nonabused children will sometimes engage in sexual doll play. Ceci and Bruck believe that the dolls should not be used for evaluating or diagnosing children who may have been abused or raped. Because the use of these dolls is not standardized, additional research should be conducted before accepting the validity of the results (Ceci and Bruck 1995).

Even if the dolls themselves are not suggestive, some researchers argue that therapists and other professionals can use them in suggestive ways, depending on how they are introduced to the child and what types of questions are asked. Cathy Maan suggests that training should be provided to all professionals involved in using these dolls to treat children who have been sexually abused (Maan 1994). Maan reports that the American Professional Society on the Abuse of Children has developed preliminary guidelines on ways to use these dolls in investigating cases of sexual abuse of children. She cites five uses that the organization views as acceptable:

1. As an icebreaker to help initiate discussions with children about sexual matters.
2. As anatomical models (for example, to assess children's knowledge of bodily functions).
3. To help children demonstrate rather than describe their experiences. This is especially important if the children's verbal skills are limited, or if they are too embarrassed to describe their experiences.
4. As a stimulus for children's memories. (For example, features of the dolls such as pubic hair or genitalia may help sexually abused children remember the details of the abuse.)
5. As a screen. Exposure to the dolls represents an opportunity for children to spontaneously disclose aspects of their sexual abuse. (ibid., 3)

Some sexual abuse investigators find the use of dollhouses beneficial, especially with preschoolers. These dollhouses should be fairly sturdy and large and can provide a context in which the child can describe the abusive behavior. The child can position dolls within the dollhouse to show where the abuse took place, and it may help them to remember certain events. The use of dollhouses also can provide another opportunity for the investigator to get to know the child, and to provide an understanding of how the child thinks about family and family activities (Faller 1993).

Interviewing the Mother

If the child has been sexually abused by the father or stepfather, the mother is often put in an extremely stressful situation, caught between her husband and her child. However, interviewing the mother is critically important in determining her ability to support the child. As Faller states:

> A major purpose of the initial interview with the mother is to assess her ability to provide support for the child. Mothers whose children have been sexually victimized by someone who is close to them, such as a spouse, are placed in a very difficult position. Often they have no inkling of the abuse until confronted by a professional. Mothers who are consciously aware of the victimization and condone or accept it are extremely rare. However, some mothers ignore signs of sexual abuse, for a variety of reasons, or are preoccupied with matters other than their children's well-being. . . .
>
> [I]nitial denial is common. . . . Mothers should not be disparaged because they require time and sometimes treatment to believe their children have been sexually abused. Only when denial persists for months in the face of compelling evidence, and the victim is blamed, should the mother be considered unworkable. (ibid., 34)

Kempe and Kempe also believe that the mother should be helped to recognize and understand her own emotions and feelings. They observe that "the mother often feels criticized and pressured by both professionals and friends to divorce her husband in order to appear to be a good mother" (Kempe and Kempe 1984, 148). Mothers should be encouraged to take their time, to try to sort out and understand everything that is happening to them, and to determine what is in their own best interest as well as that of the child.

Information to be gathered from the mother includes past history of abuse or neglect, past history of sexual abuse, current living situation, education level, employment history, parenting skills, style of discipline, relationship with spouse or partner, sexual history, history of substance abuse or mental illness, criminal history, and beliefs about the allegations of sexual abuse of the child. This same information should be gathered from the offender.

Confronting the Abuser

For people who admit, as adults, that they were abused as children, and for people who recover repressed memories of abuse as children, some therapists believe that healing from these experiences can occur only if they confront the abuser. However, confrontation is often a serious undertaking, to be considered very carefully and thoughtfully. Mike Lew suggests that for some people it could be a "logical next step in recovery; for others it could be a dangerous and self-destructive act" (Lew 1988, 228). He believes that confrontation means facing the abuse and standing up to it, not necessarily having a direct encounter with the abuser. "Confrontation is not the goal of recovery, it is a tool for recovery. Its value lies in how it is used. You deserve to take enough time to make the best decision for yourself. You can change your mind about the confrontation at any time during this process" (ibid., 231).

In her book with Katherine Ketchum, Dr. Elizabeth Loftus, a psychologist and leading expert in the field of memory, discusses the fact that many people who have retrieved repressed memories of abuse with the help of therapists are then asked whether they want to confront the abuser with those memories:

> She can either continue with therapy, working to resolve her grief and rage in a private, noncombative way, or she can choose to stand up to the abuse (and stand up for herself) by confronting her abusers. The decision to confront is never promoted as easy or risk-free. Most incest-survival authors warn that confrontations should be considered only if and when the survivor is fully prepared and well along the road to recovery. (Loftus and Ketcham 1994, 171)

Most people who consider confronting their abusers are told to build up their support systems (of friends and relatives), to rehearse the meeting, and to analyze their reasons for wanting to confront the abuser. Once they face their abuser, they are often met with denial and outrage on the part of the accused. Lew suggests that the accuser remember that he or she is not required to provide proof or to convince the abuser or the rest of the family that the abuse actually did happen. The only purpose should be to free the person abused—in essence, to "take back your power, to prove to yourself that you will not be frightened or controlled any longer, and thus to guarantee that you will never be a victim again" (Lew 1988, 231).

Laws concerning the sexual exploitation of children have been passed in all states, and in 1977 the U.S. Congress passed the Federal Protection of Children against Sexual Exploitation Act, which has been amended several times since it first became law.

In 1984 the U.S. Attorney General's Task Force on Family Violence issued its recommendations, which would minimize the trauma to the victim of violence while still protecting the rights of the accused. The recommendations included using the same prosecutor throughout the court process, allowing hearsay evidence at preliminary hearings to minimize the number of times the victim is required to testify, allowing the child's testimony to be presented on videotape, using anatomically detailed dolls to describe abuse, appointing a special volunteer advocate for the child, legally presuming that children are competent witnesses, permitting flexible courtroom settings, controlling press coverage, and limiting court continuances of each case (U.S. Attorney General's Task Force on Family Violence 1984).

Recidivism

Arguments have been made for incarcerating the perpetrator for the remainder of his or her life, believing that there are no successful means of treating people who sexually abuse children. Other experts believe that at least some perpetrators can be saved—that is, they can be successfully treated.

The primary issue in treating sexual offenders is whether or not they can be treated and safely released back into society. Little research has been conducted on this topic; many of the studies focus on offenders being caught and convicted a second or third time. Because the focus is on being convicted again, many experts believe that the studies do not adequately measure the reoccurrence of sexual abuse; most sexual abuse of children is not reported and does not come to the attention of the proper authorities. Also, many offenders, especially family members, are never convicted and sent to prison, which makes studying them extremely difficult.

Finkelhor also questions the generalizability of results obtained from criminal justice system subjects:

> A major problem with research on sexual abusers has to
> do with the fact that almost all such research is based on

subjects recruited from the criminal justice system, either incarcerated offenders or probationers in treatment. This fact certainly casts doubt on the generalizability of almost all known findings about sexual abusers. Incarcerated offenders or probationers in treatment constitute at most a very tiny and unrepresentative fraction of all sexual abusers. . . . Thus those sex abusers who are convicted or even seen within the criminal justice system are a small fraction of all offenders, and probably those who were most flagrant and repetitive in their offending, most socially disadvantaged, and least able to persuade criminal justice authorities to let them off. It seems virtually certain that such a group cannot be deemed representative of offenders. (Finkelhor 1986, 138)

Several studies found that men who sexually abused boys or were exhibitionists were more likely to repeat their offenses than those who sexually abused girls (Frisbee and Dondis 1965). Other researchers also have found that those who sexually abuse boys often start the abuse earlier and are more committed to their pedophilia as a lifestyle (Quinsey et al. 1995; Groth 1979). In 1980, Meyer and Romero discovered that only two factors predicted recidivism: a prior arrest for a sex offense and a history of indecent exposure (Meyer and Romero 1980).

Brian Abbott studied the reoffense rates of incest offenders eight years after treatment. He studied seventy-two offenders who were accepted into the Child Sexual Abuse Treatment Program (CSATP) in San Jose, California. These offenders had a parent/child–type relationship with the abused children (father, stepfather, adoptive father, uncle, grandfather, etc.); a bond of trust had existed between the child and the offender, and the offender did not show any evidence of a primary sexual attraction to children. The offenders were treated in the CSATP: twenty-six completed the program, twenty were discharged because of lack of progress, and twenty-six left the program prematurely. Recidivism rates were studied over an eight-year period. The reoffense rate for the overall sample was 5.5 percent. All reoffenders came from the group who were discharged from the program for lack of progress. Abbott concludes:

These findings indicate that treating the incest offender in the community in conjunction with a county jail sentence and probation supervision does not significantly jeopardize community safety and, in fact, the offender is less likely to re-offend than if committed to state prison, with or without treatment. This finding is of importance in light of the fact that it is much more cost-effective to treat the offender in the community rather than committing him to state prison either with or without treatment. (Abbott 1991, 27–28)

In another study, researchers found that 19 percent of those abusers who sexually abused their own children, compared with 29 percent of abusers who abused other children, were recidivists—that is, they continued to abuse children after they were initially caught (Smith et al. 1985).

Bedarf (1995) analyzed recidivism rates of sex offenders and found that as early as 1950, before there was widespread knowledge of sex offenders, the recidivism rate was only 7 percent. In 1965, only 10 percent of the 3,000 sex offenders followed for up to twenty-four years were subsequently convicted of another sexual offense. In the 1970s, mental health professionals believed that sex offenders had high recidivism rates, while law enforcement personnel and criminologists were re-examining their beliefs that sex offenders had high recidivism rates. Many of these studies examined all sex offenders, not just those involved in child sexual abuse.

A 1994 study of data from prisons in fifteen states examined recidivism rates for sex offenders; the 9,691 offenders released represent two-thirds of all male sex offenders released from all state prisons in the United States. An analysis of the data indicated that 4,295 of the sex offenders released had been convicted of child sexual abuse. When compared with the 9,691 sex offenders released and the 262,420 non–sex offenders released during the study period, the researchers found that the child sexual abusers were more likely to be rearrested for sexually abusing a child (Langan et al. 2003).

A meta-analysis of recidivism studies conducted by Hanson and Bussiere found that the overall recidivism rate for sex offenders who abused children was 12.7 percent, while the rate for rapists was 18.7 percent (Hanson and Bussiere 1998). Within the group of sex offenders who abuse children, men who were convicted of the sexual abuse of a family member were less likely to reoffend than men who sexually abused an unrelated child (Quinsey et al. 1995).

Chemical Castration

One suggested means to prevent offenders from offending again is chemical castration or some other type of hormonal treatment that suppresses the offender's sexual drive. For example, the drug medroxyprogesterone acetate (Depo Provera), which has primarily been used for birth control by women, and cyproterone, which has been used to control prostate cancer, both suppress the male sex drive.

Beginning in the 1990s, state legislatures as well as the governments in some foreign countries enacted legislation that requires certain sex offenders to submit to chemical castration in order to be released back into society. California passed a law in 1996 that mandated chemical castration for repeat child sex offenders. Florida's law, passed in 1997, provides offenders with the option of choosing physical castration, while Georgia's law requires sexual offenders who have molested children to take hormone shots that lower their sex drives. Montana's law, passed in 1997, allows judges to impose chemical castration for repeat rapists and child molesters.

Groups such as the ACLU argue against both chemical and physical castration of sex offenders in prison, claiming that it is unconstitutional. Castration interferes with an individual's right to procreate and the right to refuse medical treatment. Under the law in some states, the judge ultimately determines whether the offender should be castrated; if chemically castrated, it is the judge who will determine if and when the offender stops using the drug. To many, mandatory chemical castration is not medical treatment but, rather, cruel and unusual punishment. Also, its effectiveness is questionable, since some offenders may be able to counteract the drug's effects with other drugs. Also, the administration of the drugs does not get to the underlying psychological reasons for the deviant behavior (Spalding 1997).

Other researchers believe that chemical or physical castration—or the use of both—is the best way to protect the public from repeat sexual offenders. Many offenders will serve their time and be released from prison; because the success rate for rehabilitating sex offenders is low, most sexual offenders will likely be back on the streets to molest another child. In addition, many see castration as treatment for the offender rather than as punishment.

Repression/False Memories

The subject of repressed memories continues to be controversial. In the past several years, many articles and books have been written about adults who recall—often with the help of a therapist—one or more incidents of sexual abuse that they experienced as a child but have just recently remembered. Therapists who work with these adults, as well as other experts in the field, truly believe that the memories are real; how could someone recall these experiences, often quite vividly and in great detail, if they did not really happen? Yet other experts, as well as the families of these "victims," often believe that the accounts are fabricated. They question how anyone could forget something as serious as sexual abuse; many believe that therapists, using a checklist of symptoms of child sexual abuse, incorrectly identify the client's current problems as child sexual abuse.

Therapists who believe in repressed memories often are looking for something that happened in a person's childhood to explain why the person currently suffers from depression, obesity, anxiety, anorexia, or an assortment of other problems. They use a checklist that includes such symptoms as difficulty falling or staying asleep, nightmares, feeling different from other people, fear of the dark, fear of trying new experiences, and eating disorders. The therapists discover that their clients have a number of these characteristics, and they suggest sexual abuse as a possible cause of the clients' problems. Many clients will at first deny that they were sexually abused as children, but, desperate to find a cause for their problems and open to therapists' suggestions, they may start thinking about the possibility of abuse. With their therapist's help and over time, many clients start to believe that they were indeed sexually abused as children and begin to remember specific instances of abuse.

The mental health profession has been divided over the concept of repressed memories. Some researchers and clinicians believe that childhood sexual abuse can be determined by a set profile, a group of characteristics that can be checked off a list, and that repressed memories are valid indicators of such abuse. Victims of sexual abuse can be treated only by confronting these memories, believing them, and working to overcome their life problems. Other clinicians and researchers are less ready to acknowledge the validity of repressed memories in identifying abuse victims. They believe that therapists may inadvertently help a person believe that he or she was sexually abused as a child based on minimal evidence—especially if a checklist of various characteristics is used.

The American Psychological Association (APA) believes that most adults who were sexually abused as children remember the abuse, even though they may not understand exactly what happened or why. Researchers who study the dynamics of human memory agree that memories can be forgotten and, after a certain amount of time has passed, can be recalled. Memories can also be suggested to a person and then "remembered" as a true event. Further research into repressed and recovered memories is needed to better understand this controversial topic. In the meantime, until more is known about memory and repressed memory, the APA believes that psychiatrists must focus on helping their clients resolve their problems without letting their own personal beliefs influence the patient (American Psychological Association 2006).

People who believe that repressed memories of early childhood sexual abuse are true believe that many traumatic memories are hidden away in our unconscious minds, although some of the emotions associated with them work their way into our conscious lives and can have a major effect on how we see life and cope with its many problems. They believe that the mind buries these terrible memories; when we are better able to cope with them, usually with the help of therapists, we are able to pull these memories from the hidden recesses of our brains and recall these experiences in great detail. Only by bringing these memories into our conscious minds are we able to work them out—and help resolve many of our current problems that have been created by these experiences.

Sigmund Freud was convinced that emotions can be powerful enough to block memory, that traumatic memories can be repressed and may never become conscious. He compared the recovery of repressed memories to excavating an ancient buried city, one layer at a time. Using the case of Lucy R., Freud demonstrated his theory that "an idea must be intentionally repressed from consciousness" in order for hysterical symptoms to develop in a person (Freud and Breuer 1895). Even though Freud changed his mind regarding his theory about hysteria (that women become hysterical because of something that happened to them sexually in early life), Judith Herman believes that the "legacy of Freud's inquiry into the subject of incest was a tenacious prejudice, still shared by professionals and laymen alike, that children lie about sexual abuse" (Herman 1981, 11).

Ellen Bass and Laura Davis believe that repressed memories are often found in victims of childhood sexual abuse (Bass and Davis 1994). E. Sue Blume also believes that repression is a common characteristic among all survivors of childhood sexual abuse (Blume 1990).

For many researchers and other professionals in the field of child sexual abuse, it is easy to believe that children may repress these memories, especially if the abuse is committed by the child's father. Fathers are supposed to be the protectors of the family—they are not supposed to hurt their own children. Many people believe that there can be nothing worse for a child to bear than to have been sexually abused by the person that he or she trusts the most.

Dr. Elizabeth Loftus believes that, despite decades of research on various aspects of memory, no scientific evidence currently exists to support the idea that memories of trauma are routinely repressed and reliably recovered years later. Her research has "helped to create a new paradigm of memory, shifting our view from the video-recorder model, in which memories are interpreted as the literal truth, to a reconstructionist model, in which memories are understood as creative blendings of fact and fiction" (Loftus and Ketcham 1994, 5).

Many experts, including Loftus, understand the importance of memory and our belief that we can trust our memories, that they are reliable and can help us make sense of our lives. Most people do not want to believe that their minds, their memories, can play tricks on them, that they can distort their reality and provide a false sense of history, of what has happened in their lives.

Michael Yapko also questioned the validity of repressed memories. He believes that culture and current social conditions play a role in the growth of the belief in repressed memories:

> [T]he epidemic of allegations of child sexual abuse does not exist independently of the culture in which the allegations are made. In the past, when therapists were convinced that abuse reports were sheer fantasy, there wasn't much of an abuse problem. Now that the media and the mental health profession have announced that it is widespread, we are beginning to see the phenomenon

in more and more instances.... [In] ever-increasing numbers, therapists all across the country are actively or passively encouraging clients to identify themselves as victims of abuse—or, to be "politically correct," as "abuse survivors." (Yapko 1994, 19–20)

Yapko also discusses another aspect of therapy and the appeal of "discovering" that a client has been sexually abused as a child. This discovery provides a scapegoat for the individual, someone else who can be blamed for one's problems or failures (Yapko 1994).

Yapko and others are concerned about the innocent people whose lives are changed forever when repressed memories of childhood sexual abuse surface. So-called victims who accuse family members of horrendous acts of abuse destroy families and themselves. Confronting and accusing a family member of sexual abuse, based solely on the basis of repressed memories, has devastating effects on both the accuser and the family member being accused. If the allegation of abuse is not true, the family members usually are devastated by these allegations and by the inevitable destruction of the family. Many family members do not understand the concept of repressed memories: "Either you remember something or you don't" is the feeling of many people when confronted with this issue.

Psychologist Carol Tavris, in an article on incest in the *New York Times Book Review,* takes on Ellen Bass and Laura Davis, who wrote *The Courage to Heal,* and others who believe in repressed memories and repressed memory therapy. She finds fault with the incest-survivor recovery movement:

The problem is not with the advice they offer to victims, but with their effort to create victims—to expand the market that can then be treated with therapy and self-help books. To do this, survival books all hew to a formula based on an uncritical acceptance of certain premises about the nature of memory and trauma. They offer simple answers at a time when research psychologists are posing hard questions.... Uniformly these books persuade their readers to focus exclusively on past abuse as the reason for their present unhappiness. Forget fighting with Harold and the kids, having a bad job or no job, worrying about money. Healing is defined as your realization that you were a victim of sexual abuse and that it explains everything wrong in your life. (Tavris 1993, 1)

Based on current research on repressed memory, no definitive conclusions can be drawn about the validity of such memories. Researchers will continue to study them to determine whether these memories are real or only a result of suggestion by therapists and other trusted adults.

Community Notification Laws

Community notification laws have a short history resulting from the efforts of local communities responding to the abduction of children—especially two well-known children, Jacob Wetterling and Megan Kanka. In 1989, Jacob, his brother Trevor, and Aaron, a friend of the brothers, were riding their bicycles when they were stopped by a masked man with a gun. The man asked the boys their ages and released Trevor and Aaron—telling them to run toward the woods and not look back. By the time the boys turned around, Jacob and the man had disappeared. Even though the police reached the crime scene within minutes of Jacob's disappearance, they were unable to locate Jacob or his abductor. Hundreds of local law enforcement personnel, FBI agents, and volunteers searched for clues, but Jacob was never found. In 1994 the U.S. Congress passed the Jacob Wetterling Crimes against Children and Sexually Violent Offender Registration Program (as part of the Violent Crime Control and Law Enforcement Act of 1994), which requires states to implement a registry of sex offenders and crimes against children.

On July 29, 1994, seven-year-old Megan Kanka was invited into Jesse Timmendequas's home to see his puppy. He took her to his room, began to touch her inappropriately and, when she tried to run, raped her and strangled her with a belt. Her body was found the following day in a field at Mercer County Park, New Jersey. The murder outraged Mercer County, especially when the public was informed that Timmendequas was a convicted sex offender who could live wherever he wanted without his neighbors knowing about his record as a sex offender.

Megan's family and neighbors launched a campaign for legislation that would notify community organizations and neighbors when a convicted sex offender was moving into their neighborhood. New Jersey governor Christine Todd Whitman signed the first group of laws, named Megan's Law, just three months after Megan's death. Every state now has a version of Megan's Law on their books. A national version of Megan's Law was signed by President Clinton in 1996; it amended the Jacob Wetterling Crimes against Children and Sexually Violent Offender Registration Program, requiring states to create their own systems for registering all sex offenders in their jurisdictions with the local police and adding a provision for community notification.

Guidelines for community notification laws have been developed in all states and include notification based on three levels of risk. Level 1 is for those offenders who have a low risk of reoffending. Information can be shared with other law enforcement authorities and any victim or witness to the offense. Level 2 is for medium-risk offenders and usually adds schools, day-care centers, businesses and other organizations, and community groups to the list of those who should be notified when a sex offender moves into the neighborhood. Level 3 is for high-risk offenders, the most dangerous offenders, those who are most likely to reoffend. The general public is usually notified when a level 3 offender moves into the neighborhood.

The effectiveness of these laws has been hotly debated. On the one hand, communities are notified when potential sex offenders move into their neighborhoods, providing them with heightened awareness of the potential danger to their children. They allow parents and neighbors to keep an eye on their children. On the other hand, they can prevent convicted sex offenders, who have technically paid their debt to society, to resume a "normal" life, including finding a job and a place to live. They can promote vigilantism, as neighbors may work to prevent the offender from moving into their neighborhood or provoke actual attacks on the offender. For example, in the state of Washington, after Joseph Gallardo, a convicted child sexual abuser, decided to move back to his old neighborhood following his release from prison, the neighbors held a protest and burned down his home. Other sex offenders have received death threats, been assaulted, and been forced to move from their neighborhood (Montana 1995).

Some experts suggest that by forcing sex offenders out of some neighborhoods, they encourage them to relocate to areas where the notification laws aren't strongly enforced. They also make it difficult for offenders to readjust to freedom and to reintegrate themselves into society. Some professionals believe that sex offenders are never truly rehabilitated and that therefore these community notification laws reinforce the idea that the sex offender will never be able to change. If they aren't able to work their way back into society, they may turn again to children for companionship (ibid.).

There have been several challenges to these community notification laws in various states, often based on issues of equal protection, double jeopardy, and cruel and unusual punishment. Challenges based on equal protection argue that the law classifies sex offenders separately from all other criminals, which violates equal protection; proponents argue that classifying sex offenders separately promotes public safety. Challenges based on double jeopardy argue that the offenders have paid their debt to society and should not continue to be punished. Challenges based on cruel and unusual punishment are similar to the double jeopardy challenges, in that the offender has already paid for his crime and should not be punished forever.

Another issue surrounding community notification laws is the threat of vigilantism against offenders. There have been instances of community members banding together and chasing the offender out of their neighborhood. Threats against the lives of some offenders have been made, and many offenders have been attacked or murdered. In 1997 in California, an offender whose name was released to the public had his car fire-bombed. Other offenders have had people shooting at their houses, fire-bombing their homes, and physically attacking them. In 2006, two men in Maine were gunned down by a man who had obtained information about them from the state's registry of sexual offenders. Pursuant to a 2006 Missouri State Supreme Court decision, the ongoing duty to register for pre-1995 offenses was invalidated; however, all other provisions remain in effect.

Juvenile Offenders and Community Notification

There are special considerations and concerns when the offender is a juvenile. The success rate for treatment of juveniles who commit sex crimes against other children is fairly high—several studies have demonstrated that juvenile offenders who have participated in treatment programs have a recidivism rate of between 7 and 13 percent over five years, compared with a recidivism rate of between 15 and 50 percent for nonsexual offenses. However, the reporting requirement of community notification laws makes it difficult for juveniles to recover and reclaim their lives; they are marked as sex offenders, ridiculed, and shunned by neighbors. Young people generally have a harder time overcoming the shame conveyed by being named as a sexual offender; the juvenile justice system generally focuses on rehabilitation, but young offenders often find it difficult to focus on rehabilitation when the community is rallying against them (Wind 2003).

Prevention

Prevention efforts are an important part of teaching children how to protect themselves and in lowering the number of new child sexual abuse cases. Most professionals in the field believe that prevention is important, although they may differ on the best means of prevention. Current issues of concern in this area include the effectiveness of the ways in which researchers measure the success of these programs, potential side effects of the programs, the degree to which these programs are geared to the developmental levels of the child, the degree of parental involvement in such programs, the means of presenting information to the child, and the differing perspectives of victims and offenders (Roberts and Miltenberger 1999).

In evaluating programs, several studies have shown that programs geared at elementary school–age children have shown some positive gains. One review of twenty-five studies reported that children exposed to these programs have shown significant gains in knowledge about child sexual abuse and what to do if someone abuses them (Finkelhor and Strapko 1992). The National Committee for the Prevention of Child Abuse summarized the successes of prevention programs:

> With respect to the children, participants who have received these instructions demonstrate an increase in knowledge about safety rules and are more aware of what to do and who to turn to if they have been or are being abused. However, children have greater difficulty in accepting the idea that abuse may occur at the hands of someone they know. Also, relatively little is known about whether any of the concepts presented in the classroom settings translate into behavioral changes that would prevent sexual assault. Parents and teachers who

have attended the informational meetings which generally precede the classroom presentations report greater understanding of the problem of sexual abuse and greater confidence in how to respond to a child's disclosure. Further, while not preventing initial maltreatment, the programs do create an environment in which children can more easily disclose prior or ongoing maltreatment. As with all prevention programs, these gains are not universal across all participants; some children, parents, and teachers remain uninformed following the presentations. (National Committee for the Prevention of Child Abuse 1986, 1–2)

Generally, research suggests that children younger than five years old are not able to retain information presented to them about sexual abuse and make a connection between the information and anything that might ever happen to them. Some children are just too young or immature to understand many of the concepts about sexual abuse that are presented to them. Many instructions are difficult for young children to understand. The National Committee for the Prevention of Child Abuse agrees:

Many child development specialists and concerned advocates feel these instructions place an inappropriate burden on young children to be self-protective. They argue that most preschoolers cannot distinguish between appropriate and inappropriate touch, nor can they take the actions necessary to protect themselves from harm. Rather than targeting the child for intervention, proponents of this position suggest that parents need to be reached and made more aware of their responsibility to protect their children. On the other hand, other experts stress that it is important to integrate safety concepts into a child's educational process beginning at the earliest possible age. (ibid., 2)

Many programs, even those for older children, have found that when they retested children on the information about sexual abuse they had been given, many retained little information over time, especially after a period of eight months to a year had passed.

Conte suggests that, until researchers better understand the process by which children are coerced into being sexually abused, prevention programs will have limited success:

There has not yet been a systematic study of the victimization process toward the end of identifying new concepts or skills that might be useful in preventing child
sexual abuse. The more that is learned about the coer-
cive process that sexual abuse is, the more questions are
raised about whether current prevention activities are
likely to be all that useful to children exposed to this coercion. Nothing that current prevention efforts teach, for
example, is likely to be helpful in overcoming the fear
instilled in children by the violent dismemberment of a
living animal before them, with the threat that they or
ones they love will be similarly treated if they tell about
their abuse. (Conte 1986, 34)

Early prevention programs focused on teaching children to
stay away from strangers, believing that most sex offenders were
strangers. However, as more research focused on perpetrators, investigators began to realize that children were more likely to be
abused by someone they know. As a result, prevention programs
began to focus on offenders known to the children.

Based on a review of twenty-seven control group studies on
the effectiveness of existing school-based, child sexual abuse prevention programs, Davis and Gidycz found that children who
participated in prevention programs at school were more likely to
improve their knowledge and skills concerning sexual abuse than
were nonparticipants (Davis and Gidycz 2000). While this and
other studies focus on the effectiveness of prevention programs in
teaching children about sexual abuse, few studies have been conducted on whether these and other prevention programs actually
prevent a child from being sexually abused.

Finkelhor and his colleagues conducted a national telephone
survey of 2,000 children between the ages of ten and sixteen
years. They found that children who participated in school-based
prevention programs demonstrated greater knowledge concerning sexual abuse and also were more likely to exhibit protective
behaviors and use protective strategies when threatened with
abuse (Finkelhor and Dziuba-Leatherman 1995). In a follow-up
study the next year, Finkelhor and his colleagues contacted many
of the 2,000 children previously studied and again found that
children who had participated in school-based programs concerning sexual abuse prevention were more likely to use protective strategies. However, there was no indication that those pre-

vention programs actually helped children avoid becoming victims of sexual abuse (Finkelhor et al. 1995).

Later studies have provided some indication that school-based programs may help children to avoid becoming victims of sexual abuse. Gibson and Leitenberg, in a study of 825 female undergraduates, found that women who had not participated in a school-based prevention program were almost twice as likely to have been sexually abused as a child as those who had participated (Gibson and Leitenberg 2000). In another, smaller study, Ko and Cosden surveyed high school students and found that those who had participated in a child abuse prevention program (not specifically on sexual abuse, but on the broader topic of child abuse) were no less likely to be sexually abused than those who had not participated in such a program (Ko and Cosden 2001).

Sexual Abuse Committed by Clergy

While most of the attention concerning clergy abuse has been focused on the Catholic Church, other denominations also have issues with their clergy committing sexual abuse of children. For example, in 2004, nine victims who accused a governing body of the Lutheran Church in Marshall, Texas, of concealing a former pastor's past sexual abuse history were awarded almost $37 million by a Texas jury. The former pastor, who was the church's pastor from 1997 to 2001, had been convicted on child pornography charges and sentenced to five years in federal prison. He was more recently sentenced to 397 years in state prison after being convicted on eleven counts of multiple sex crimes against children.

In 1984, one of the first public cases of clergy abuse was filed in Louisiana. The priest, Gilbert Gauthe, was sentenced to twenty years in prison after pleading guilty to thirty-nine counts of sexual battery. The following year, as more incidents were reported and cases filed, a report was drafted by three individuals familiar with the Gauthe case. The report estimated the legal and financial liability as a result of sexual abuse of minors by priests and provided guidelines on ways to respond to the allegations of abuse.

The U.S. Conference of Catholic Bishops drafted the Charter for the Protection of Children and Young People in response to the growing awareness of the problem of child sexual abuse by Catholic priests. They created two entities to address the problem:

the National Review Board and the Office of Child and Youth Protection.

One of the mandates of the National Review Board was to evaluate the "causes and context" of this crisis, and in 2004 the board issued its report (U.S. Conference of Catholic Bishops 2004). While most priests in the United States "fulfill their roles honorably and chastely," the board found that "there were credible allegations that several thousand priests, comprising four percent of priests in ministry over the last half-century, committed acts of sexual abuse of minors" (ibid., 4). Specifically, the research indicated that 4,392 priests were accused of sexually abusing a minor between 1950 and 2002—or 4 percent of the 109,694 priests active during that period. Some 10,667 minors were abused, and 81 percent of them were male. The number of allegations appeared to have peaked in the 1970s, decreasing thereafter. Analyzed by number of allegations per priest, the results indicated that 56 percent of the accused priests had one allegation made against them; 27 percent had two or three allegations; 14 percent had four to nine; and 3 percent had ten or more allegations made against them. In terms of the type of abusive behavior reported (not all allegations were described), 27 percent of the priests allegedly performed oral sex on the children, and 25 percent engaged in penile penetration or attempted penetration.

Most of the time when abuse was alleged, the diocese did take some type of action. However, not all priests were removed from contact with minors; some were simply transferred to another diocese where they could again engage in abusive behavior. The study found that slightly more than 100 priests actually served time in prison for sexually abusing a minor. In many other cases, the abuse was not reported to civil authorities.

Following the Gauthe case that first brought widespread attention to allegations of abuse in the Catholic Church, lawsuits were filed throughout the country. The Church could no longer hope that the incidence of sexual abuse by priests was localized in a few dioceses. Lawsuits were filed across the country, including Santa Fe, Boston, Dallas, New York, Phoenix, and Los Angeles, but the news focused primarily on the archdiocese of Boston. Father John Geoghan was transferred from one parish to another, even though many allegations had been made against him; the first allegation was made in 1979 and continued into the 1990s. He was indicted in 1999 on child rape charges and in 2002 was convicted of indecent assault and battery and sentenced to ten years in prison where, in 2003, he was murdered. Another priest, Father Paul Shanley, even caught the attention of the Vatican in 1978, after he had made several comments in public that appeared to support homosexual conduct with minors. He was alleged to have abused several young boys but was allowed to remain in the ministry until 1996. The archbishop of Boston at the time, Cardinal Law, later admitted that he had transferred priests accused of sexual abuse of minors to other parishes. He later apologized and resigned as archbishop in 2002. That same year, Pope John Paul II met with cardinals from the United States and leaders of the Conference to the Vatican to discuss the problems of priests and the sexual abuse of minors.

In 2002 the USCCB adopted the Charter for the Protection of Children and Young People as well as the Essential Norms, which set standards for how to deal with sexual abuse of minors, including the permanent removal from the ministry of any priest who sexually abuses a minor. In effect, the Church instituted a zero-tolerance policy that called for the removal of a priest for any act of sexual abuse—no matter what the abusive behavior entailed. The zero-tolerance policy even applied to priests who had reported themselves in order to get help; the Church realized that these measures were necessary to deal with the problem of sexual abuse committed by priests and the growing news media attention.

In its report, the National Review Board also had something to say about celibacy and about homosexuality. The report indicated that, while the authors did not believe that celibacy led to the sexual abuse of minors, the Church needed to do a better job in explaining celibacy and in preparing young priests for a celibate life. On the issue of homosexuality, the report's authors were concerned because most of the targets of the sexual abuse were boys; therefore, they assumed that the priests who committed most of the abuse were homosexual. The report's authors believed that they "must call attention to the homosexual behavior that characterized the vast majority of the cases of abuse observed in recent decades. That eighty-one percent of the reported victims of child sexual abuse by Catholic clergy were boys shows that the crisis was characterized by homosexual behavior" (ibid., 80).

This scandal has damaged the Church's credibility and authority, and it will have to change its attitude and work to regain the trust that has been lost. The Review Board believes that there are several steps that the Church can take to ensure children's safety and to regain trust and respect. These recommendations include: (1) further study of the causes and context of sexual abuse, (2) careful screening of candidates to the priesthood, (3) increased sensitivity and better response to allegations of sexual abuse, (4) better accountability of Church leaders, (5) increased communication and cooperation with civil authorities, and (6) better and more meaningful participation of the Christian laity (U.S. Conference of Catholic Bishops 2004). According to other observers, the Church must clearly describe the actions it will take to prevent additional occurrences of sexual abuse, as well as show more remorse for its past behavior and more compassion to its victims (Robertson 2005).

Statutes of Limitations

Over the past several years, there has been increasing debate over extending the civil and criminal statutes of limitations in child sexual abuse cases. In essence, all states have time limits for filing a lawsuit to recover damages. On the criminal side of the law, federal, state, or local governments have a certain amount of time to bring charges against individuals for alleged offenses (as opposed to murder, which is the only criminal offense that does not currently have a statute of limitations associated with it). On the civil side, plaintiffs have a certain amount of time in which to bring charges against a party whom they believe has injured them in some way. In cases of child sexual abuse, there are both civil and criminal options to punishing the perpetrator.

Proponents of these limits have good reasons for supporting them. Statutes of limitations for criminal offenses force law enforcement agencies to investigate alleged crimes in a timely manner, ensure that evidence is collected before it becomes stale or is destroyed, ensure that the alleged offender has a speedy trial, and protect the public from alleged criminals who otherwise could be out on the streets committing additional crimes before they are charged and prosecuted. In addition, witnesses may move out of the area, disappear, or forget the details of their testimony if too much time passes before a case is investigated and brought to trial.

Opponents believe that the current court system is set up to protect defendants' rights to timely evidence collection and a speedy trial. Many also believe that in many cases, especially in cases of child sexual abuse, the abuse is not disclosed immediately, or is repressed, and victims need additional time to think about bringing charges against the perpetrator.

Generally, in civil cases, the statute of limitations begins to run at the time of the offense; however, sometimes the offense is not readily apparent, and in those cases, legislatures have created a means by which the statute can be frozen, or tolled, especially when the victim suffers some type of mental deficiency, has not reached the age of majority, or is not aware of the harm caused. In such cases, the statute of limitations begins when the plaintiff becomes aware or should become aware of the offense and the damages. Most states currently suspend the statute of limitations when the person is a minor.

The problem with statutes of limitations in cases of child sexual abuse originally centered on adults who were abused as children but did not tell anyone until years afterward. It became more apparent when individuals began to recall memories of sexual abuse that had been repressed for many years. This issue is still hotly discussed, as more individuals are coming forth and admitting that they have been abused by Catholic clergy or others and had told no one because they were afraid, embarrassed, or pressured to keep quiet.

At least twenty-eight states currently have extended the statute of limitations regarding child sexual abuse, and some others are considering doing so. See Chapter 6 for more information on each state's statute.

Online Predators

The growing popularity of the Internet, especially among children and teens, also brings with it a growing population of predators that use the Internet to locate potential sexual abuse victims, as well as to locate child pornography. See Chapter 3 for a discussion of issues relating to Internet solicitations and child pornography (Internet and child pornography reach beyond the physical borders of the United States). One issue currently in the news is the role of police and other adults who pose as juveniles online to catch online predators.

Statistics vary on the number of solicitations that juveniles receive online, but some researchers believe that as many as 20 percent of children are solicited each year (Finkelhor et al. 2000). While some of these solicitations may be relatively harmless, others can pose a greater danger to young children and teens, and may include involvement with adults that can lead to sexual abuse or exploitation.

Results from the National Juvenile Online Victimization Study indicate that law enforcement agencies are successful in stopping some offenders before they molest a child. While some people believe that having a police officer pose as a juvenile in order to catch a potential abuser is entrapment, the prosecution of these individuals has for the most part been successful. While some offenders raise entrapment as a defense, judges and juries have largely not been in agreement.

References

Abbott, Brian R. 1991. *Sexual Re-offense Rates among Incest Offenders Eight Years after Leaving Treatment.* San Jose, CA: Giarretto Institute.

Allen, Craig. 1991. *Women and Men Who Sexually Abuse Children: A Comparative Analysis.* Orwell, VT: Safer Society.

American Psychological Association. 2006. "Questions and Answers about Memories of Childhood Abuse." http://www.apa.org/topics/memories.html.

August, R., and B. Foreman. 1988. "A Comparison of Sexually and Non-Sexually Abused Children's Behavioral Responses to Anatomically Correct Dolls." *Child Psychiatry and Human Development* 20, no. 1: 39–47.

Bass, Ellen, and Laura Davis. 1994. *The Courage to Heal: A Guide for Survivors of Child Sexual Abuse.* 3d ed. New York: HarperPerennial.

Bedarf, Abril R. 1995. "Examining Sex Offender Community Notification Laws." *California Law Review* 83: 885.

Berliner, Lucy, and Jon R. Conte. 1990. "Effects of Disclosure and Intervention on Sexually Abused Children." Final report to NCCAN of grant #90CA1181. Seattle: University of Washington Sexual Assault Center.

Blume, E. Sue. 1990. *Secret Survivors: Uncovering Incest and Its Aftereffects in Women.* New York: Ballantine.

Broussard, S., N. G. Wagner, and R. Kazelskis. 1991. "Undergraduate Students' Perceptions of Child Sexual Abuse: The Impact of Victim Sex, Perpetrator Sex, Respondent Sex, and Victim Response." *Journal of Family Violence* 6: 267–278.

Cameron, Paul, William Cobrun, Jr., Helen Larson, Kay Proctor, Nels Forde, and Kirk Cameron. 1986. "Child Molestation and Homosexuality." *Psychological Reports* 58: 327–337.

Ceci, Stephen, and Maggie Bruck. 1995. *Jeopardy in the Courtroom: A Scientific Analysis of Children's Testimony.* Washington, DC: American Psychological Association.

Ceci, Stephen J., and Richard D. Friedman. 2000. "The Suggestibility of Children: Scientific Research and Legal Implications." *Cornell Law Review* 86: 33.

Conte, Jon. 1986. *A Look at Child Sexual Abuse.* Chicago: National Committee for Prevention of Child Abuse.

Davis, M., and C. Gidycz. 2000. "Child Sexual Abuse Prevention Programs: A Meta-Analysis." *Journal of Clinical Child Psychology* 29, no. 2: 257–265.

Denov, Myriam S. 2003. "The Myth of Innocence: Sexual Scripts and the Recognition of Child Sexual Abuse by Female Perpetrators." *Journal of Sex Research* 40, no. 3: 303–308.

Faller, Kathleen Coulborn. 1993. *Child Sexual Abuse: Intervention and Treatment Issues.* Washington, DC: National Center on Child Abuse and Neglect.

Finkelhor, David. 1986. *A Sourcebook on Child Sexual Abuse.* Newbury Park, CA: Sage.

Finkelhor, D., N. Asdigian, and J. Dziuba-Leatherman. 1995. "The Effectiveness of Victimization Prevention Instruction: An Evaluation of Children's Responses to Actual Threats and Assaults." *Child Abuse and Neglect* 19, no. 2: 141–153.

Finkelhor, David, and J. Dziuba-Leatherman. 1995. "Victimization Prevention Programs: A National Survey of Children's Exposure and Reactions." *Child Abuse and Neglect* 19, no. 2: 129–139.

Finkelhor, David, and Lisa M. Jones. 2004. *Explanations for the Decline in Child Sexual Abuse Cases.* Washington, DC: Office of Juvenile Justice and Delinquency Prevention.

Finkelhor, David, Kimberly J. Mitchell, and Janis Wolak. 2000. *Online Victimization: A Report on the Nation's Youth.* Alexandria, VA: National Center for Missing and Exploited Children.

Finkelhor, David, and Nancy Strapko. 1992. "Sexual Abuse Prevention Education: A Review of Evaluation Studies." In *Child Abuse Prevention,* edited by D. Willis, E. Holder, and M. Rosenberg. New York: John Wiley.

Freud, Sigmund, and Josef Breuer. 2004 [1895]. *Studies on Hysteria.* New York: Penguin Classics.

Freund, K., G. Heasman, I. G. Racansky, and G. Glancy. 1984. "Pedophilia and Heterosexuality vs. Homosexuality." *Journal of Sex and Marital Therapy* 10: 193–200.

Frisbee, L. V., and E. H. Dondis. 1965. *Recidivism among Treated Sex Offenders*. Sacramento: California Department of Mental Hygiene.

Gallagher, Bernard. 2000. "The Extent and Nature of Known Cases of Institutional Child Sexual Abuse." *British Journal of Social Work* 30: 795–817.

Gibbons, Michael, and Dana Campbell. 2003. "General Aspects of Recreation Law: Liability of Recreation and Competitive Sport Organizations for Sexual Assaults on Children by Administrators, Coaches and Volunteers." *Legal Aspects of Sport* 13: 185–229.

Gibson, L., and H. Leitenberg. 2000. "Child Sexual Abuse Prevention Programs: Do They Decrease the Occurrence of Child Sexual Abuse?" *Child Abuse and Neglect* 24, no. 9: 1115–1125.

Glaser, D., and C. Collins. 1989. "The Response of Young, Non-Sexually Abused Children to Anatomically Correct Dolls." *Journal of Child Psychology and Psychiatry* 30: 547–560.

Groth, Nicholas. 1979. *Men Who Rape*. New York: Plenum.

Groth, Nicholas, and T. S. Gary. 1982. "Heterosexuality, Homosexuality, and Pedophilia: Sexual Offenses against Children and Adult Sexual Orientation." Pp. 143–152 in *Male Rape: A Casebook of Sexual Aggressions*, edited by A. M. Scacco. New York: AMS.

Hammerschlag, Margaret R. 2002. *Sexually Transmitted Diseases and Child Sexual Abuse*. Washington, DC: Office of Juvenile Justice and Delinquency Prevention.

Hanson, R. K., and M. Bussiere. 1998. "Predicting Relapse: A Meta-analysis of Sexual Offender Recidivism Studies." *Journal of Consulting and Clinical Psychology* 66, no. 2: 348–362.

Hendrie, Caroline. 1998. "A Trust Betrayed: Sexual Abuse by Teachers." *Education Week* (December 2, 9, 16).

Herman, Judith L. 1981. *Father-Daughter Incest*. Cambridge: Harvard University Press.

Hollenberg, Elizabeth, and Cynthia Ragan. 1991. *Child Sexual Abuse: Selected Projects*. Washington, DC: National Center on Child Abuse and Neglect.

Jampole, L., and M. K. Weber. 1987. "An Assessment of the Behavior of Sexually Abused and Non-Sexually Abused Children with Anatomically Correct Dolls." *Child Abuse and Neglect* 11: 187–192.

Jennings, Diane, and Robert Tharp. 2003. "Betrayal of Trust." *Dallas Morning News* (May 4, 5, 6).

Jenny, C., T. A. Roesler, and K. L. Poyer. 1994. "Are Children at Risk for Sexual Abuse by Homosexuals?" *Pediatrics* 94: 41–44.

Katz, Nancie. 2002. "Jail for Coach in Sex Abuse," *New York Daily News* (July 16), p. 2.

Kaufman, K. L., D. R. Hilliker, and E. L. Daleiden. 1996. "Subgroup Differences in the Modus Operandi of Adolescent Sexual Offenders." *Child Maltreatment* 1: 17–24.

Kempe, Ruth S., and C. Henry Kempe. 1984. *The Common Secret: Sexual Abuse of Children and Adolescents.* New York: W. H. Freeman.

Ko, S., and M. Cosden. 2001. "Do Elementary School-Based Child Abuse Prevention Programs Work? A High School Follow-Up." *Psychology in the Schools* 38, no. 1: 57–66.

Langan, Patrick A., Erica L. Schmitt, and Matthew R. Durose. 2003. *Recidivism of Sex Offenders Released from Prison in 1994.* Washington, DC: Bureau of Justice Statistics.

Lew, Mike. 1988. *Victims No Longer: Men Recovering from Incest and Other Sexual Child Abuse.* New York: Harper and Row.

Loftus, Elizabeth, and Katherine Ketcham. 1994. *The Myth of Repressed Memory: False Memories and Allegations of Sexual Abuse.* New York: St. Martin's.

Maan, Cathy. 1994. "Current Issues in Using Anatomical Dolls." *Violence Update* 4: 1–4.

McConaghy, Nathaniel. 1998. "Paedophilia: A Review of the Evidence." *Australian and New Zealand Journal of Psychiatry* 32, no. 2: 252–265.

Meyer, L., and J. Romero. 1980. *Ten-Year Follow-up of Sex Offender Recidivism.* Philadelphia: Joseph Peters Institute.

Montana, Jenny. 1995. "Note: An Ineffective Weapon in the Fight against Child Sexual Abuse: New Jersey's Megan's Law." *Journal of Law and Policy* 3: 569–602.

Monto, M., G. Zgourides, and R. Harris. 1998. "Empathy, Self-Esteem, and the Adolescent Sexual Offender." *Sexual Abuse: A Journal of Research and Treatment* 10: 127–140.

National Committee for the Prevention of Child Abuse. 1986. *Child Assault Prevention with Preschoolers: What Do We Know?* Chicago: National Committee for the Prevention of Child Abuse.

Quinsey, V. L., et al. 1995. "Actuarial Prediction of Sexual Recidivism." *Journal of Interpersonal Violence* 10: 85.

Richardson, G., T. P. Kelly, S. R. Bhate, and F. Graham. 1997. "Group Differences in Abuser and Abuse Characteristics in a British Sample of Sexually Abusive Adolescents." *Sexual Abuse: A Journal of Research and Treatment* 9: 239–257.

Righthand, Sue, and Carlann Welch. 2001. *Juveniles Who Have Sexually Offended: A Review of the Professional Literature.* Washington, DC: U.S. Department of Justice.

Roberts, Jennifer A., and Raymond G. Miltenberger. 1999. "Emerging Issues in the Research on Child Sexual Abuse Prevention." *Education and Treatment of Children* 22, no. 1: 84-103.

Robertson, Kathleen R. 2005. "Dark Days for the Church: Canon Law and the Response of the Roman Catholic Church to the Sex Abuse Scandals." *Washington University Global Studies Law Review* 4: 161–185.

Sgroi, Suzanne. 1998. *Vulnerable Populations: Evaluation and Treatment of Sexually Abused Children and Adult Survivors.* Lexington, MA: Lexington.

Shakeshaft, Charol. 2003. "Educator Sexual Abuse." *Hofstra Horizons* (Spring): 10–13.

Shakeshaft, Charol, and Audrey Cohan. 1995. "Sexual Abuse of Students by School Personnel." *Phi Delta Kappan* 76, no. 7: 513–520.

Sivan, Abigail B., D. P. Schor, G. K. Koeppl, and L. D. Noble. 1988. "Interaction of Normal Children with Anatomical Dolls." *Child Abuse and Neglect* 12: 295–304.

Smith, Peggy, Marvin Bohnstedt, Elizabeth Lennon, and Kathleen Grove. 1985. *Long-Term Correlates of Child Victimization: Consequences of Intervention and Non-Intervention.* Washington, DC: National Center on Child Abuse and Neglect.

Spalding, Larry Helm. 1997. "Chemical Castration: A Return to the Dark Ages." http://www.aclufl.org/about/newsletters/1997/chem.cfm.

Stein, Nan D., Nancy Marshall, and Linda R. Tropp. 1993. *Secrets in Public: Sexual Harassment in Our Schools.* Wellesley, MA: Wellesley Centers for Women.

Tavris, Carol. 1993. "Beware the Incest-Survivor Machine." *New York Times Book Review* 78 (January 3): 1.

U.S. Attorney General's Task Force on Family Violence. 1984. *Final Report of the U.S. Attorney General's Task Force on Family Violence.* Washington, DC: U.S. Government Printing Office.

U.S. Conference of Catholic Bishops (USCCB). 2004. *A Report on the Crisis in the Catholic Church in the United States.* Washington, DC: U.S. Conference of Catholic Bishops.

Wind, Timothy E. 2003. "The Quandary of Megan's Law: When the Child Sex Offender Is a Child." *John Marshall Law Review* 37: 73–124.

Wishnietsky, Dan H. 1991. "Reported and Unreported Teacher-Student Sexual Harassment." *Journal of Educational Research* 84, no. 3: 164–169.

Yapko, Michael D. 1994. *Suggestions of Abuse: True and False Memories of Childhood Sexual Trauma.* New York: Simon and Schuster.

3

Worldwide Perspective

According to UNICEF's 2004 report on the state of the world's children, there are 2.2 billion children in the world. Some 1.9 billion of them live in developing countries, and 1 billion of them live in poverty.

This chapter will explore the characteristics of child sexual abuse around the world. It will examine how child sexual abuse is defined and dealt with in other countries. There are similarities in the characteristics of child sexual abuse among the developed countries, including the European countries, Canada, Australia, and New Zealand. The focus and characteristics of child sexual abuse in developing countries may differ from that of developed countries, and those differences will be explored. Cultural and religious differences also play a role in definitions, identification, treatment, and punishment of child sexual abuse. Finally, major issues that are of worldwide concern will be examined, including child pornography, child prostitution, and sex tourism.

International Laws and Conventions

There are many international laws and conventions that protect children from abuse and exploitation, including sexual abuse and sexual exploitation. A brief description of the major laws and conventions is provided here. The United Nations has been a major player in the development of many of the international laws and conventions currently in existence. The major ones include the following:

The UN Convention on the Rights of the Child, ratified by every country (as of 2005) except Somalia and the United States, is the most comprehensive treaty on children's rights. It was adopted in 1989 and entered into force in 1990. According to Article 19, children have the right to protection "from all forms of physical or mental violence, injury or abuse, neglect or negligent treatment, maltreatment or exploitation including sexual abuse, while in the care of parent(s), legal guardian(s), or any other person who has the care of the child." Article 32 recognizes "the right of the child to be protected from economic exploitation and from performing any work that is likely to be hazardous . . . or to be harmful to the child's health or physical, mental, spiritual, moral, or social development." Article 34 specifically requires state parties to protect their children from sexual exploitation, urging them to implement measures to prevent the inducement of a child into sexual activity, prostitution, pornography, or other unlawful sexual practices. Articles 35 and 36 require state parties to ensure the protection of children against abduction, sale, or trafficking, and against any form of exploitation prejudicial to the child's welfare.

The International Covenant on Civil and Political Rights (ICCPR) entered into force in 1966. It provides for the protection of children against violence and other forms of abuse. For example, Article 8 protects all persons from being held in slavery or servitude; all forms of the slave trade are prohibited, and no one can be required to perform forced or compulsory labor. Article 24 requires that all children have the right to all forms of protection as required by their status as minors.

The Convention against Torture and Other Cruel, Inhuman or Degrading Treatment or Punishment was adopted in 1984 and entered into force in 1987. It protects all persons, including children, from torture or cruel, inhuman, or degrading treatment or punishment.

The Protocol to Prevent, Suppress and Punish Trafficking in Persons, Especially Women and Children, Supplementing the UN Convention against Transnational Organized Crime entered into force in September 2003. Its purpose is to prevent and combat trafficking in persons, especially women and children; to protect and assist victims; and to promote cooperation among state parties in meeting its objectives.

The Optional Protocol to the Convention on the Rights of the Child on the Sale of Children, Child Prostitution and Child Pornography was adopted in May 2000 and entered into force in January 2002. It recognized the growing use of children in prostitution and pornography and prohibits the sale of children, child prostitution, and child pornography.

Other Conventions

The Hague Convention on Jurisdiction, Applicable Law, Recognition, Enforcement and Co-Operation in Respect of Parental Responsibility and Measures for the Protection of Children entered into force in January 2002. State parties are required to take measures to protect children in the areas of parental responsibility and contact, protection and care, custody disputes, their representation, and protection of their property.

The Yokohama Global Commitment 2001, adopted by the Second World Congress against Commercial Sexual Exploitation of Children, requested that states "take adequate measures to address negative aspects of new technologies, in particular child pornography on the Internet, while recognizing the potential of new technologies for the protection of children from commercial sexual exploitation, through dissemination and exchange of information and networking among partners."

The Convention Concerning the Prohibition and Immediate Action for the Elimination of the Worst Forms of Child Labour (ILO Convention No. 182) defines the use, procurement, or offer of a child for prostitution, for the production of pornography, or for pornographic purposes.

The 2002 outcome document of the UN General Assembly's twenty-seventh special session, *A World Fit for Children,* asked states to "raise awareness of the illegality and harmful consequences of sexual exploitation and abuse, including through the Internet," and to "take necessary measures, including through enhanced cooperation between Governments, intergovernmental organizations, the private sector and non-governmental organizations to combat the criminal use of information technologies, including the Internet, for the purposes of the sale of children, for child prostitution, child pornography, child sex tourism, paedophilia and other forms of violence and abuse against children and adolescents" (UN General Assembly 2002, 18).

Regional Laws and Conventions

The Economic Community of West African States (ECOWAS), in its 2001 Declaration and its Plan of Action on Trafficking in Persons, appealed to its member states to focus attention on implementing existing international agreements for eliminating trafficking in persons, including children, and on criminal justice responses to trafficking. It suggested that each member state establish a National Task Force on Trafficking in Persons.

The African Union, during the 2002 session of its Labour and Social Affairs Commission, identified the elimination of child trafficking as an organizational priority.

The African Charter on Human and Peoples' Rights, adopted in 1981 and entered into force in 1986, requires, in Article 18, that the state "shall ensure the elimination of every discrimination against women and also ensure the protection of the rights of the woman and the child as stipulated in international declarations and conventions."

The African Charter on the Rights and Welfare of the Child, adopted in 1990 and entered into force in 1999, contains several articles relating to the protection of the child from all types of sexual abuse. Article 15 protects the child from "all forms of economic exploitation." Article 16 directs state parties to protect the child from "all forms of torture, inhuman or degrading treatment and especially physical or mental injury or abuse, neglect or maltreatment including sexual abuse." Article 17 protects children who are detained from torture or other inhuman treatment and requires that they be separated from adults while in detention. Article 21 protects children from harmful social and cultural practices, prohibiting child marriage and the betrothal of girls and boys, specifying that the minimum age of marriage is eighteen years. Article 27 protects children against all forms of sexual exploitation and sexual abuse, specifically any sexual activity, child prostitution, and child pornography. Article 29 prohibits the abduction, sale, or trafficking of a child for any reason.

Incidence and Prevalence of Child Sexual Abuse

Children throughout the world can be exposed to violence and abuse. War zones and refugee camps are two areas that are often in the headlines. However, children throughout the world are at risk for sexual abuse in other areas as well: schools, orphanages, at home, at work, and on the streets. Perpetrators include family members, neighbors, law enforcement personnel, teachers, and strangers. A 1996 study of violence against children in eighteen countries conducted by Human Rights Watch found that children throughout the world were exposed to varying levels and types of violence, including sexual abuse. While in police custody children are beaten and sexually abused, and young girls who live on the streets have reported that they are sometimes forced to provide sex to the police in order to avoid being arrested or as a condition of their release from police custody. In juvenile correctional institutions children are exposed to physical and sexual assaults, forced labor, harassment, torture, and other forms of abuse. In schools, children, especially girls, are at risk for sexual abuse from other students and from teachers. In refugee camps and war zones, women and children are at high risk for sexual abuse (Human Rights Watch 2001a).

The following sections provide a survey of child sexual abuse research from various countries. For organizational purposes, the countries are divided into developed and developing countries according to UN definition. Developed countries are those countries that are considered capitalist and industrial, and include countries in North America, Europe, Japan, Australia, and New Zealand. Developing regions include Africa, the Caribbean, Central and South America, Asia (excluding Japan), and Oceania (excluding Australia and New Zealand).

Developed Regions/Countries

Sexual abuse of children in developed/industrialized countries—such as Western Europe, Canada, Australia, New Zealand, and Japan—is similar to that in the United States. These countries have similar issues and laws concerning the sexual abuse of children.

The developed countries generally define a child as a person under the age of eighteen years, following the definition provided in the UN Convention on the Rights of the Child. Table 3.1 provides information concerning age of majority, age of consent for sexual activity, and age of consent for marriage in selected countries.

TABLE 3.1
Age of Majority, Age of Consent for Sexual Activity, and Age for Consent for Marriage for Selected Countries

Country	Age of Simple Majority	Age of Consent for Sexual Activity	Age of Consent for Marriage
Albania	14	Not specified	16 – female 18 – males
Argentina	18	15	21
Armenia	18	16	18 – males 17 – females 16 – females under exceptional circumstances
Australia	18	16	18 16 – with parental purpose
Austria	18	Not specified	18
Azerbaijan	18	Not specified	18 – males 17 – females
Bahamas	18	16	18
Bahrain	21	Only through marriage	15 21 if girl does not have parental consent
Barbados	18		16
Belarus	18	18	18
Belgium	18	16	18
Bhutan		18	
Bolivia	18	14 – females 16 – males	16 – males 14 – females
Bosnia Herzegovina	18	15	18 16 if court allows
Brazil	21	females – after puberty	16 – with parental consent
Brunei	18	16	18
Bulgaria	18	Not specified	16
Burundi	females – 18 males – 21	Not specified	18 – females 21 – males
Cambodia	18	16	18 – females 20 – males

(continues)

TABLE 3.1 *(continued)*
Age of Majority, Age of Consent for Sexual Activity, and Age for Consent for Marriage for Selected Countries

Country	Age of Simple Majority	Age of Consent for Sexual Activity	Age of Consent for Marriage
Canada	Fixed by province	14	Fixed by province
China	18	Not specified	22 — males 20 — females
China (Hong Kong)	18	16	21
Colombia	18	12 — females 14 — males	14 — females 16 — males
Croatia	18	14	18
Czech Republic	18	15	18
Denmark	18	15	18
Djibouti	18	18	18
Dominica	18	16	18
Egypt	21	18	16
Finland	18	16	18
France	18	15	18 — males 15 — females
Germany	N/A	N/A	18
Gibraltar	17	16	18
Greece	18	15	18
Guatemala	18	14 — females 16 — males	18
Guinea	21	15	17 — females 18 — males
Guyana	18	16	18
Hungary	18	14	18 16 — with parental consent
Iceland	18	14	18
India	18	18	18 — males 21 — females
Indonesia	18 — males 15 — females	19 — males 16 — females	18 — males 15 — females
Ireland	18	17	18
Italy	18	14	18
Jamaica	18	N/A	18 16 — with parental consent
Japan	20	13	18 —males 16 — females

(continues)

TABLE 3.1 *(continued)*
Age of Majority, Age of Consent for Sexual Activity, and Age for Consent for Marriage for Selected Countries

Country	Age of Simple Majority	Age of Consent for Sexual Activity	Age of Consent for Marriage
Kenya	18	16	21
Latvia	18	16	18
Lebanon	18	15	18 – males 15 – females
Lesotho	21	14	18 – males 16 – females
Lithuania	18	Not specified	18 15 – by decision of court
Malta	18	18	16
Mauritania	18	16	21
Mexico	18	18	16 – males 14 – females
Monaco	21	15	21
Mongolia	N/A	16	18
Myanmar	16	N/A	20
Netherlands	18	N/A	18
Norway	18	16	18
Oman	18	Not allowed prior to marriage	Not specified; generally 18
Pakistan	18 – male 16 – female	18 – male 16 – female	18 – male 14 – female
Panama	18	14 – males 12 – females	16 – males 14 – females
Peru	18	16 – 18	18
Poland	18	15	18 – females 21 – males
Portugal	18	18	16
Puerto Rico	18	14	16
Romania	18	15	16
Saudi Arabia	18	Not allowed prior to marriage	18
Singapore	21	16	18
Slovakia	18	15	18
Slovenia	18	15	18 16 – certain conditions
South Africa	21	Not specified	21
Swaziland	21	12 – females 14 – males	21 earlier with parental consent

(continues)

TABLE 3.1 *(continued)*
Age of Majority, Age of Consent for Sexual Activity, and Age for Consent for Marriage for Selected Countries

Country	Age of Simple Majority	Age of Consent for Sexual Activity	Age of Consent for Marriage
Sweden	18	15	18
Switzerland	18	16	18
Syria	18	13	17
Tanzania	16	18	18
Thailand	18	N/A	17
Turkey	18	Not specified	17
Ukraine	18	Established by medical examiner	18 – males 17 – females
Uruguay	18	N/A	14 – males 12 – females
Uzbekistan	16	16	17
Venezuela	18	Not specified	18

In the United Kingdom, estimates of the number of children sexually abused are difficult to acquire because of the lack of reporting for a variety of reasons, including fear, shame, and embarrassment. According to one report, approximately 70,000 crimes were reported between 1980 and 2001 that involved gross indecency with a child and unlawful sexual intercourse (National Criminal Intelligence Service 2005). Some experts believe that as many as 95 percent of all cases of child sexual abuse go unreported. As of 2005, the NCIS also reported that more than 18,000 individuals were listed on sex offender registries (ibid.).

Several studies have been conducted concerning the incidence and prevalence of child sexual abuse in Australia (Goldman and Goldman 1988; Higgins and McCabe 1994; Fleming 1997; Mazza et al. 1996; Martin 1996; Goldman and Padayachi 1997; Swanston et al. 1997; Dinwiddie et al. 2000; Nelson et al. 2002). In one study of child abuse and neglect cases reported in 1993–1994, researchers found that 28,711 cases of child abuse were substantiated: 19 percent of those were sexual abuse, and 74 percent of all sexual abuse cases involved abuse of a young girl.

Reviewing all of the studies conducted, Andrews, Gould, and Corry determined that the adjusted prevalence rate for sexual abuse was 5.1 percent in males and 27.5 percent in females. The mean age at the beginning of the abuse was ten years, and most abuse occurred before the age of twelve. In 40 percent of the reported incidents, the abuser was a family member, and was known to the child in 75 percent of the cases (Andrews et al. 2002).

In a study of child abuse and family violence in Western Australia's Aboriginal communities, researchers found that child sexual abuse in those communities arises "from multiple causes, many of which related to cultural disintegration, unresolved community trauma and racial abuse" (Stanley et al. 2002, 11). Many cases are probably not reported to the authorities, for fear of reprisals or embarrassment. Another study indicated that of the 4,073 Aboriginal children in out-of-home care in June 2001, approximately 80 percent had been sexually abused (Stanley et al. 2002).

The Canadian Incidence Study of Reported Child Abuse and Neglect was conducted in 1998 and was the first nationwide study of child abuse and neglect in that country. Findings indicated that there were approximately 21.52 investigations of child abuse and neglect per 1,000 children in Canada, and 45 percent of those abuse allegations were substantiated. Some 10 percent of the investigations concerned child sexual abuse, and 38 percent of those were substantiated. The study found that the most common forms of sexual abuse included touching and fondling of the genitals, completed sexual activity, and adults exposing their genitals to children.

Medical personnel in New South Wales have been required to report suspected cases of physical and sexual abuse of children since 1977. In 1987, teachers, counselors, social workers, and early childhood workers were added to the list of mandated reporters. Doctors, nurses, and police personnel have been required to report since 1993 in Victoria. Teachers and school principals were added to the list in 1994, and by 1995 reports had increased by 58 percent. Queensland medical personnel were mandated to report in 1937. In South Australia, medical personnel, nurses, dentists, pharmacists, psychologists, police, probation officers, social workers, teachers, family day-care workers, and governmental and nongovernmental workers in the fields of health, welfare, education, child care, and residential services to children were mandated reporters as of 1993 (ibid.).

The 1995 results of a study of the prevalence of child sexual abuse in Spain indicated that prior to the age of seventeen years, 15 percent of males and 22 percent of females had been abused (Lopez et al. 1995).

Developing Regions/Countries

The developing countries consist of less industrialized countries, many of which do not have reporting systems in place to track cases of child abuse, especially child sexual abuse. See Table 3.2 for information concerning reporting systems in selected countries. Definitions of child sexual abuse may vary from country to country, depending on cultural and social values.

For many children in developing countries, survival is foremost on their minds. They live in poverty, often not attending school but working to help support the family; this is especially true for girls. Parents work hard to support their families, often with the help of the children, but the cycle of poverty is difficult to escape. The government's attention is not focused on child sexual abuse, because it rarely makes the headlines. Children who have no parents are often left to fend for themselves. The age of consent may also be lower in developing countries than in developed countries; for example, the age of maturity for girls in Pakistan is sixteen.

Studies of the prevalence and incidence of child sexual abuse have been conducted with limited samples in many countries. For example, in Nicaragua, a random sample of literate men and women between the ages of twenty-five and forty-four years in the city of Leon were interviewed concerning sexual abuse when they were children. Results indicated that 20 percent of the men and 26 percent of the women reported that they had been sexually abused as children (Olsson et al. 2000).

Prior to 1997, no studies had been conducted on the sexual abuse of children in Pakistan; a 1997 study focused on one province of the country. At the time, the local newspapers had reported forty-six cases of child sexual abuse over a three-month period, including sexual assaults, rapes, incest, and exposure to pornographic materials. Generally, child sexual abuse was considered to be a domestic affair and police rarely interfered. The study reported in 2001 included seventy-four children in three out of four provinces who had been sexually abused: thirty boys and forty-four girls. They ranged in age from five to eighteen,

TABLE 3.2
Child Abuse Records and Policies in Selected Countries

Country	Official Records Maintained by Government	Official Government Policy Regarding Child Abuse and Neglect	Elements of Policy Regarding Reported Abuse
Argentina	No	Yes	Mandated reporting by certain professionals
Armenia	No	No	
Australia	Yes	No	
Bahrain	Yes	Yes	Voluntary reporting of suspected abuse
Brazil	No	Yes	Mandated reporting by certain professionals
Bulgaria	Yes	Yes	Mandated reporting by certain professionals
Cameroon	No	Yes	No mandatory reporting
Canada	Yes	Yes	Mandated reporting by certain professionals
China	No	Yes	Mandated reporting by certain professionals
Colombia	Yes	Yes	Mandated reporting by certain professionals
Congo	Yes	Yes	Mandated reporting by certain professionals
Côte D'Ivore	No	Yes	No mandatory reporting
Denmark	No	Yes	Mandated reporting by certain professionals
Egypt	No	Yes	Mandated reporting by certain professionals
El Salvador	Yes	Yes	Mandated reporting by certain professionals
England	Yes	Yes	Mandated reporting by certain professionals
Estonia	No	Yes	Mandated reporting by certain professionals
France	Yes	Yes	Mandated reporting by certain professionals
Georgia	Yes	No	N/A
Germany	Yes	Yes	Voluntary reporting
Ghana	yes	Yes	Mandated reporting by certain professionals
Hong Kong	Yes	No	N/A
Hungary	Yes	Yes	Mandated reporting by certain professionals

(continues)

TABLE 3.2 *(continued)*
Child Abuse Records and Policies in Selected Countries

Country	Official Records Maintained by Government	Official Government Policy Regarding Child Abuse and Neglect	Elements of Policy Regarding Reported Abuse
India	No	Yes	Voluntary reporting
Indonesia	No	Yes	Voluntary reporting
Israel	No	Yes	Mandated reporting by certain professionals
Italy	Yes	Yes	Mandated reporting by certain professionals
Jordan	Yes	Yes	Mandated reporting by certain professionals
Kenya	Yes	Yes	Voluntary reporting
Krygyzstan	No	Yes	Voluntary reporting
Latvia	No	Yes	Mandated reporting by certain professionals
Lebanon	No	Yes	Voluntary reporting
Liberia	No	Yes	Voluntary reporting
Malaysia	Yes	Yes	Mandated reporting by certain professionals
Mauritius	Yes	Yes	Mandated reporting by certain professionals
Mexico	Yes	Yes	Mandated reporting by certain professionals
Mongolia	No	Yes	Voluntary reporting
Nepal	No	Yes	Mandated reporting by certain professionals
Netherlands	Yes	No	N/A
New Zealand	Yes	Yes	Voluntary reporting
Nigeria	No	Yes	No reporting requirements
Pakistan	No	No	N/A
Palestinian Territory	Yes	Yes	Mandated reporting by certain professionals
Peru	Yes	Yes	Mandated reporting by certain professionals
Philippines	Yes	Yes	Mandated reporting by certain professionals
Poland	No	No	N/A
Portugal	Yes	Yes	Mandated reporting by certain professionals
Romania	Yes	No	N/A

(continues)

TABLE 3.2 *(continued)*
Child Abuse Records and Policies in Selected Countries

Country	Official Records Maintained by Government	Official Government Policy Regarding Child Abuse and Neglect	Elements of Policy Regarding Reported Abuse
Russian Federation	No	No	N/A
Rwanda	Yes	Yes	No reporting requirement
Saudi Arabia	No	No	N/A
Scotland	Yes	Yes	Voluntary reporting
Serbia and Montenegro	No	No	N/A
Singapore	Yes	Yes	Voluntary reporting
Slovak Republic	Yes	Yes	Mandated reporting by certain professionals
South Africa	Yes	Yes	Mandated reporting by certain professionals
Spain	No	Yes	Mandated reporting by certain professionals
Sri Lanka	Yes	Yes	Voluntary reporting
Sweden	No	Yes	Mandated reporting by certain professionals
Switzerland	Yes	Yes	Mandated reporting by certain professionals
Syria	No	No	N/A
Thailand	No	Yes	Mandated reporting by certain professionals
Ukraine	Yes	Yes	Mandated reporting by certain professionals
United States	Yes	Yes	Mandated reporting by certain professionals

including twenty-six children who were thirteen or younger when they were first abused. Perpetrators included immediate family, acquaintances, neighbors, teachers, shopkeepers, and strangers (UN Economic and Social Commission for Asia and the Pacific 2001).

In a study conducted in Ethiopia, Kenya, and Uganda on violence against girls, the researchers studied a variety of forms of violence, including physical, psychological, and sexual violence perpetrated against young girls. Three research teams selected

500 young women from a variety of social classes and groups in the capital cities of each country. Sexual violence included verbal abuse, rape, sexual harassment, exploitation, trafficking, and harmful traditional practices including genital mutilation. The most common form of sexual abuse was being spoken to in a sexual manner, experienced by more than 85 percent of the girls in Uganda, 65 percent in Kenya, and over 50 percent in Ethiopia. Indecent sexual touching was experienced by 53 percent of the girls in Uganda, 44 percent in Kenya, and 42 percent in Ethiopia. Forty-two percent of the girls in Uganda, 30 percent in Ethiopia, and 26 percent in Kenya had been raped (African Child Policy Forum 2006).

Similar to findings for the developed countries, children in developing countries are sexually abused not only at home but also at other, seemingly safe locations outside the home. Several specific locations are discussed below.

In School

In 1998, according to UNICEF, almost two-thirds of the 130 million children not attending school in developing countries were girls. When girls do attend school, they are often subjected to various types of abuse, including sexual abuse. Boys may also be at risk of sexual abuse, but girls more frequently experience sexual assault, abuse, sexual harassment, and rape by classmates and teachers.

In South African schools, a Human Rights Watch study found that the incidence of rape, sexual assault, and sexual harassment of girls was widespread, and that both teachers and male students were the offenders. Girls were raped in school bathrooms, in empty classrooms and hallways, and in hostels and dormitories. They were frequently fondled, subjected to aggressive sexual advances, and verbally degraded. The atmosphere created by the abuse was difficult for many of the girls to withstand; some quit school because of the abuse or fear of abuse. Others were determined to stay in school, wanting the education and believing that the abuse was the price they had to pay to be educated (Human Rights Watch 2001d).

The reactions of those in authority often were not very sympathetic to the girls brave enough to report the sexual abuse. School officials treated the schoolgirls who reported being sexually abused by their male classmates or teachers with indifference, disbelief, or hostility. Parents in South Africa repeatedly told Human Rights Watch that schools asked them not to get the police involved or to draw publicity to problems of sexual violence at school. In one instance, a school principal persuaded a parent to drop rape charges against a teacher, promising "to take care of the matter." Nothing was done, and the teacher continued to teach at the school (ibid.). In another instance, it was found that a teacher accused of raping a student had been reported at other schools for similar offenses. None of the schools had reported him to the police, however, leaving him free to continue his pattern of abuse in new schools and against other children (Human Rights Watch 2001a).

Some countries, including South Africa, may require girls to submit to virginity examinations before being allowed to attend school. In Turkey, a 2001 decree required girls studying in government-sponsored medical high schools to undergo virginity examinations, specifically for those girls "known to be having sex or engaging in prostitution." Girls who fail these examinations, which entail intimidation and pain, are expelled from school. The examinations, which had been banned since 1999, also violate the "girls' right to bodily integrity. In the past, girls have attempted suicide rather than submit to this abusive examination" (ibid., 17).

In Orphanages

Orphanages are another place where sexual abuse of children has been reported. Children in orphanages, especially the sick and abandoned, may not have anyone protecting them from abuse. A study of abuse in an orphanage in Shanghai found that, when workers in Shanghai's orphanage tried to expose abuses, they were demoted and harassed. The orphanage director, accused of abusing and raping children in the orphanage, used his control over bonuses, staff assignments, and housing allocations to harass his opponents and reward supporters. A speech therapist was suspended from her duties and transferred to a position cleaning bathrooms and windows. An orphanage driver was attacked and badly beaten by a group of employees loyal to the director. Eventually, all of the critical staff were forced from their jobs (Human Rights Watch 1996b).

At Work

According to the International Labor Organization (ILO), there are approximately 250 million children between the ages of five and fourteen who work in developing countries, and almost half of them work full-time. In India children often work as bonded laborers, working off the debts of their families. Girls were subjected to sexual abuse, and those working inside Indian factories were frequently targeted for sexual assault by the factory owners. The practice was so prevalent that it was difficult for these girls later to get married. Because of the high rate of abuse, everyone assumed that the factory girls had been "touched"— that is, molested or raped by their employers. As a consequence, they were shunned as potential brides (Human Rights Watch 1998).

In Kenya, a study of girls working as housemaids found that, of twenty-five girls aged nine to sixteen years who were interviewed in depth, eighteen were HIV-positive. Of those eighteen, most had worked in several homes and reported being sexually abused in all or most of them. Fifteen of the girls said that their first sexual experiences were coerced and were with their employer or someone in his family or circle of friends (Human Rights Watch 2001b). Kenya is estimated to have about 1 million children who have lost parents to AIDS, and many more whose parents are ill with the disease. In Kenya and many other African countries, these AIDS-affected children are likely to have to leave school and seek work, and they may wind up on the streets or in jobs that put them at risk of violence, including sexual abuse (Human Rights Watch 2001a).

In a 1998 study in Sri Lanka, Human Rights Watch interviewed approximately seventy children who were domestic workers. Several of the Sri Lankan girls who were interviewed also experienced sexual abuse at the hands of their employer, their employer's children, or their employer's friends. Such abuse is frequently known to agents who arrange for the children's employment. One agent told Human Rights Watch of how he had recruited more than a thousand children for domestic service when he knew that the primary purpose of the recruitment was sexual (ibid.).

In Ecuador, where Human Rights Watch interviewed forty-five children who had worked on banana plantations in early

2001, researchers found that girls working in banana packing plants routinely experience sexual harassment in the workplace. "He goes around touching girls' bottoms. . . . I was taking off banana plastic coverings, and he touched my bottom. He keeps bothering me," one twelve-year-old girl said, speaking of one of her supervisors. "He gave my cousin the nickname 'whore.'" Another twelve-year-old girl said that the boss of the packing plant makes lewd remarks "when we bend down to pick up plastic bags" (ibid.).

Boys and girls can also be put to work in small shops or factories. Boys from Bangladesh, for example, are often sent to work in manufacturing industries and sweatshops in India and Pakistan. Others, including the disabled, are used for organized begging (UNICEF 2003).

By Marriage

In many countries, some girls are taken for forced marriage. In 2002 the government of the United Kingdom reported that, in the previous 18 months, it had dealt with more than 240 cases of forced marriage and helped with the repatriation of 60 young people. Not all victims were female; in about 1.5 percent of cases, the unwilling partner was the husband. Forced marriage is also a huge problem in many African countries, including Ethiopia, Gambia, and Nigeria (ibid.).

In War

During armed conflicts, children may be subjected to rape, sexual assault, and other violent crimes. For example, in Sierra Leone, children have been murdered, mutilated, tortured, beaten, raped, and enslaved for sexual purposes. Some of the atrocities committed by the rebel Revolutionary United Front (RUF) were unthinkable. Infants and children were thrown into burning houses, the hands of toddlers as young as two were severed with machetes, and girls as young as eight were sexually abused (Human Rights Watch 1999a). A newspaper reporter in Sierra Leone told Human Rights Watch, "There was rampant raping. I saw a fifteen-year-old girl raped right before me. They left her, but they captured others, and among them was a seven-year-old girl (Human Rights Watch 2001a).

In Colombia, thousands of children have been recruited into guerrilla forces and pro-government, military-backed paramilitaries. The Colombian paramilitaries have recruited children as young as eight years old, and according to some estimates, up to 50 percent of some paramilitary units are made up of children. Girls are reportedly subjected to high levels of sexual abuse by adult members of the paramilitaries (ibid.).

In Refugee Camps

Women and girls in refugee camps are vulnerable to rape, sexual assault, and other forms of sexual violence. While investigating the conditions of Burundian refugees in Tanzania refugee camps in 1998 and 1999, Human Rights Watch found that girls were subject to high levels of sexual abuse. In 1997, the International Rescue Committee conducted a survey of 3,800 women and girls; researchers found that approximately 26 percent of girls and women between the ages of twelve and forty-nine reported having been subjected to violence either during flight from Burundi or while in the camp. They found that girls were often attacked while carrying out routine daily tasks such as gathering firewood, collecting vegetables, farming, or seeking local employment (Human Rights Watch 2000).

Human Rights Watch received a number of testimonies from girls who had been raped in or near the Tanzanian camps. A fifteen-year-old girl reported that she was raped by two Tanzanian villagers in April 1999 while in the forest gathering firewood with a female friend. A sixteen-year-old girl was raped in October 1999, while collecting firewood outside a camp, by a refugee she described as a fifteen-year-old boy. Another sixteen-year-old girl was raped by two men while traveling to visit her uncle with her younger brother. "The two men took off my clothes, in the presence of my brother. They blindfolded me and raped me, one after the other. I would like the assailants to be punished for raping me." Although all three of these girls reported the rapes to the police, only one of the assailants was apprehended. He was released and subsequently fled (Human Rights Watch 2001a).

Many children are victimized not only by the initial abuse but also by the failure of authorities to take effective action against the perpetrator, or by acts of retaliation in response to their attempts to seek justice.

In Police Custody

Human Rights Watch found that children in the juvenile ward of a Pakistani prison rioted after members of the prison staff beat a thirteen-year-old boy for complaining of sexual abuse by the head warden. A legal aid center reported that such cases were far from isolated, and that they received many reports of sexual abuse of juveniles by both prison staff and adult inmates (Human Rights Watch 1999b).

In Jamaica, a fifteen-year-old Jamaican girl who ran away from home was picked up by police as a child "in need of care and protection" and taken to the local police station. During her second night in the lockup, she said that a police officer came to her and asked her age. When she told him, he asked if she had ever had sex. She said no, and he then tied her down with a belt, and raped and beat her (ibid.).

When children are put into adult prisons, they are frequently abused physically and sexually. Even in developed countries, children are sexually abused while in police custody and in prison. For example, in the United States a sixteen-year-old sentenced to eight years for arson was sent to an adult prison and within a week was raped by fellow prisoners (Human Rights Watch 2001c).

On the Streets

Children living on the streets are also at high risk for physical and sexual abuse. For example, a study in Bulgaria found that police harass and beat street children, extort money and sex from them, and demand oral sex from young girls (Human Rights Watch 1996a). Another study in Guatemala revealed similar abuse by police; young girls reported being raped by police and threatened by the police if they reported the rape. One girl reported that the police threatened to imprison her for marijuana if she reported the rape to anyone (Human Rights Watch 1997).

Worldwide Issues

Sexual abuse of children is found throughout the world, and there are certain issues that are better examined as global issues rather than issues related to individual countries or groups of countries. These areas include child pornography, child prostitution, and sex-trafficking.

The Internet and Child Pornography

The Internet has become an effective and efficient source of information in general, and a dynamic educational tool for children and adults. It is also a resource and vehicle for reproducing and disseminating child pornography, and providing a means for soliciting and procuring children for sex. Its speed, ease of use, availability, and low cost have speeded the growth and distribution of child pornography. Governments around the world are working to develop effective safeguards for protecting children from solicitations and restricting or banning child pornography.

Child pornography has become a multibillion-dollar international industry, generating more than $3 billion annually. All Western nations publicly denounce child pornography as being depraved and immoral. Participation is difficult to track and largely underground. Prior to the Internet, access to child pornography was complicated and could be expensive. However, today it is considered a worldwide problem, and pictures of children are traded around the world. The Internet has become a vast resource for pedophiles looking for child pornography; it has made these images readily accessible, and easy to produce and distribute.

The growing popularity of digital and video cameras, and even cell phone photo capabilities, has made it relatively simple and inexpensive to produce child pornography. As of July 2005, there were approximately 938 million people accessing the Internet and more than 35 million websites, with the numbers continuing to grow. There were approximately 4.2 million pornographic websites, including 372 million pornographic pages, and more than 100,000 websites that offer child pornography (TopTenREVIEWS 2006).

Some countries go into great detail in defining child pornography, while others, especially those countries with little access to the Internet, provide less detail in their definitions. For example, child pornography legislation in South Africa is highly detailed, while legislation in Barbados refers only to "photographs" when describing child pornography.

One factor to be considered in examining child pornography is how various countries and legislation define a child—this generally is a chronological age, but social and cultural factors also affect the definition. The UN Convention on the Rights of the Child and many countries in the West define a child as a person under the age of eighteen years. However, the age of consent for sexual activity varies from country to country; it is sixteen or fourteen in some jurisdictions (see Table 3.1). For example, in Australia and its territories, for the purposes of pornography, a child is defined as a person under the age of sixteen years in the Crimes Amendment (Child Pornography) Act 2004. The age of consent in the United States varies from state to state, being as low as fifteen in some jurisdictions. Often Western jurisdictions are likely to view children as dependent on their parents until the age of eighteen, while in other cultures childhood does not last that long.

Another factor is what constitutes pornography. Definitions of child pornography also vary among jurisdictions. A basic definition is "the visual depiction of children involved in sexually explicit activities" (Levesque 1999, 62). Article 2 of the Optional Protocol to the Convention on the Rights of the Child on the Sale of Children, Child Prostitution and Child Pornography defines it as "any representation, by whatever means, of a child engaged in real or simulated explicit sexual activities or any representation of the sexual parts of a child for primarily sexual purposes." The Interpol standing working group on offenses against minors defines child pornography as "the consequence of the exploitation or sexual abuse perpetrated against a child. It can be defined as any means of depicting or promoting sexual abuse of a child, including print and/or audio, centred on sex acts or the genital organs of children" (Fournier de Saint Maur 1999).

Some jurisdictions suggest that child pornography contains obscene material; others suggest that it just contain sexualized behavior. These differing criteria mean that it is quite possible for a picture to be regarded under laws that emphasize sexual qualities as child pornography but to fail in jurisdictions where obscenity or public morality definitions prevail (Taylor and Quayle 2003). For example, in the United States, pictures of naked children, not in any sexual or sexualized pose, are not generally considered to be pornography.

Suggestions that child pornography is acceptable if the child consents to the photographs being taken are not valid, because children are considered not able to consent to participating in child pornography or any other sexual activity.

Functions of Child Pornography

Some research suggests that viewing child pornography leads to the sexual abuse of real children, while other research indicates that those who view or use child pornography have never abused a child and never intend to do so. Some offenders may use images of child pornography to help them overcome their fears and inhibitions and go out and sexually abuse children, while others may fulfill their desires by viewing the pornographic images and never need or want to abuse a child (Quayle and Taylor 2002; Marshall 2000; Jenkins 2001).

In a study of thirteen men who were convicted of various child pornography offenses—that is, images were found on their computers—Taylor and his colleagues found six ways in which the men used the images they had found on the Internet. The men used the images for sexual arousal, as collectibles, to facilitate social relationships, to avoid reality (real life), as therapy, and as an anonymous source of a wide variety of materials. Several of the men used the images as a way of arousing themselves, creating fantasies to go along with the images; the wide availability and ease of access gave several of these men a sense of justification and legitimacy—that if the images are readily available, they must be all right to use. Others collect images, completing sets of images as if they were stamp or baseball card collections, which also appeared to give them legitimacy in the minds of the offenders.

Some of the men found that child pornography helped them to meet others like themselves—especially in chat rooms—and reinforced their behavior, making them believe that their actions were legitimate. Such contacts also helped to provide additional sources of child pornographic images. These relationships may also help the offender avoid real life, by creating enough contact or actual friendships on the Internet that he does not feel isolated. Some of the men interviewed claimed that by accessing the images on the Internet, they do not feel the need to go out and find actual children to abuse, implying that they would sexually abuse children if they did not view pornography. Finally, some of the men indicated that the Internet has made it easier to access child pornographic materials: it is anonymous, and there is more variety available than before the advent of the Internet (Taylor et al. 2001).

Legislation against Child Pornography

Laws have been enacted by the U.S. Congress and the states to protect children from pornography and predators on the Internet. The constitutionality of many of these laws has been challenged, and some have been overturned. While the First Amendment does not protect pornography that involves real children, virtual child pornography creates a different problem. Morphing permits an image that is not obscene to be transformed into a pornographic image; this technique actually can create a computer-generated image of a child from adult pornography images.

The first attempt by the U.S. Congress to regulate transmission of pornography to children was the Communications Decency Act of 1996, which "prohibited the transmission in interstate or foreign commerce of obscene or indecent images to any recipient under the age of eighteen. The CDA also prohibited knowingly sending or displaying patently offensive material in a manner that was available to persons under eighteen. . . . The Supreme Court eventually struck down the CDA as a content-based regulation of speech that was unconstitutionally vague and overbroad" (Martin 2002).

Following the ruling that struck down the CDA, Congress passed the Child Online Protection Act (COPA). COPA prohibits any individual or entity from knowingly making a communication using the World Wide Web for commercial purposes when that communication is available to minors and is harmful to minors. Congress intended COPA to limit the scope of the content prohibition to commercial speech on the Web that is harmful to minors. The Supreme Court heard the case and in 2004 upheld the lower court injunction against enforcing COPA (*Ashcroft v. ACLU*, 542 U.S. 656 [2004]).

With the advent of digital-imaging technology, real children were not required in the production of child pornography. There are two types of computer-generated pornography: computer-altered and virtual. Computer-altered images are images of actual children that have been altered in some way—for example, pictures of innocent children in which their clothes have been removed or they are posed in provocative positions. Virtual images are created by the computer without using photographs of real children.

As a result of this new technology, Congress passed the Child Pornography Prevention Act of 1996 (CPPA) to prevent the production of virtual child pornography. In the U.S. Senate report on the CPPA, photo imaging and related technologies allow people to produce "visual depictions of children engaging in sexually explicit conduct which are virtually indistinguishable to an unsuspecting viewer from unretouched photographs of actual minors engaging in such conduct" (S. Rep. No. 104–358, at 8 [1996]). The CPPA defined child pornography as "any visual depiction, including any photograph, film, video, picture, or computer, or computer-generated image or picture, whether made or produced by electronic, mechanical, or other means, of sexually explicit conduct."

In 2002, the U.S. Supreme Court held that the ban on virtual child pornography in the CPPA abridges the freedom to engage in a substantial amount of lawful speech and is therefore overbroad and unconstitutional under the First Amendment.

Many initiatives are under way to combat and prevent online child pornography. They range from legislative measures, the starting point to addressing the phenomenon with a human rights perspective, to the establishment of specialized units within law enforcement agencies, action plans, working groups, codes of conduct, hotlines, and awareness-raising campaigns (Petit 2004).

In England and Wales, for the purposes of child pornography, a child is defined as being under the age of sixteen under the Protection of Children Act of 1978. The act prohibits four aspects of child pornography: taking or permitting to be taken an indecent photograph of a child, or manipulating an image to appear to be an indecent photograph, showing or distributing such photographs, having in one's possession such photographs, and publishing an advertisement for such a photograph (Protection of Children Act, 1978, c. 37, § 1 [Eng.]). The Criminal Justice and Public Order Act of 1994 further defined a photograph to include negatives, films, video recordings, and stored data (Criminal Justice and Public Order Act, 1994, c 33 § 84[3][b]). In addition, possession of child pornography is prohibited by Section 160 of the Criminal Justice Act of 1988 (Criminal Justice Act, 1988, c. 33 § 160 [Eng.]).

The United Kingdom has also created the Paedophile On Line Investigation Team (POLIT), which was formed in 2003 as part of the National Crime Squad as the single point of contact in the United Kingdom for supporting, coordinating, and assisting national and international investigations of Internet-related child abuse, including sexual abuse. Between January 2004 and July 2005, POLIT received more than 2,500 referrals. The team also developed ChildBase, a sophisticated database to help identify victims of abuse, as well as the abusers themselves. Software helps to detect whether the victim or abuser is known to other law enforcement agencies; faces can be mapped and compared against images already in the database. As of August 2005, the ChildBase database contains approximately 220,000 images of abuse, involving approximately 20,000 children from around the world.

The National Crime Squad also participates in the Virtual Global Taskforce (VGT), which is developing several initiatives to reduce the incidence of child sexual abuse via the Internet. The taskforce is an international partnership among law enforcement agencies and industry in Australia, Canada, the United Kingdom, the United States, and Interpol. Their website acts as a gateway for information concerning child sexual abuse; it allows individuals to report instances of online sexual abuse in various countries, and offers links to other resources.

The forty-three member states of the Council of Europe, along with four nonmember states (Canada, Japan, South Africa, and the United States), were concerned about all types of criminal activity, including child pornography, occurring on the Internet and other computer networks. As a result, in 2001 they enacted the Convention on Cybercrime, which entered into force in 2004; it is the first international treaty to address several types of crimes that are committed on the Internet. The convention defines prohibited conduct, including child pornography. It includes descriptions of basic national legal procedures and human rights safeguards that all member nations should include in their legal systems, and it suggests several areas where international cooperation is appropriate.

In England, although Internet service providers (ISPs) are required to remove illegal content from their servers when they become aware of that material, they are not required to search their servers for such material. Some ISPs are working on ways to find illegal content on their servers. For example, the Demon Internet, an ISP in the United Kingdom, has developed and tested a system that automatically extracts child pornography and other illegal material from Usenet groups. Their engine scans more than 25,000 newsgroups, looking for material that has been reported to the Internet Watch Foundation (IWF), and then removes it from the newsgroups.

IWF is an independent organization based in the United Kingdom that gathers information on illegal child abuse images found on the Internet. Working with all the major search engine organizations, the IWF has become the primary hotline for reporting indecent images on the Internet. They forward information regarding substantiated complaints to the National Criminal Intelligence Service/Interpol for dissemination to appropriate law enforcement agencies. Almost 20,000 complaints were made to the IWF in 2003, and some type of action was taken in 17 percent of the complaints. In 2004 more than 17,000 complaints were made, and action was taken in 20 percent of them. Most of the illegal content was found on websites (90 percent), with the remainder on Usenet groups (2 percent), proprietary groups (1 percent), and other sources (7 percent). Some 40 percent of the websites containing illegal content were located in the United States; 31 percent were in Russia, 12 percent in Europe, 13 percent in Asian countries, 1 percent in the United Kingdom, and 3 percent in other countries (*Internet Watch Foundation Annual Report 2004*).

The Hotline for Child Pornography on Internet in The Netherlands requests that Internet users who find child pornography sites report them to the hotline. The national commissioner of police in Denmark established an Internet home page where individuals can report information on suspected distribution of child pornography directly to the police.

In addition to child pornography, the Internet also serves as a means for child sexual abusers to locate children who can be lured into performing various sexual acts. Whether the predator searches for a child in person or over the Internet, the process is similar—the predator targets a child, initiates a friendship, provides gifts to the child, and does whatever else he or she believes is necessary to earn the child's trust. The advantage of the Internet to the predator is that it is anonymous—no one is there to observe the predator and child together and question the relationship.

The National Center for Missing and Exploited Children provided funding for a survey on Internet victimization of youth in 1999. Four types of victimization were examined: sexual solicitation and approaches, aggressive sexual solicitation, unwanted exposure to sexual materials, and harassment. The survey results indicated that one child out of five had received a sexual approach or solicitation over the past year; one in thirty-three had received an aggressive sexual solicitation; one in four had an unwanted exposure to sexual materials, including pictures of naked people or people having sex; and one in seventeen was threatened or otherwise harassed. Girls were targeted more than boys (66 percent to 34 percent), and 77 percent were fourteen or older. The youngest age group, ten to thirteen years old, constituted 22 percent of the solicitations but were more distressed by the contact than the older children. The characteristics of the perpetrators were not always known; when known, they were more often male (67 percent, to 19 percent female) and under eighteen years of age (48 percent, to 24 percent eighteen years of age or older). This does not fit the stereotype of "dirty old men" in search of young children. In addition, only 25 percent of the children who were approached on the Internet told a parent, and 40 percent who reported an unwanted exposure told a parent. The authors concluded that

> the survey presents a complex picture about Internet relationships. Many young people are forming close friendships through the Internet, and some are forming close friendships with adults. Most such relationships appear to have no taint of sexual exploitation and appear to be positive and healthy. The fact that our survey found few sexually oriented relationships between youth and adult does not mean they never occur. They certainly do occur, but probably at a level too infrequent to be detected by a survey of this size. They seem to be few in a much larger set of seemingly benign friendships. (Finkelhor et al. 2000)

Another study focusing on ways in which juveniles become victims of sex crimes initiated through the Internet surveyed a random sample of 2,574 federal, state, and local law enforcement agencies between October 2001 and July 2002. The researchers found that 76 percent of the juveniles were between the ages of thirteen and fifteen; all were twelve years old or older. Three-fourths of the victims were female. Almost all (99 percent) of the offenders were male; approximately three-fourths (76 percent) were twenty-six years old or older. The offenders most often initiated the contact in chat rooms (76 percent), and spent between one and six months communicating with the juvenile. Communications included online contact through the chat room, telephone conversations (79 percent), sending pictures to victims (48 percent), offers of money or gifts, including jewelry, teddy bears, cell phones, and digital cameras. Most of the offenders were open in their desires—80 percent talked about sexual topics, while many others lured victims by posing as their friends or as owning or managing modeling agencies. Eighty-three percent of the offenders met face-to-face with the victims, who willingly went with them—to a hotel, movie, or restaurant; 89 percent of the encounters included oral sex, sexual intercourse, or other sexual activity with the victim. Forty-one percent spent at least one night with the victim. These findings indicate that, contrary to popular opinion and many prevention efforts, predators using the Internet are not always pedophiles who attempt to lure the child into meeting them by disguising their real intent. The authors suggest that a major challenge for prevention is determining the best methods for reaching the population of young teens who are willing to participate voluntarily in sexual relationships with adults whom they meet online (Wolak et al. 2004).

Chat rooms are increasingly used by predators to meet and groom children for eventual sexual encounters. Some countries have enacted legislation regarding such grooming or luring practices and are cooperating to monitor chat rooms and protect children. For example, the National Crimes Squad in the United Kingdom is working with the FBI in the United States and officers in Australia to monitor chat room conversations. The Virtual Global Task Force, composed of international police chiefs, has set up a fake child pornography website to identify and catch pedophiles.

Queensland (Australia) has a law that specifically targets adults who groom children using a variety of electronic means, including e-mail and Internet chat rooms. It is an offense for an adult to use any electronic communication to solicit a child under the age of sixteen for the purposes of engaging in a sexual act. The government of Australia followed Queensland's lead and, in 2004, enacted an antigrooming law specifically targeting the use of telecommunications to groom a child for sexual purposes.

Virtual Child Pornography

Another issue that arises with regard to child pornography and the Internet is whether virtual child pornography can be considered child pornography in the sense that it is harmful to children. Virtual child pornography is computer-generated; no child is being harmed in the making of virtual child pornography. In the United States, the Supreme Court ruled in 2002 (*Ashcroft v. Free Speech Coalition,* 535 U.S. 234 [2002]) that provisions in the Child Pornography Prevention Act that ban simulated or virtual child pornography are unconstitutional.

Many individuals and organizations believe that virtual child pornography is harmful to children. Child pornography, according to many, causes child abuse; therefore it does not matter that no child is harmed in the making of the pornography, because individuals viewing the images may be more likely to abuse children sexually. Just as perpetrators use images of child pornography to seduce children, trying to show them that "other children do it, so it must be all right," they can use these virtual images to encourage real children to participate in sexual activities. If virtual pornography is permitted, then it may be impossible to prove in court whether an image is real or simulated; some predators may be found not guilty on the basis of reasonable doubt.

Others argue that virtual child pornography is a good thing. If pedophiles are busy creating virtual images of children in various sexual poses and activities, then they will not be using and abusing real children. Therefore, children will be safe from sexual exploitation. However, most legislators and other professionals in the field of child sexual abuse believe that child pornography, virtual or real, harms children; some state legislators are considering banning virtual pornography, and attempts at the federal level continue.

Child Prostitution

According to UNICEF, there are roughly 10 million child prostitutes throughout the world. Many of these children get coerced into prostitution because their families are poor and need the income, because they have no family, or because they are trafficked.

Increasing population in Pakistan, as in many other developing countries, has put stress on the economic development of the country. Despite these pressures, however, "Pakistani society has stood for high value, respect and dignity of human life. Because of its strong social structure, cultural values and norms, women generally enjoy respect and regard in society. As a Muslim state, Pakistan forbids the practice of prostitution, and it is viewed as a social stigma. Although prostitution is not legal in Pakistan, its practice in certain segments of society where poverty forces women to earn their livelihood through prostitution cannot be denied" (UN Economic and Social Commission for Asia and the Pacific 2001).

Commercial sexual exploitation of children is below the radar in Pakistan but is known to exist, although statistics are hard to come by. A 2001 study found three basic categories of sexual exploitation—girls who were sold or married for profit, female prostitutes, and male prostitutes. The researchers believe that, for various reasons including societal norms and values, the serious problem of child sexual abuse and sexual exploitation remains a hidden social problem in Pakistan. It also appeared that because of sociocultural taboos, public displays of affection between an adult male and a male child were often accepted, while such expressions between an adult male and girl child were not tolerated. This may be a contributing factor to the existence of commercial sexual exploitation of boys. The age at which children are first commercially exploited ranged from twelve to fifteen years (37.1 percent), with one boy as young as six years old being reported. The research indicates that the family was the primary contributing factor in forcing 26.6 percent of the children into a life of prostitution and sexual exploitation. The secondary pathway into prostitution and abuse was "friends" who either forced or enticed the child.

Child Trafficking

Many purposes exist for trafficking in children, according to the traffickers—from general migration, especially in Africa and parts of Asia, to labor, sex, and child marriage. Trafficking generally requires the movement of people from one country, known as the country of origin, to another country, known as the country of destination. In some cases, they travel through another country, the transit country, before they reach the destination. Third World countries are often countries of origin, while the more developed countries are more likely to be destination countries.

Countries of origin have traditionally been more aware of child trafficking. Transit countries are more likely to perceive trafficking as a non-national issue, and that is a major obstacle to the control of national borders and coastlines. Countries of destination tend to show some indifference, as the problem originated in another country and does not concern their own children. They tend to view the problem as outside of their jurisdiction.

The trafficking in children has become a global phenomenon, and it is of growing concern for the international community as a whole—governments, international agencies, nongovernmental organizations, and the news media. The links between trafficking and the worst forms of exploitation of children are very apparent—in the Southeast Asia region, for example, the number of younger children who are being trafficked is rising alongside a clear increase in the number of child prostitutes.

Any study of trafficking must take into account cultural and other factors unique to each country. Poverty is certainly one factor, but weak governments, armed conflicts, and attitudes toward women and children are just some of the other factors. Families are tempted with false promises of a better life or an immediate cash payment for a child. Traffickers may tell the parents that their child will receive a good education and a secure job. In some cases the parents may suspect the truth, but their extreme poverty and lack of knowledge of trafficking may blind them to the truth of the situation.

Countries in which gender discrimination is strong or sanctioned are more likely to be open to trafficking of women and children, which may be seen as being morally acceptable. Cultures in which women and children are seen as inferior and weak are prime candidates for traffickers. Poor families may be encouraged to sell their children outright or hire them out; girls are more likely than boys to be subject to this practice, as they are not perceived as valuable to the family.

At the regional level, there is an increasing acknowledgment of the importance of a human rights approach in the development of laws to address trafficking. This is supported by the adoption of the African Charter on the Rights and Welfare of the Child and the initiative to finalize the optional protocol to the African Charter on Human and Peoples' Rights concerning the rights of women. It is also reflected in the critical work of the African Committee on the Rights and the Welfare of the Child, which, at its first session in 2001, identified the need for a human rights–based response to the problem of trafficking (Innocenti Research Centre 2003).

Ritual Abuse

Ritual abuse is generally seen as the prolonged, sadistic abuse in a secret group setting, usually under the aegis of Satanism, Christianity, witchcraft, and numerous pagan or other belief systems (see Chapter 1 for an overview of ritual abuse). Children are usually the victims, and the abuse can be physical, emotional, or sexual in nature. Attention to ritual abuse and its victims began in the United States following the publication of *Michelle Remembers*, a book about the author's alleged escape from a satanic cult when she was a child.

The day-care center abuse cases, beginning with the McMartin case, increased public attention to and awareness of this topic. In the late 1980s and early 1990s, allegations of ritual abuse began to appear in England, Australia, New Zealand, and a few other, primarily English-speaking countries. In 1991 the health secretary of the British government ordered a study of ritual abuse, following allegations of children being forced to participate in various activities during occult and other mysterious ceremonies. Some estimates of the number of children in England subjected to some type of ritual abuse were as high as 4,000. The study, conducted by Professor Jean La Fontaine, studied 967 cases that alleged organized ritual abuse and 86 cases of alleged ritual abuse between 1988 and 1991 in England. Allegations of human sacrifice were made in 35 cases, but no evidence was found to support the allegations. In 28 cases, allegations were made of individuals wearing ceremonial robes while participating in the rituals, but only two of those allegations proved true. As was the case with similar interviewing techniques used in the United States, this study found that the interviews with the children were not well done, and that questioning was often aggressive and suggestive (La Fontaine 1994).

In 1988, a case involving allegations of ritual abuse made headlines in New South Wales, when a mother claimed that her three-year-old daughter was being abused while at a day-care center. During the investigation, which included interviews with most of the children attending the center, many of the children claimed that they had been abducted; assaulted with various objects, including knives, pins, and hammers; sexually abused; given drugs; and forced to watch animal sacrifices and other forms of ritual abuse. The magistrate judge dismissed all of the charges on the grounds that the information gathered by investigators had been contaminated by the use of leading questions (Guilliatt 1996). Following the publicity of this case and other similar cases, however, new allegations began to appear throughout Australia.

Concerns over ritual abuse began to appear in New Zealand in 1991, when the Ritual Action Network was established. Members included social workers, counselors, and at least one police officer. Funded in part by the government, the group ran workshops concerning ways to recognize ritual abuse. Soon after one of their first workshops, a mother accused Peter Ellis, a day-care center worker at the Christchurch Civic Crèche, of sexually abusing her son. During an investigation, parents of the children were given a list of ritual abuse symptoms and began to ask their children questions about their experiences. Following intensive interviews with the children, stories surfaced of rituals involving human and animal sacrifice, insertion of various items into children's body cavities, forcing children to stand naked while female workers danced in a circle around them, and other bizarre activities. Ellis was convicted in 1993 of abusing seven of the children in the day-care center and served seven years in prison.

Castration of Repeat Sex Offenders

The debate over castration—either through drugs or actual physical castration—of sex offenders is not limited to the United States. Many countries had policies regarding castration long before the United States began to consider this method of control of sexual offenders. For example, Sweden has allowed castration since legislation was enacted in 1944. Individuals must be over twenty-three years old and must be considered a threat to society if not treated; they also must consent to the procedure, and it must be performed by a licensed physician (Russell 1997).

Denmark was the first country in Europe to enact legislation regarding castration. Enacted in 1929 and amended in 1935, it authorized castration without the permission of the offender, but that provision was removed in 1967. It can now be performed only by informed consent.

The Czech Republic's law, enacted in 1966 and amended in 1991, permits castration to be performed only on a voluntary basis and after being approved by a special committee.

Norway's castration law was passed in 1977. An individual may be castrated if it can be demonstrated that he is a continuing threat to society because of abnormal sexual urges (ibid.).

References

African Child Policy Forum. 2006. *Violence against Girls in Africa: A Retrospective Survey in Ethiopia, Kenya and Uganda.* Addis Ababa: African Child Policy Forum.

Andrews, Gavin, Bronwyn Gould, and Justine Corry. 2002. "Child Sexual Abuse Revisited." *Medical Journal of Australia* 176: 458–459.

Dinwiddie, S., A. C. Heath, M. P. Dunne, et al. 2000. "Early Sexual Abuse and Lifetime Psychopathology: A Co-twin Control Study." *Psychology and Medicine* 30: 41–52.

Finkelhor, David, Kimberly J. Mitchell, and Janis Wolak. 2000. *Online Victimization: A Report on the Nation's Youth.* Arlington, VA: National Center for Missing and Exploited Children.

Fleming, J. M. 1997. "Prevalence of Childhood Sexual Abuse in a Community Sample of Australian Women." *Medical Journal of Australia* 166: 65–68.

Fournier de Saint Maur, Agnes. 1999. "Sexual Abuse of Children on Internet: A New Challenge for INTERPOL." Paper presented at the Conference on Sexual Abuse of Children, Child Pornography and Paedophilia on the Internet: An International Challenge, January 18–19.

Goldman, J. D. G., and U. K. Padayachi. 1997. "The Prevalence and Nature of Child Sexual Abuse in Queensland, Australia." *Child Abuse and Neglect* 21: 489–498.

Goldman, R. J., and J. D. G. Goldman. 1988. "The Prevalence and Nature of Child Sexual Abuse in Australia." *Australian Journal of Sex, Marriage and Family* 9: 94–106.

Guilliatt, Richard. 1996. *Talk of the Devil.* Melbourne: Text Publishing.

Higgins, D. J., and M. P. McCabe. 1994. "The Relationship of Child Sexual Abuse and Family Violence to Adult Adjustment: Toward an Integrated Risk-Sequelae Model." *Journal of Sex Research* 31: 255–267.

Human Rights Watch. 1996a. *Children of Bulgaria: Police Violence and Arbitrary Confinement.* New York: Human Rights Watch.

Human Rights Watch. 1996b. *Death by Default: A Policy of Fatal Neglect in China's Orphanages.* New York: Human Rights Watch.

Human Rights Watch. 1997. *Guatemala's Forgotten Children: Police Violence and Arbitrary Detention.* New York: Human Rights Watch.

Human Rights Watch. 1998. *The Small Hands of Slavery: Bonded Child Labor in India.* New York: Human Rights Watch.

Human Rights Watch. 1999a. *Getting Away with Murder, Mutilation and Rape: New Testimony from Sierra Leone.* New York: Human Rights Watch.

Human Rights Watch. 1999b. *Prison Bound: The Denial of Juvenile Justice in Pakistan.* New York: Human Rights Watch.

Human Rights Watch. 2000. *Seeking Protection: Addressing Sexual and Domestic Violence in Tanzania's Refugee Camps.* New York: Human Rights Watch.

Human Rights Watch. 2001a. *Easy Target: Violence against Children Worldwide.* New York: Human Rights Watch.

Human Rights Watch. 2001b. *In the Shadow of Death: HIV/AIDS and Children's Rights in Kenya.* New York: Human Rights Watch.

Human Rights Watch. 2001c. *No Escape: Male Rape in U.S. Prisons.* New York: Human Rights Watch.

Human Rights Watch. 2001d. *Scared at School: Sexual Violence against Girls in South African Schools.* New York: Human Rights Watch.

Innocenti Research Centre. 2003. *Trafficking in Human Beings, Especially Women and Children, in Africa.* Florence, Italy: UNICEF Innocenti Research Centre.

Internet Watch Foundation Annual Report. 2004. Cambridge: Internet Watch Foundation.

Jenkins, Phillip. 2001. *Beyond Tolerance: Child Pornography on the Internet.* New York: New York University Press.

La Fontaine, Jean S. 1994. *The Extent and Nature of Organized and Ritual Abuse: Research Findings.* London: Her Majesty's Stationery Office.

Levesque, Roger J. R. 1999. *Sexual Abuse of Children: A Human Rights Perspective.* Bloomington: Indiana University Press.

Lopez, F., E. Carpintero, A. Hernandez, M. J. Martin, and A. Fuertes. 1995. "Prevalence and Sequelae of Childhood Sexual Abuse in Spain." *Child Abuse and Neglect* 19, no. 9: 1039–1050.

Marshall, W. L. 2000. "Revisiting the Use of Pornography by Sexual Offenders: Implications for Theory and Practice." *Journal of Sexual Aggression* 67: 67–77.

Martin, G. 1996. "Reported Family Dynamics, Sexual Abuse, and Suicidal Behaviours in Community Adolescents." *Archives of Suicide Research* 2: 183–195.

Martin, Richard. 2002. "State Regulation of Pornographic Internet Transmissions: The Constitutional Questions Raised by Senate Bill 144." *Florida State University Law Review* 29: 1109–1138.

Mazza, D., L. Dennerstein, and V. Ryan. 1996. "Physical, Sexual and Emotional Violence against Women: A General Practice-Based Prevalence Study." *Medical Journal of Australia* 164: 14–17.

National Criminal Intelligence Service (NCIS). 2005. "United Kingdom Threat Assessment of Serious and Organised Crime 2003: Sex Offences against Children Including Online Abuse." http://www.ncis.co.uk /ukta/2003/threat09.asp (accessed May 14, 2006).

Nelson, E. C., A. C. Heath, P. A. F. Madden, et al. 2002. "Association between Self-Reported Childhood Sexual Abuse and Adverse Psychosocial Outcomes." *Archives of General Psychiatry* 59: 139–145.

Olsson, Ann, Mary Ellsberg, Staffan Berglund, Andres Herrera, Elmer Zelaya, Rodolfo Pena, Felix Zelaya, and Lars-Ake Persson. 2000. "Sexual Abuse during Childhood and Adolescence among Nicaraguan Men and Women: A Population-Based Anonymous Survey." *Child Abuse and Neglect* 24, no. 12: 1579–1589.

Petit, Juan Miguel. 2004. "Report on the Rights of the Child." Report submitted by the Special Rapporteur on the sale of children, child prostitution, and child pornography. New York: UN Economic and Social Council.

Quayle, Ethel, and Max Taylor. 2002. "Child Pornography and the Internet: Perpetuating a Cycle of Abuse." *Deviant Behavior: Interdisciplinary Journal* 23: 331–333.

Russell, Stacy. 1997. "Castration of Repeat Sexual Offenders: An International Comparative Analysis." *Houston Journal of International Law* 19: 425–459.

Stanley, Janet, Katie Kovacs, Adam Tomison, and Kyllie Cripps. 2002. *Child Abuse and Family Violence in Aboriginal Communities—Exploring Child Sexual Abuse in Western Australia*. Melbourne: Australian Institute of Family Studies.

Swanston, H. Y., J. S. Tebbutt, and B. I. O'Toole. 1997. "Sexually Abused Children 5 Years after Presentation: A Case-Control Study." *Pediatrics* 100: 600–608.

Taylor, M., G. Holland, and E. Quayle. 2001. "Child Pornography, the Internet and Offending." *ISUMA, The Canadian Journal of Policy Research* 2 (Summer): 94–100.

Taylor, Max, and Ethel Quayle. 2003. *Child Pornography: An Internet Crime*. New York: Brunner Routledge.

TopTenREVIEWS. 2006. "Internet Pornography Statistics." Available at: http://internet-filter-review.toptenreviews.com/internet-pornography-statistics.html (accessed September 29, 2006).

UN Economic and Social Commission for Asia and the Pacific. 2001. *Sexually Abused and Sexually Exploited Children and Youth in Pakistan.* New York: United Nations.

UN General Assembly. 2002. "A World Fit for Children." Resolution adopted by the General Assembly, May 10.

UNICEF. 2003. *End Child Exploitation: Stop the Traffic!* New York: UNICEF.

Wolak, Janis, David Finkelhor, and Kimberly Mitchell. 2004. "Internet-Initiated Sex Crimes against Minors: Implications for Prevention Based on Findings from a National Study." *Journal of Adolescent Health* 35: 424–430.

4

Chronology

Sexual relations between adults and children have a long history. In early Christian history, women were considered the property of first the father and then the husband; female children were also considered property and had no rights. The early church considered twelve the age at which a young girl could be married; future husbands would examine these young girls much as they would measure the value of a horse.

Both the Bible and the Talmud encouraged men to have sexual relations with young girls. They were allowed to do this through socially sanctioned marriage, concubinage, and slavery. As Florence Rush wrote: "The Talmud held that a female child of 'three years and one day' could be betrothed by sexual intercourse with her father's permission. Intercourse with one younger was not a crime but invalid" (Rush 1980, 17).

In Hindu law and tradition, a girl must be married before puberty; if she is not married before she starts menstruating, she and her family are doomed to a tragic afterlife. A female child is born without a soul, and her only salvation is to be married before her first menstrual period. This, along with being a faithful and obedient wife, will often guarantee that she will have a peaceful afterlife.

In ancient Greece pubescent girls were forced to marry men usually between fifteen and twenty years older than themselves, and boys from noble families, at age ten, were required to have adult male lovers, who also would act as the boys' teachers and counselors. An adult man would court a young boy, and, once the boy's father had approved of and selected one lover for his son, the lover was allowed by law to "possess the boy by rape" (ibid., 50).

The remainder of this chapter presents a chronological list of major events in the more recent history of child sexual abuse.

900   Lady Murasaki writes *Tales of Gengi,* the story of her experiences with royal Japanese court manners. She was adopted by Prince Gengi of Japan at the age of ten. She was obviously more than a daughter to him, and in describing the situation, she says that if she were truly his daughter, "convention would not have allowed him to go on living with her on terms of such complete intimacy" (Lady Murasaki 1955, 146).

1179   The Catholic Church begins to sentence clerics who have molested boys and young men to a monastic life (France 2004).

1500s   Legislation is enacted in England that begins the process of protecting young children from sexual abuse. Boys are protected from forced sodomy, while girls under ten years of age are protected from forcible rape.

1576   Jurists in England rule that a female child can consent to sex at age ten and can be married at age twelve. Thus, having sexual relations with a female child under the age of ten is a felony, and having sexual relations with a female child between the ages of ten and twelve is a misdemeanor. It is still common for men to make exceptions to this rule, and female children generally are given little or no protection. Prior to this ruling, sexual relations with a child under the age of three according to Hebrew practice, and sex with a child under the age of seven according to canon law, are considered invalid, meaning that it was not believed to have occurred and was therefore ignored.

1600   The Piarist schools are founded in Rome by José de Calasanz, a priest who came to Rome from Spain, as the first free schools for poor children, established primarily to teach children vocational skills.

1646   Pope Innocent X abruptly closes the Piarist schools after allegations are made of sexual abuse of the children by teachers (Liebreich 2004).

1672   In Connecticut, a father is found guilty of incestuous acts with his daughter and is executed. However, the child is also blamed as partially responsible and is punished for her role in the incest; she is sentenced to a whipping (Oates 1990).

1828   In India, Ram Mohan Ray tries to eliminate child marriage but is not able to gather enough followers or to persuade the legislature to enact such a law. Child marriage has a long Hindu tradition, and was a common practice among many Hindu families in India.

1870s   In London, more than 20,000 children live on the streets, many of them dying of illness and starvation. Boys usually survive by stealing and girls by becoming prostitutes.

1877   The American Humane Association is founded as the only national organization working to protect both children and animals from abuse, neglect, cruelty, and exploitation. Their Children's Division works to break the cycle of abuse through training, risk assessment, research, and policy development programs initiated to provide effective child protective systems. They begin their efforts by working to protect animals and add children to their repertoire when they realize that no other organization exists to help and protect children.

1879   The London Committee for the Suppression of the Traffic of British Girls for the Purpose of Continental Prostitution is set up by Alfred Dyer and Benjamin Scott and is joined by several prominent members of the campaign against the Contagious Diseases Acts.

1883   The British Criminal Law Amendment Bill is passed by the House of Lords; the House of Commons passes it in 1885. The legislation raises the age of consent for girls from thirteen to sixteen years. Some of the provisions are enacted in response to what some referred to as "a moral panic about the sale of children into prostitution" (Smart 1989).

1897   Sigmund Freud begins to doubt the validity of his theories on hysteria, in which he first believed that many of his female clients had been sexually abused by their fathers, resulting in hysteria. He had theorized that these women were seduced by their fathers and then as adults experienced a variety of symptoms, including loss of appetite, vomiting, sneezing, and temporary blindness. He now believes that many of his patients were not sexually abused by their parents; they were merely attracted to the opposite-sex parent when they were very young. He will later develop his theory of the Oedipus complex, in which he theorizes that children are sexually attracted to their opposite-sex parent.

1910   Reginald Wright Kauffman writes *The House of Bondage,* in which he describes women who become prostitutes, the current social attitudes that lead children into prostitution, how they are seduced into it, and how they have difficulty escaping from it.

     In the United States, child protection agencies start a campaign against sexual attacks on young girls. The focus is on attacks by strangers, and the girls are often blamed as sex delinquents rather than being seen as victims. Many people believe that the young girls are the seducers and that most men cannot help but be lured by them.

1917   The Code of Canon Law of the Catholic Church condemns priests who exploit minor children, as well as those who solicit sexual favors during confession.

1920s   Sociologists start studying delinquent girls and discover that many have been victims of sexual abuse within their families. Up until this time, many experts believed that strangers, not family members, were the primary abusers of young girls.

1924   The first Declaration of the Rights of the Child is passed by the League of Nations. In its five brief articles it does not provide specific rights for children but offers only aspirations—that children should be cared for and protected: if they are hungry, they should be fed, and they should be the first to receive relief during times of distress.

1927   Many sources indicate that more than 80 percent of the people in India participate in child marriages. Katherine Mayo writes *Mother India*, a book about the lower status of women and the abuse that young girls are subjected to in child marriages. Because she is an outsider (she is American), many Indians attack her, claiming that she does not understand the reasons for child marriage and that she has manipulated the facts; she is also accused of racism. Nevertheless, her descriptions of what happens to child brides, based on a review of hospital records and interviews with medical personnel, are horrifying to most people outside of India. She describes the ruptured vaginas, lacerated bodies, peritonitis, venereal disease, and death of young women who are the victims of what most people consider sexual abuse. Many Indians, including poet Rabindranath Tagore, respond to her criticisms by condoning child marriage and denying that it is abusive to the young girls (Mayo 1927).

1937   Dr. Lauretta Bender and Dr. Abram Blau, after studying children who have been sexually assaulted, conclude that children are not necessarily innocent in cases of sexual abuse. They also hypothesize that these children may not be irreparably harmed by the sexual relations with an adult. Bender and Blau believe that in some cases the children are the actual seducers, rather than the adults—that these young girls either looked seductively at the men or dressed provocatively, and that the men were the victims (Bender and Blau 1937).

1950   In order to protect young girls, Israel forbids a father or groom from setting up a marriage with a girl who has not yet reached her sixteenth birthday. The Israelis later realize that this is not against the law according to the Talmud, and in 1960 they will strengthen this law by declaring that any person contracting a marriage for a young woman under the age of seventeen, no matter what the ancient law stipulates, will be subject to imprisonment or fines or both.

1953   Dr. Alfred Kinsey and his colleagues publish their landmark study of sexual behavior, *Sexual Behavior in the Human Female*. The researchers seem surprised to find that one in four women they interviewed report some sort of undesired sexual contact or experience initiated by an adult man. In cases of what we would today call sexual abuse, Kinsey also believes that men are in danger of being persecuted by females intent on protecting children and themselves. By punishing the offender, the law often damages everyone involved more than any pain the sexual abuse causes. For example, Kinsey and his colleagues cite cases in which men are thrown in jail for exposing themselves: their families are left destitute, their wives divorce them, and the children often become wards of the court. They believe that this is much more damaging than the physical and emotional pain inflicted on the child by the sexual abuse (Kinsey et al. 1953).

1954   Olympia Press publishes *Lolita* by Vladimir Nabokov. It is banned in many public libraries and denounced by many critics. The story centers on an aging European pedophile, Humbert Humbert, and Lolita, a twelve-year-old American who is kidnapped by Humbert, drugged, and sexually abused by him. He imprisons her, watches her every move, and thwarts her attempts at escape, until she finally gets away.

1959   The second Declaration on the Rights of the Child is passed by the United Nations. It indicates that children have the right to "special safeguards." Principle 9 provides that children "shall be protected against all forms of neglect, cruelty and exploitation."

1962   Seven couples who advocate legalizing sex with children start the Rene Guyon Society. They work toward getting this policy enacted into law but do not allow anyone who claims to have had sex with children to join their organization, because that behavior is still illegal. They advocate for policies that would allow children to have sexual relations with other children as well as to allow sex between children and adults. Their motto is "Sex by year eight or else it's too late."

C. Henry Kempe, a pediatrician from Denver, Colorado, and his colleagues, in an article in the *Journal of the American Medical Association*, describe the battered child syndrome, including characteristics of physically abused children that all physicians should be able to determine and that should help them more easily identify abused children. This is the first formal recognition of child abuse in the medical community. This article results in a surge of research on abuse— physical, sexual, and psychological—and brings national attention to the seriousness and extent of child abuse (Kempe et al. 1962).

The Catholic Church secretly sends "Instruction on the Manner of Proceeding in Cases of Solicitation" to the world's bishops. This document provides lengthy directions for trying a priest accused of sexual abuse and spells out punishments ranging from suspension of duties to excommunication and defrocking or laicization.

1963   California becomes the first state to enact a mandatory reporting law regarding the reporting of child abuse, including child sexual abuse. Physicians, teachers, and certain other professionals have greater responsibilities toward children and their protection.

1964   The Sex Information and Educational Council of the United States (SIECUS) is founded and is the first organization to provide honest and straightforward information about sex to parents, children, and teachers. Among other activities, it denounces all acts of sexual exploitation and sexual abuse. However, the organization also believes that children often are unable to report events accurately, may willingly participate in the sexual activity, may actually precipitate sexual relations, and for the most part are not significantly harmed by exposure to fondling and exhibitionism.

1967   All states in the United States have now adopted statutes regarding child abuse.

1969   The Children's Division of the American Humane Association, under the direction of Vincent DeFrancis, publishes the results of its study of sexual crimes perpetrated against children in Brooklyn and the Bronx, New York. They studied a sample group of 250 cases reported to police and child protection agencies. This is one of the first studies to estimate the prevalence and incidence of sexual abuse of children and to take into consideration the emotional trauma done to the child by such abuse (DeFrancis 1969).

1970   Parents Anonymous, a national self-help group for parents to help prevent child abuse, is founded. The national organization offers a variety of services to local chapters, including parent support groups, parent education workshops, and advocacy and public awareness activities. The organization will offer more than 2,100 groups this year for children and their parents at no charge to the families.

The National Commission on Obscenity and Pornography publishes a report concluding that pornography is not necessarily harmful to children or adults. Pornography may actually encourage open discussions between parents and children about sex. It is "not a factor in the causation of crime" and as a result "is not a matter of public concern" (*Report of the Com-*

mission on Obscenity and Pornography 1970, xi). This report does not discuss the exploitation of children who appear in all types of child pornography and denies that children are victimized by pornography.

1971   Henry Giarretto establishes one of the first model treatment programs, now known as the Child Sexual Abuse Treatment Program, in Santa Clara County, California. The Juvenile Probation Department (JPD) in Santa Clara, the designated reporting agency for all cases of child sexual abuse, has difficulty providing coordinated services to sexually abused children and their families. Members of the JPD ask Giarretto, a marriage and family counselor, to help establish a pilot project to provide counseling to the children and their families. At the end of the eight-week pilot project period, everyone who is involved in the project recognizes the benefits of this program. It is expanded to include the coordination of services required by the family, such as financial advice and legal assistance, and to help facilitate the reunification of the family.

1972   The C. Henry Kempe National Center for the Prevention and Treatment of Child Abuse and Neglect is established. Its purpose is to provide a clinically based resource for training, consultation, program development and education, and research into all forms of child abuse and neglect. The center is committed to multidisciplinary approaches to improve the recognition, treatment, and prevention of all forms of abuse and neglect, including sexual abuse.

1973   The Runaway Youth Act is passed by the U.S. Congress. It authorizes the spending of $8 million to develop shelters for children who have run away from home. Many people believe that this will help protect the estimated 1 million children living on the streets and protect them from becoming prostitutes, getting involved in drugs and alcohol, or becoming involved in pornography.

1974   The National Center on Child Abuse and Neglect (NCCAN) is established by the Child Abuse Prevention and Treatment Act (Public Law 93–247) as the primary federal agency charged with helping states and communities address the problems of child maltreatment. NCCAN oversees all federal child abuse and neglect efforts and allocates child maltreatment funds appropriated by Congress. They are responsible for conducting research on the causes, prevention, and treatment of child abuse and neglect; collecting, analyzing, and disseminating information to professionals concerned with child abuse and neglect; increasing public awareness of the problems of child maltreatment; and assisting states and communities in developing programs relating to the prevention, identification, and treatment of child abuse and neglect.

Marian Wright Edelman organizes the Children's Defense Fund (CDF) to protect America's youth. She wants to provide a strong and effective voice for all children, to educate the nation about the needs of children, and to encourage the support of children before they get sick, are abused, drop out of school, or get into trouble.

1976   Alfred M. Freedman and his colleagues write *Modern Synopsis of Comprehensive Textbook of Psychiatry II*, a psychiatric text used in many medical schools. It proclaims that "the occurrence of mother-son incest bespeaks more severe pathology than does father-daughter incest" (Freedman et al. 1976, 772).

NCCAN supports the first comprehensive incidence study of child abuse and neglect. Known as the National Incidence Study, in its written report, published in 1981, it estimates that 44,700 cases of child sexual abuse, or 0.7 per 1,000 children, were known to professionals during the period from April 1979 to March 1980 (National Center on Child Abuse and Neglect 1981).

In Louisiana, two fathers complain that Father Gilbert Gauthe inappropriately kissed their young sons. Bishop Gerard Frey orders Father Gauthe into psychotherapy, but the bishop never suspends or censures Gauthe in any way.

1977 The federal Protection of Children against Sexual Exploitation Act of 1977 is passed by the U.S. Congress. This law prohibits the production of any sexually explicit material that uses a child under the age of sixteen if the material will cross interstate lines. Penalties include ten years in prison and a $10,000 fine. This law focuses on the transporting, shipping, or mailing of child pornography, and little can be done to prevent someone from giving this type of material away or in other ways exchanging it for something else. The law prevents only the sale of this type of material. Many experts realize that this law does very little to stop the growing market for child pornography.

1978 The North American Man/Boy Love Association (NAMBLA) is formed. Members advocate for sexual relations between men and boys, arguing that children should be sexually liberated because children are fully capable of entering into sexual relations with appropriate knowledge and understanding of what is happening. They also believe that the age of consent laws in all states should be abolished.

The Protection of Children Act of 1978 is passed in the United Kingdom. This law makes it an offense for a person to take, or permit to be taken, any indecent photograph of a child, or to distribute or show such photographs, or to possess such photographs, or advertise them to others.

1979 The Illusion Theater in Minneapolis, Minnesota, produces the first live-theater program focusing on the prevention of sexual abuse. Children are the primary audience for this program, which focuses on letting

1979
(cont.)
children know that it is not acceptable if someone abuses them sexually, that it is not their fault, and that, if they have any questions or if they have been sexually abused, it is all right to talk to another adult about it.

Sociologist Diana Russell conducts the first truly random study to estimate the extent of sexual abuse of children. She interviews more than 900 women from the San Francisco area about their sexual experiences as children. Her findings indicate that 38 percent of the women had been sexually abused as children (Russell 1986).

1980
Michelle Remembers is published, the story of Michelle Smith and her escape from a satanic cult. The publication of this book triggers many reports from other people of satanic cults and ritual abuse, and it leads to growing interest and controversy regarding satanic cults.

Florence Rush publishes *The Best Kept Secret: Sexual Abuse of Children,* one of the first comprehensive studies on child sexual abuse. Rush, with detailed research and analysis, shows that child sexual abuse is not the occasional deviant act of some stranger, but a common occurrence in many families. With a historical overview of the sexual abuse of children, she shows how sexual abuse is still condoned in today's society.

Five sexual abuse treatment and training institutes are funded by the National Center on Child Abuse and Neglect (NCCAN). These include: (1) the Joseph J. Peters Institute in Philadelphia, Pennsylvania, (2) the Knoxville Institute for Sexual Abuse Treatment in Knoxville, Tennessee, (3) the Child Abuse Unit for Studies, Education, and Services (CAUSES) in Chicago, Illinois, (4) the Sexual Assault Center at the Harborview Medical Center in Seattle, Washington, and (5) the Institute for the Community as Extended Family (ICEF) in San Jose, California. Each of these institutes is founded to add to the knowledge of child sexual abuse and to demonstrate ways to disseminate this information nationally to professionals.

Several parishioners in St. John Parish in Henry, Louisiana, complain to Bishop Frey that Father Gilbert Gauthe spends more time with young boys than his adult parishioners. They are also concerned because he frequently has removed children from class for weekend sleepovers. Bishop Frey does not become concerned over this complaint, and because it is unsigned, he dismisses the letter as unreliable. He subsequently names Father Gauthe to be the diocesan chaplain for the Boy Scouts.

1981   The Boy Scouts publish the *Scoutmaster Handbook,* their first publication to include information about sexual abuse. The discussion focuses on men infiltrating troops for the sole purpose of sex, but the emphasis of the document is on young boys who are searching for sex, not adults who molest children.

Even though the allegations of sexual abuse committed by Father John Geoghan are well known, the archdiocese of Boston places him back into the ministry as an assistant pastor at St. Brendan's Church in Dorchester, Massachusetts. The pastor at St. Brendan's is unaware of the earlier allegations against Father Geoghan and welcomes his arrival. In addition, the archdiocese does not tell Geoghan to stay away from children. Not knowing of Geoghan's past, the pastor at St. Brendan's makes Father Geoghan responsible for the altar boys and CCD (Confraternity of Christian Doctrine) classes.

1982   In a case before the U.S. Supreme Court, *Ferber v. New York,* the plaintiff is a bookstore owner who was convicted, under New York state law, of promoting the sexual performance of a child under the age of sixteen after he sold two films of boys masturbating to an undercover police officer. This is the first time that the U.S. Supreme Court has considered the problem of

1982
(cont.)

child pornography, and it upholds the state law, ruling that "states are entitled to greater leeway in the regulation of pornographic depictions of children" (*New York v. Ferber*, 458 U.S. 747 [1982]). See Chapter 6 for a more detailed description of this and other relevant Supreme Court cases.

1983

Dr. Roland Summit publishes an article about the Child Abuse Accommodation Syndrome, in which he convincingly argues that children tend to remain silent about their experiences of sexual abuse. Many therapists and prosecutors believe that, if children deny that anything has happened to them, they are hiding the truth. This theory will come into play in later trials and convictions of several day-care employees at preschools throughout the country (Summit 1983).

A two-and-a-half-year-old child alleges that his teacher at the McMartin Preschool in southern California has hurt his bottom. Subsequent investigations at this preschool and others in the same area find at least 350 children who claim to have been sexually abused while attending preschool. After repeated questioning by authorities, children say that they have watched other children being sexually abused as well as being sexually abused themselves. Allegations include fondling, exposure to vaginal, oral, and anal sex, and ritualistic and satanic acts of abuse. After seven years of legal proceedings and much news media attention, no one is convicted.

On September 26, two young girls and their mothers go to the police department in Jordan, Minnesota, and tell the officers that James John Rud, a twenty-seven-year-old trash collector, has sexually abused the two young girls. Within six months, the case will attract national attention. Two-dozen men and women, many of them well respected in the community, will be charged in a conspiracy of sex, torture, and murder. The victims are their own children. The children will eventually allege acts of not only sexual abuse but also murder. The stories seem incredible, and many lawyers insist that the children have made everything up. What appear as strong cases against some parents end up as bizarre stories that no one believes; the prosecutor's behavior in all of the cases is soundly criticized, and all charges are eventually dropped. This is a classic case of charges of sexual abuse being made only to have the children's imaginations and the public's fear take over. In the end, people believe that some children were indeed sexually abused, but everyone involved in the case got carried away and overreacted. Many families are hurt financially and emotionally, but nothing is resolved.

An organization named VOCAL (Victims of Child Abuse Laws) is started in Minnesota by people who claim to have been falsely accused of sexually abusing children. It is started as a result of the many people charged with sexually abusing children in Jordan, Minnesota, who believe that they have been railroaded by the legal system and want to offer support to others who have been falsely accused.

The Catholic Church revises the Code of Canon Law. Several of the canons refer to child sexual abuse: clerics are prohibited from having sexual contact with minors, and punishment is described if the cleric disobeys this policy (Canon 1395). Canons 1717, 1718, and 1719 describe the requirements for investigations into cases in which a cleric is accused; Canon 1922 restricts an accused cleric's activities.

1984   The U.S. Congress passes the Child Protection Act, which expands the Protection of Children against Sexual Exploitation Act of 1977. It eliminates the requirement for a commercial transaction, strengthens prosecuting authority against the producers and distributors of child pornography, and raises the statutory age of a minor to eighteen. This legislation is an attempt to answer the Supreme Court's decision in *New York v. Ferber* by eliminating the requirement that child pornography be obscene to be criminal.

1984
(cont.)

The U.S. Senate holds its first hearing on the importation of child pornography from foreign countries.

The Attorney General's Task Force on Family Violence presents its final report. They find that many children typically endure up to twelve or more separate interviews through the course of court hearings in cases of child sexual abuse. The task force makes several recommendations to minimize the trauma to the victim of violence while still protecting the rights of the accused. They recommend using the same prosecutor throughout the court process, allowing hearsay evidence at preliminary hearings to minimize the number of times that the victim is required to testify, allowing the child's testimony to be presented on videotape, using anatomically detailed dolls to describe abuse, appointing a special volunteer advocate for the child, legally presuming that children are competent witnesses, allowing flexible courtroom settings, controlling press coverage, and limiting court continuances of each case.

A grand jury in Schriever, Louisiana, indicts Father Gilbert Gauthe on thirty-four counts of aggravated crimes against nature, immoral acts, producing child pornography, and aggravated rape. This indictment draws national attention to the sexual abuse of children being committed by priests.

1986

The Children's Justice Act is passed by the U.S. Congress and becomes law. It provides funds to the states to train law enforcement personnel in ways to manage child abuse. To receive funding, each state must establish an interdisciplinary task force that includes medical and mental health professionals, child advocates, judges, and attorneys. The purpose is to improve the chances of prosecution while reducing the trauma to the victims.

The Child Sexual Abuse and Pornography Act of 1986, Public Law 99–628, 100 Stat. 3510 (1986), is passed by the U.S. Congress. This legislation bans the production of and advertisements for child pornography.

A conference is held in Nairobi in which twenty-two countries participate. The participants created the African Network for the Prevention and Protection against Child Abuse and Neglect.

1987 The first documented case of ritual sexual abuse in England is reported in Congleton in Cheshire. Seven children in an extended family are believed to have been sexually abused, and the diaries kept by their foster parents reveal stories of witch parties, the murder of babies, and the killing of animals.

1988 The Boy Scouts introduce "Youth Protection Guidelines," a course on sexual abuse for professional and volunteer leaders. The course, presented on videotape, describes what sexual abuse of children is and how troop leaders can work to prevent the sexual abuse of Boy Scouts. Presenters include David Finkelhor and Kenneth Lanning, both sex abuse experts. Information is provided on new rules developed by the organization to combat the sexual molestation of scouts, such as requiring more than one adult leader on all trips, limiting conversations between an adult and a scout to areas where they can be observed by other people, and prohibiting an adult from sharing a tent with a young scout.

Kelly Michaels is found guilty and sentenced to forty-seven years in prison in one of the most bizarre and disturbing day-care cases in the country. Children attending the Wee Care preschool in Maplewood, New Jersey, allege that Michaels, their teacher, would gather them together at nap time and lead them through the church that housed Wee Care into a choir room. In this room, she made them remove their clothes and often removed her own clothing as well. The children report that they were forced to engage in sexual acts, to eat feces and urine, and to lick peanut butter off her genitals. Many of the children also accuse Michaels of putting kitchen utensils and Lego toys into their vaginas and rectums. None of the staff members say that they suspected any of

1988
(cont.)
these activities. In 1993, Michaels's conviction is overturned and all charges dropped.

The National Network of Children's Advocacy Centers is formed in response to the need for a coordinated effort to provide services to children who are sexually abused. The National Network consists of member and affiliate programs that provide technical assistance, training, and networking for communities that want to establish a children's advocacy center. These centers offer coordinated, multidisciplinary services to children who have been abused, particularly those who have been sexually abused, and their families. Each center offers a variety of services, usually coordinated by a case management team. The National Network establishes minimum standards that each member program must meet to be part of the network.

The U.S. Congress passes the Child Protection and Obscenity Enforcement Act, which prohibits the use of computers to transport, distribute, or receive child pornography. The act requires "all persons producing material containing visual depictions made after February 6, 1978, showing actual explicit sexual activity to determine the true age of the performers, to maintain records containing this information, and to affix to each copy of the material a statement about where these records could be found."

1989
The United Nations adopts the Convention on the Rights of the Child (UNCRC), which, among other items, prohibits child prostitution, child trafficking, and other illegal sexual practices with children under the age of eighteen years.

1990
In a case argued before the U.S. Supreme Court, *Osborne v. Ohio* (495 U.S. 103 [1990]), the plaintiff is convicted of possessing four photographs of a naked boy. The U.S. Supreme Court rules in the state's favor, indicating that the state can constitutionally forbid the possession of child pornography.

The U.S. Supreme Court rules in *Maryland v. Craig* (497 U.S. 836 [1990]) that a Maryland law that allows children to provide testimony in a sexual abuse case using closed-circuit television outside of the courtroom with only the prosecutor and defense attorney present does not violate the defendant's right to confront his accuser.

The Victims of Child Abuse Act is passed by the U.S. Congress. It allows children testifying in court to use anatomically correct dolls to demonstrate what happened to them, presumes children to be competent witnesses, protects children's privacy, allows children to testify via closed-circuit television or by using videotaped testimony, authorizes the appointment of a guardian ad litem to protect the best interests of the child, and provides for victim impact statements from the children. Speedy trials are encouraged, as are the use of multidisciplinary teams to treat and help the sexually abused child. The statute of limitations for beginning prosecution of child sexual abuse allegations is also extended until the child reaches the age of twenty-five.

An international campaign to End Child Prostitution in Asia Tourism (ECPAT) is started.

1991   A Predatory Offender Registration Statute is enacted in Minnesota as a result of the brutal abduction of eleven-year-old Jacob Wetterling. Individuals who have been convicted of a variety of child-related offenses are required to register as predatory offenders when they are released from prison.

1992   A former priest, James Porter, estimates that he sexually abused as many as 100 children when he was a priest. Defrocked in 1974, he is living with his wife and children in Minnesota when the allegations arise. In the end, 101 people come forward, claiming that he abused them when they were children. The publicity concerning the allegations against him draws attention to priest abuse of children and leads to a growing

1992 *(cont.)*	number of cases against priests and the Catholic Church.
1993	Former priest James Porter is indicted by a grand jury on forty-six counts of sodomy and indecent assault on thirty children in Massachusetts. Porter pleads guilty and is sentenced to eighteen to twenty years in the state prison.

President Bill Clinton signs into law the National Child Care Protection Act, sponsored by Representative Patricia Schroeder (D-CO), to create a national database of convicted child molesters. Youth organizations will be able to submit the names of their employees and volunteers to a state agency that is designated to run these names through the database of molesters, as well as through the FBI's database of convicted criminals, which includes murderers and kidnappers.

The New Jersey Court of Appeals rules that Kelly Michaels from the Wee Care preschool in Maplewood did not receive a fair trial, in part because the judge's questioning of the children was not impartial. The ruling states that the judge questioned the children in his chambers, and while the jury watched on closed-circuit television he played ball with them, sometimes held them on his lap and knee, whispered in their ears and had them whisper in his ear, and encouraged and complimented them. The state appeals the decision, and the New Jersey Supreme Court affirms the appellate court's ruling.

The Boston archdiocese of the Catholic Church puts in place written policies on handling sexual abuse complaints that are made against Catholic clergy.

At their semiannual meeting, the U.S. bishops' main agenda topic is sexual misconduct. They create an ad hoc subcommittee on sexual abuse, made up entirely of bishops. The subcommittee is given a broad mandate, including the power to ask Rome for the power to laicize sex offenders. The bishops also adopt a brief resolution that establishes a new national policy for dealing with individual allegations of abuse. It focuses on removing clergy promptly once the allegations against them are proved, reporting confirmed instances of abuse to civil authorities when required by law to do so, and informing the community when appropriate.

The Council of Representatives of the American Psychological Association votes to establish a working group to review current research into memories of childhood abuse and to identify future research and training needs.

1994   In the United States, agents from the U.S. Immigration and Customs Enforcement Agency's Operation Predator program arrest 237 individuals in what is believed to be one of the largest investigations into Internet child pornography at the time. More than 1,000 individuals are arrested in Australia, Canada, China, Denmark, Finland, Japan, Liechtenstein, The Netherlands, New Zealand, Norway, Sweden, Switzerland, and the United Kingdom. An Internet billing company, Regpay, is charged with providing credit card billing services to fifty child pornography websites, with operating at least four of its own child pornography websites, and with money laundering.

On July 29, Megan Kanka stops to talk to her neighbor, Jesse Timmendequas (a convicted sex offender), about his new puppy. She is never seen alive by her family again. Timmendequas would later confess to sexually abusing her and then killing her.

The U.S. Congress passes the Jacob Wetterling Crimes against Children and Sexually Violent Offender Registration Program (as part of the Violent Crime Control and Law Enforcement Act of 1994), requiring states to implement a registry of sex offenders and crimes against children.

1994
(cont.)
The International Bureau for Children's Rights is created to address violence against children throughout the world. One of their aims is to ensure that signatories will guarantee that the rights of every child within their borders are protected. The bureau's International Tribunal for Children's Rights provides coordinated intervention in behalf of children by lawyers, judges, criminologists, and human rights experts.

1995
At least four states (Florida, Missouri, Ohio, and Oklahoma) pass laws that require convicted sex offenders to be electronically monitored for the remainder of their lives. Laws vary according to the type of sex offender and the type of monitoring device required—electronic or GPS.

Cardinal Hans Hermann Groer, the archbishop of Vienna, is accused of repeatedly molesting young boys at an all-male Catholic high school in Austria. He rejects the allegations but is forced to resign.

1996
Megan's Law is signed by President Bill Clinton. It amends the Jacob Wetterling Crimes against Children and Sexually Violent Offender Registration Program, requiring all states to create their own systems for having sex offenders in their jurisdiction register with the local police. It also adds a provision for community notification. The hope is that Megan's Law will help the public better protect themselves from sexual offenders, and that it would discourage offenders from abusing again.

The U.S. Congress passes the Communications Decency Act, which makes it a crime for anyone to post indecent or obscene materials on the Internet. The law is challenged by the American Civil Liberties Union on First Amendment grounds. The U.S. District Court for the Eastern District of Pennsylvania enters a preliminary injunction against enforcement. The case reaches the U.S. Supreme Court, which affirms the lower court decision, finding that "provisions of the CDA prohibiting transmission of obscene or indecent communications by means of telecommunications device to persons under age 18, or sending patently offensive communications through use of interactive computer service to persons under age 18, were content-based blanket restrictions on speech, and, as such, could not be properly analyzed on First Amendment challenge as a form of time, place, and manner regulation" (*Reno v. American Civil Liberties Union*, 521 U.S. 844 [1997]).

The Child Pornography Prevention Act of 1996 is enacted into law. It bans "sexually explicit pornographic images of children that 'appears to be' or 'conveys the impression' that a minor is depicted." The law is later overturned (*Ashcroft v. Free Speech Coalition*, 535 U.S. 234 [2002]).

The Internet Watch Foundation (IWF) is established as an independent organization based in the United Kingdom that works to resolve problems of illegal material on the Internet. The IWF forwards information regarding substantiated complaints to the National Criminal Intelligence Service/Interpol for dissemination to appropriate law enforcement agencies.

The Australian Catholic Church agrees to settle 126 cases and pays U.S.$1.7 million in compensation, as well as another $850,000–$1.1 million for victims' counseling. The Church also apologizes to the victims ("Australian Church Apologizes for Abuse," BBC News, June 8, 2002, at http://news.bbc.co.uk/2/hi/asia-pacific/2032698.stm).

ECPAT organizes the World Congress against the Commercial Sexual Exploitation of Children in Stockholm, Sweden, to focus on ways to mobilize the world to find effective means of combating the commercial sexual exploitation of children. More than 120 countries participate; representatives are from intergovernmental organizations, NGOs, and the commercial community. An Agenda for Action is adopted that commits "governments to mobilize the business

1996
(cont.)

sector, including the tourism industry, against the use of its networks and establishments for the commercial sexual exploitation of children."

A U.S. federal grand jury indicts thirteen people from the United States, and three from Australia, Canada, and Finland, on charges of planning, organizing, and participating in the online molestation of ten-year-old girls. The defendants participated in real-time photo shoots in which they sent messages requesting photos of the girls in certain poses; one person shot the photos with a digital camera and transmitted the photos to the group. All of the defendants are members of the "Orchid Club," a private, online child pornography organization that shares sexually explicit images and videos of girls as young as five. To join the Orchid Club, members were required to know the password to access photos and online chat sessions. Initiation to the club required an aspiring member to describe a personal experience with a child (Stewart 1997).

1997

Approximately 10,000 sites can be found on the Internet that contain sexually explicit material (Miller 1999).

Father John Geoghan is arrested and charged with criminal sexual assault of a minor. He is accused of crimes against twenty-eight children.

The International Tribunal for Children's Rights holds its First Hearings in Paris, France, focusing on ways to use extraterritorial legislation to protect children from sexual exploitation. They develop several recommendations toward that end (see Chapter 6 for details).

In England, the legislature passes the Sex Offenders Act of 1997, which requires sexual offenders to register with the police but does not provide for public notification of sex offenders.

1998   The Protection of Children from Sexual Predators Act of 1998 criminalizes and increases penalties for conduct involving child sexual abuse and child pornography.

The Child Online Protection Act (COPA) is passed and requires commercial websites to collect a credit card number or other proof of age before allowing Internet users to view material deemed harmful to minors. The law is challenged on the grounds that it violates the First Amendment. The U.S. District Court grants a preliminary injunction against enforcement. The Court of Appeals affirms, and the U.S. Supreme Court affirms the lower court's ruling (*Ashcroft v. American Civil Liberties Union*, 542 U.S. 656 [2004]).

A European meeting of the International Dimension of Sexual Exploitation of Children is held in Madrid, organized by the Spanish Ministry of Justice and the International Bureau for Children's Rights to further the implementation of the Convention on the Rights of the Child and to work to develop effective means of protecting children.

The International Tribunal for Children's Rights holds its second hearings in Brazil, focusing on the development of solutions to the exploitation of children that could be implemented on regional and national levels.

In Operation Cathedral, led by Interpol, ninety-six people are arrested in twelve countries. The biggest equipment seizure involves forty-eight gigabytes of child pornography files that are seized at the home of a man in Finland. In the United Kingdom, the size of the seizure is estimated at a minimum of 250,000 images. In the United States, the biggest seizure at an individual's home is 75,000 images. Total seizures amount to 500,000 images and more than 120 videos of child pornography.

1999   The number of sites on the Internet that contain sexually explicit material has grown to between 30,000 and 60,000.

The Convention on the Rights of the Child has been ratified by 191 countries, but children are increasingly victims of violence.

The U.S. Congress provides funding and directs the National Center for Missing and Exploited Children to conduct the first national survey on risks that children face when they are on the Internet, with a focus on unwanted sexual solicitations and pornography.

The Worst Forms of Child Labour Convention is adopted by the International Labor Organization (ILO). Article 3 specifically prohibits sexual exploitation of children.

The International Tribunal for Children's Rights holds its Third Hearings in Colombo, Sri Lanka, focusing on ways in which to foster international cooperation in fighting child sexual exploitation.

2000   The Trafficking Victims Protection Act of 2000 is passed in the United States to punish traffickers, protect victims, and prevent trafficking. It also requires the U.S. Department of State to submit a report to Congress each year on foreign governments' attempts to eliminate severe forms of trafficking in persons.

In June, the U.S. Conference of Catholic Bishops drafts the Charter for the Protection of Children and Young People, in response to the growing awareness of the problem of child sexual abuse by Catholic priests. They create two entities to address the problem: the National Review Board and the Office of Child and Youth Protection.

The Child Internet Protection Act (CIPA) is enacted, mandating that public schools and libraries install filters on computers with Internet access. CIPA is ruled constitutional in 2003 (*Am. Library Ass'n v. United States*, 201 F. Supp. 2d 401 [E. D. Pa 2002], rev'd 123 S. Ct. 2297 [2003]).

In England, the body of eight-year-old Sarah Payne is found buried in a shallow grave, murdered by a pedophile. As a result of a large public outcry asking for better notification and registration of sexual offenders, the legislature amends the Sex Offenders Act of 1997 by tightening up the registration of sex offenders with the police, but it does not go as far as Megan's Law in the United States. It does not provide the public with the names or exact locations of sex offenders, but rather sets up "risk panels" to determine the risk that each offender poses to the public.

The UN Protocol, also known as the Palermo Protocol, is enacted as a supplement to the UN Convention against Transnational Organized Crime. Its primary purpose is to help prevent, suppress, and punish trafficking, especially trafficking in women and children.

The UNICEF Regional Office for West and Central Africa and the International Organization for Migration's Dakar Bureau adopt a memorandum of understanding concerning trafficking of women and children, as well as the recruitment of children into the armed forces.

2001   Interpol announces that it believes human trafficking, including trafficking in children, generates $19 billion.

The first Africa-Europe Ministerial Conference is held in Brussels in October. The issue of trafficking in women and children is identified as a major problem. Government representatives indicate their desire to develop a plan of action to deal with the issue.

The 2nd World Congress against Commercial Sexual Exploitation of Children is held in Yokohama, Japan.

2001
(cont.)

The Economic Community of West African States (ECOWAS) adopts a Declaration and Plan of Action against Trafficking in Persons during its annual summit, held in Dakar in December.

The dioceses of Orange and Los Angeles are sued by Ryan DiMaria for the abuse he suffered as a high school student at Santa Margarita High School at the hands of the school's principal, Father Michael Harris; Harris had a history of sexually abusing students. Church officials settle DiMaria's suit for $5.2 million, the largest publicly disclosed settlement ever paid by the Catholic Church to an individual claiming abuse. They also agree to a policy devised by Ryan DiMaria, who has just graduated from law school, to protect children in the future. Referred to as "Ryan's Law," it requires the Church to hire monitors for all diocesan Catholic schools, to create a toll-free number for victims to call, and to ban all priests from being alone in social settings with minors.

In Dallas, eleven former altar boys allege that Father Rudolph Kos had sexually abused them hundreds of times. Local diocesan officials reject pleas to settle the case, and instead argue at trial that Father Kos (and, by association, all priests) are actually independent contractors, not employees, and therefore responsible for their own actions. The jurors are not convinced. They believe instead Father Tom Doyle, and others who provide expert testimony, and find Church leaders grossly negligent. They hand down a $119.6 million judgment against the Church.

2002

The Vatican rejects the policy submitted by the U.S. Catholic Conference of Bishops for dealing with allegations of the sexual abuse of children because it does not conform to requirements of canon law. The bishops change the policy, but the debate will continue over whether the changes are needed and whether the policy conveys the appropriate message to victims.

Father John Geoghan goes on trial for putting his hand into the bathing suit of a ten-year-old boy. After a short deliberation, the jury finds Geoghan guilty of indecent sexual assault on a minor. The judge sentences him to nine to ten years in prison.

The Australian Catholic Church is hit with another sexual abuse scandal. George Pell, the archbishop of Sydney, is alleged to have offered to pay victims of sexual abuse for their silence in 1993. Later in the year, Archbishop Pell is accused of having abused a twelve-year-old boy in the 1960s. He denies both allegations but agrees to step down temporarily from his post while the Church investigates the charges. He is later cleared of charges.

Cardinal Bernard Law, the archbishop of Boston, travels to Rome, where Pope John Paul II accepts his resignation.

Massachusetts becomes the thirtieth state to add clergy to the list of individuals required to report suspected sexual abuse of children to the authorities. Cardinal Bernard Law in the past had opposed the requirement.

The UNICEF Medium Term Strategic Plan for 2002–2005 goes into effect. Among other items, two of its priorities are fighting HIV/AIDS and increasing protection of children from violence, abuse, exploitation, and discrimination.

The New Partnership for Africa's Development (NEPAD) is formulated and entered into by the G8 governments in their meeting in Canada. It provides the framework for helping African nations to focus on developing democracy and sound economic management, and seeks to promote peace, good governance, and human rights. It recognizes the critical role that children will play in the success of its programs.

2002
(cont.)
The U.S. Supreme Court holds that the ban on virtual child pornography in the Child Pornography Prevention Act of 1996 (CPPA) abridges the freedom to engage in a substantial amount of lawful speech and is therefore overbroad and unconstitutional under the First Amendment (*Ashcroft v. Free Speech Coalition*, 535 U.S. 234 [2002]).

2003
The Eighth Circuit Court of Appeals, in *Gunderson v. Hass* (339 F. 3d 639 [8th Cir. 2003]), upholds the requirement that a defendant who is cleared of predatory offense charges is still required to register as a predatory offender under Minnesota law because he was convicted of a nonpredatory offense that arose out of the same set of circumstances as the charged predatory offense.

The U.S. Supreme Court upholds the constitutionality of the Children's Internet Protection Act, which requires schools and libraries receiving federal funds for Internet access either to filter or to block access to visual depictions that are child pornography, obscene, or material considered harmful to minors.

The U.S. Immigration and Customs Enforcement Office begins its Operation Predator program, an initiative to safeguard children from foreign national predators, pedophiles, international sex tourists, child pornographers who use the Internet to attract children, and human traffickers. During its first two years of operations, the program arrests more than 6,000 child predators.

The Sexual Offences Act of 2003 is enacted in the United Kingdom and includes legislation to protect children against sexual assaults, indecent photographs, exploitation, pornography, and trafficking.

In the United Kingdom, the Paedophile On Line Investigation Team is created to support, coordinate, and assist national and international investigations of Internet-related child sexual abuse.

The U.S. Congress passes the Prosecutorial Remedies and Other Tools to End the Exploitation of Children Today Act of 2003 (PROTECT Act), which has been written to correct flaws in the Child Pornography Prevention Act. It bans virtual child pornography.

Gerald Thomas, a former pastor in a Lutheran church in Texas, is convicted and sentenced to 397 years in the state prison after being found guilty of eleven counts of multiple sex crimes against children. He is already serving a five-year sentence in federal prison on child pornography charges. In 2004, a Texas jury will award almost $37 million to the nine plaintiffs who accuse the Lutheran governing body of knowing about and hiding Thomas's history of abuse.

Michael Jackson is charged with ten counts of molesting a child, conspiracy, and providing alcohol to minors. In 2005 he will be acquitted on all counts.

California enacts a new law that lifts the statute of limitations for one year on civil child sexual abuse cases that are filed against individuals, as well as negligence cases filed against groups. Other states will consider similar action.

2004   More than 100,000 sites on the Internet contain sexually explicit materials.

2005   Debra Lefave, a twenty-five-year-old teacher in Florida, reaches a plea agreement with prosecutors after being charged with two counts of lewd and lascivious battery as a result of having sexual relations with a fourteen-year-old student. As part of the plea agreement, Lefave will serve three years of house arrest and seven years of probation.

An investigation of UN peacekeepers working in the Democratic Republic of Congo finds at least 150 allegations of rape and sexual abuse of women and girls, some as young as thirteen, committed by the peacekeepers.

2005   The Roman Catholic Church sends out questionnaires
(cont.)   to all faculty and students at more than 220 seminar-
           ies in the United States. The questionnaire asks about
           the existence of homosexuality in the seminaries. The
           Church indicates that this is a service to U.S. bishops
           trying to recover from the sex abuse scandal, but crit-
           ics see it as the Church's view that equates pedophiles
           with homosexuals and as a poorly disguised attempt
           to rid the Church of all homosexual priests.

           There are at least forty-five regional task forces partic-
           ipating in the Internet Crimes against Children (ICAC)
           Task Force Program. These task forces help state and
           local police to develop effective programs to respond
           to sexual enticement of children on the Internet.

           Douglas Smith, who had been with the Boy Scouts of
           America for thirty-nine years, is sentenced to eight
           years in prison after pleading guilty to one count of re-
           ceiving and distributing child pornography. Investi-
           gators had searched his home and computer and
           found 520 images of child pornography, including
           video clips.

2006   A special agent for the Wyoming Task Force on Inter-
           net Crimes against Children traces a movie depicting
           the rape of a two-year-old to a computer in Colorado.
           The agent is unable to find the computer because the
           Internet service provider (ISP) does not maintain
           records relating to specific accounts. Colorado state
           legislators are considering a bill to require all ISPs in
           Colorado to maintain their records for at least one
           year.

References

Bender, Lauretta, and Abram Blau. 1937. "The Reaction of Children to Sexual Relations with Adults." *American Journal of Orthopsychiatry* 7: 500–518.

DeFrancis, Vincent. 1969. *Protecting the Child Victim of Sex Crimes Committed by Adults.* Denver: American Humane Association.

France, David. 2004. *Our Fathers: The Secret Life of the Catholic Church in an Age of Scandal.* New York: Broadway.

Freedman, Alfred M., Harold I. Kaplan, and Benjamin J. Sadock. 1976. *Modern Synopsis of Comprehensive Textbook of Psychiatry II.* Baltimore, MD: Williams and Wilkins.

Kempe, C. Henry, F. N. Silverman, B. F. Steele, W. Droegemueller, and H. K. Silver. 1962. "The Battered Child Syndrome." *Journal of the American Medical Association* 181: 17–24.

Kinsey, Alfred C., Wardell B. Pomeroy, Clyde E. Martin, and Paul H. Gebhard. 1953. *Sexual Behavior in the Human Female.* Philadelphia: W. B. Saunders.

Lady Murasaki. 1955. *The Tales of Gengi.* New York: Doubleday Anchor.

Liebreich, Karen. 2004. *Fallen Order: Intrigue, Heresy, and Scandal in the Rome of Galileo and Caravaggio.* Berkeley, CA: Grove/Atlantic.

Mayo, Katherine. 1927. *Mother India.* New York: Harcourt, Brace.

Miller, Heather L. 1999. "Strike Two: An Analysis of the Child Online Protection Act's Constitutional Failures." *Federal Communications Law Journal* 52: 155, 159–160.

National Center on Child Abuse and Neglect (NCCAN). 1981. *Study Findings: National Study of the Incidence and Severity of Child Abuse and Neglect.* Washington, DC: U.S. Department of Health and Human Service.

Oates, R. K. 1990. "Understanding the Problem." In *Understanding and Managing Child Sexual Abuse*, edited by R. K. Oates. Sydney: Harcourt Brace Jovanovich.

Report of the Commission on Obscenity and Pornography. 1970. New York: Bantam.

Rush, Florence. 1980. *The Best Kept Secret: Sexual Abuse of Children.* New York: McGraw-Hill.

Russell, Diana E. H. 1986. *The Secret Trauma: Incest in the Lives of Girls and Women.* New York: Basic.

Smart, C. 1989. *Feminism and the Power of Law.* London: Routledge.

Stewart, Jennifer. 1997. "If This Is the Global Community, We Must Be on the Bad Side of Town: International Policing of Child Pornography on the Internet." *Houston Journal of International Law* 20: 205–246.

Summit, Roland. 1983. "The Child Sexual Abuse Accommodation Syndrome." *Child Abuse and Neglect* 7: 177, 181–188.

5

Biographical Sketches

Many people throughout the country, and the world, have contributed in some way to the field of child sexual abuse. Some have devoted their entire lives to studying the problem, while others, with broader interests, have nevertheless had an impact in this field. This chapter profiles some of the more prominent researchers, writers, political activists, offenders, and others who have been of note.

Dr. Gene Abel

Dr. Abel is the director of the Behavioral Medicine Institute of Atlanta, the largest treatment program in the southeast United States for sex offenders. Approximately 250 people are in treatment at any given time, and 90 percent of them are child molesters. Abel is also professor of psychiatry at Emory University School of Medicine and Morehouse University School of Medicine. He is internationally known for his research work with sexually aggressive people, primarily adults who sexually abuse children. He has headed six federal research projects for NIMH and has published more than 100 medical articles in numerous scientific journals. Dr. Abel also maintains a database containing the results of his research with 400 known sex offenders and over 100 normal people; this database can provide information on a variety of topics.

One of his best known accomplishments is the Abel Screen, which he developed as a method of screening people to determine those who may have a sexual interest in children or may already be sexually abusing children. It has proven to be a reliable and cost-effective technique. The screen consists of a series of four easily administered tests; the combined scores reveal twenty separate types of sexual interest. The first test consists of computer-generated slides of children, adolescents, adults, and couples; the individual rates his interest in each slide. The second test is a physiologic measure of the subject as he views the slides and is taken without the subject's knowledge. The final two tests are question-and-answer tests.

The Abel Screen can be used as the first step in evaluating someone who might be at high risk of being a sex offender and who perhaps should not be placed in environments in which children are present. If a person fails the screen, the next step in assessment is usually the administration of more intrusive measures.

Louise Armstrong

In 1978, Louise Armstrong wrote *Kiss Daddy Goodnight,* a compilation of first-person accounts of incest. Written from a feminist perspective, Armstrong believes that the primary focus in attempting to reduce the incidence of incest is to alter the cultural assumption that men have the right to control their wives and children, with the added implication that control includes sexual abuse. She demonstrated that courts often rule in favor of abusers and against the women who try to protect their children from abuse. As a political activist, she believes that political action is the primary means to change cultural attitudes. Also, she is not a fan of therapy, believing that it serves only to encourage victims to live within the system and adapt to current cultural norms. It leads to the assumption that cycles of violence are inevitable.

Armstrong is also the author of *Rocking the Cradle of Sexual Politics: What Happened When Women Said Incest,* in which she discusses incest, how she became involved in speaking out about incest, and her disagreements with the directions that research has taken concerning this topic.

Marilyn Van Derbur Atler

Marilyn Van Derbur, Miss America of 1958, in 1991 stood before a small audience at the University of Colorado Health Sciences campus (who had come to hear about plans for a new program at the Kempe National Center, which is dedicated to preventing and treating child abuse and neglect) and revealed that she was an incest survivor. She had been sexually abused as a young girl by her father, from the time she was five years old until she left home for college at the age of eighteen. Her father, Francis S. Van Derbur, was a well-known philanthropist, socialite, and Denver businessman. He died in 1984, years before his daughter revealed her secret to the world. Marilyn was one of four sisters, growing up in a family that had everything: they went skiing in the winter and rode their horses in the summer, they attended the proper schools, took music lessons, and played games. The girls also had something else, however, a father who sexually abused at least two of them.

In her four-page disclosure of childhood sexual abuse, Van Derbur wrote: "People ask me why I didn't tell what was happening to me. . . . In order to survive, I split into a day child, who giggled and smiled, and a night child, who lay awake in a fetal position, only to be pried apart by my father. Until I was 24, the day child had no conscious knowledge of the night child" (Loftus and Ketcham 1994, 79). She pushed herself hard to win her father's approval, but the day child never received much attention from her father. She graduated Phi Beta Kappa; won the Miss America pageant, sometimes making more than 200 appearances in one day; and was a member of the University of Colorado ski team. Yet her father never gave her the kind of love and attention she was looking for. When she was twenty-four years old, the memories of sexual abuse became conscious. She currently travels around the country talking to a variety of groups about incest. She has developed, with others, several videos to help educate the public about child sexual abuse and to help victims recover from their experiences.

Fred Berlin

Fred Berlin received his B.A. in psychology from the University of Pittsburgh in 1964, his M.A. in psychology from Fordham University in 1966, and both his Ph.D. in psychology (1970) and his M.D. (1974) from Dalhousie University in Canada. He completed his residency in the Department of Psychiatry and Behavioral Science at the Johns Hopkins Hospital in Baltimore, Maryland. In 1980, he founded and currently is the director of the Sexual Disorders Clinic; he is also an associate professor in the Department of Psychiatry and Behavioral Sciences of the Johns Hopkins University School of Medicine. The Sexual Disorders Clinic is currently known as the National Institute for the Study, Prevention and Treatment of Sexual Trauma.

Working with in-patients who manifest some type of sexual disorder, as well as with victims of sexual trauma, Berlin and his associates are dedicated to the prevention of sexual trauma by learning more about the abusers and their disorders as well as about the victims of sexual abuse. Over the years, Berlin and his colleagues determined that mandatory reporting of child sexual abuse usually kept undetected adult abusers from entering treatment. Mandatory reporting also deters patient disclosures about child sexual abuse that occurs during treatment, and it does not help determine the number of abused children. When reporting became mandatory in Maryland (in 1989) the rate of self-referrals dropped from about seven per year (seventy-three over a ten-year period) to zero. The researchers' conclusion was that the law, which was intended to protect children, deters abusers from coming forward and entering treatment. Berlin believes that mandatory reporting requirements should not be applied to psychiatrists.

Berlin has many publications. He has been an invited participant to the White House Conference on Child Sexual Abuse. He has spoken to a variety of groups and meetings, including the Colleges of Judges in several states, the national Symposium on the Child Victim of Sexual Abuse, and the National Conference of Catholic Bishops, where he delivered the keynote address on sexual problems in the clergy.

Lucy Berliner

Lucy Berliner, the director of the Sexual Assault Center at Harborview Hospital in Seattle, Washington, is internationally recognized for her pioneering work in assessing and treating children who have been sexually abused. Known for training other clinicians around the world in specialized intervention methods, she has written and lectured throughout the country on sexual assault. Berliner has testified in court in cases of child sexual abuse, often in which she is asked to testify as to whether she believes that a child has been abused. She has mixed feelings about providing this type of testimony. Because no standards exist among mental health workers for evaluating these cases, judges can look at several evaluations from different professionals and believe that one is better than another; this can lead to inconsistency in the outcome of these cases. She also worries about therapists who believe that they have special insights in these cases, as well as about other professionals—including those in the legal field—who believe that therapists do indeed have special insights. "Any individual mental health professional has to be darn careful about setting themselves up to say, 'I have some special ability and insight into the truth that no one else has.' I mean all you are doing is forming an opinion that will be a piece of the mosaic" (Hechler 1988, 162). Berliner has a master's degree in social work.

Douglas Besharov

Douglas Besharov is currently a research scholar at the American Enterprise Institute for Public Policy Research and a professor at the University of Maryland School of Public Policy. He was the first director of the National Center on Child Abuse and Neglect in the U.S. Department of Health and Human Services from 1975 to 1979 (then the Department of Health, Education and Welfare). He received his law degree from New York University. Well known for his thoughts on inappropriate investigations in child sexual abuse cases and on removal of children from their homes, he was a keynote speaker at the first VOCAL

(Victims of Child Abuse Laws) conference. He has written extensively on the problems with mandatory reporting laws, which have led to an increase in the number of child sexual abuse reports made to authorities. He believes that by convincing the public that children are being sexually abused and that any suspicion of abuse must be reported, children have been made more vulnerable than ever before. According to Besharov, the rate of unfounded reports of sexual abuse has risen by more than 65 percent, which means that more time is spent investigating reports; many of those reports may not be investigated in a timely manner, and therefore those children who really are being abused may be in greater danger of additional abuse before investigators can help them.

Barbara Blaine

Beginning in 1969, when she was thirteen years old, Barbara Blaine was sexually abused by Father Chet Warren, a Catholic priest. He continued to molest her for four years, and told her not to tell anyone because no one would understand or believe her. She kept her secret until 1974, when she attended a Catholic retreat and told another priest about Father Warren. The priest responded by telling her that Jesus would forgive her, acting as though the abuse were her own fault. Despite that priest's response, the retreat gave her a newfound strength and increased her self-esteem. In 1985, she told her family about the abuse; her mother, a devout Catholic, went directly to the Church, expecting them to take care of the situation. Father Warren was sent to therapy, denied the allegations of abuse, and eventually was dismissed from the Church, although he was not formally laicized through official church proceedings. Blaine later found out that Father Warren had abused others and that the Church was aware of his behavior as early as 1970.

Blaine told her story on various talk shows; she never revealed the priest's name until she appeared on the *Oprah Winfrey Show*, at which time she finally revealed his name. She continued to meet other victims of sexual abuse by priests and in 1989 founded Survivors Network for Those Abused by Priests (SNAP), an activist organization working to help survivors deal with their abuse (see Chapter 7 for a description of SNAP).

John Briere

Dr. Briere is associate professor of psychiatry and psychology at the Keck School of Medicine at the University of Southern California and director of the Psychological Trauma Program at LAL-USC Medical Center. He received an M.A. from California State University and his Ph.D. from the University of Manitoba. He is a past president of the International Society for Traumatic Stress Studies and the author of many books, articles, and psychological tests relating to trauma-related distress and interpersonal violence. The focus of his research includes victims of violence, psychological trauma, long-term effects of child abuse, and psychological assessment of post-traumatic states.

In *Child Abuse Trauma: Theory and Treatment of the Lasting Effects*, Briere examined the long-term effects of all forms of child abuse, including sexual abuse, and described how this abuse affects the victim's psychosocial functioning as an adult.

Focusing their attention on the controversy over repressed memories of sexual abuse, Briere and Jon Conte, a clinical social worker and researcher, reported the results of a study to determine the role of repressed memory in sexual abuse trauma. They studied 450 patients who reported having been sexually abused as children, and among their findings was the fact that more than half of the patients reported no memory of their abuse between the time it occurred and their eighteenth birthday. Briere and Conte concluded that amnesia appears to be a common phenomenon among survivors of sexual abuse. However, Briere appears to have modified his thoughts recently on repressed memory (see Chapter 2 for a discussion of repressed memories in child sexual abuse cases).

Sandra Butler

In *Conspiracy of Silence: The Trauma of Incest*, Sandra Butler focused attention on a topic that, until the book's publication in 1978, was not discussed publicly. Written from a feminist perspective, it has become a classic reference on child sexual abuse perpetrated by a family member, providing a historical perspective on the issue. When she was conducting research for the book, she thought that professionals treating victims of incest could answer questions that she had after reviewing the literature on the topic. What she found was what she referred to as a "conspiracy of silence": she believed that women's reality is created and defined by men and clinicians, scholars, and theorists who are trained by men. A "conspiracy of silence" is created by this belief system, and feminists "must break out part of the silence by speaking the truth of our lives and experiences so that the theory, the funding, the clinicians, and the criminal justice personnel will be made to respond to us with clarity, respect, and immediacy" (from "Incest: Whose Reality, Whose Theory," undated, found at http://www.trc-cmwar.ca/articles).

Butler is an associate professor in the School of Social Work at the University of Maine. She is a former codirector of the Institute for Feminist Training, which focuses on training in feminist psychological theory and practice, political activism, and cross-cultural perspectives. She received her M.S.W. from Washington University and her Ph.D. from the University of Washington.

Jon R. Conte

A clinical social worker and researcher, Jon Conte is currently an associate professor and the associate dean of academic affairs at the School of Social Service Administration at the University of Chicago. He has taught in the School of Social Work at the University of Washington. He frequently lectures at both national and international meetings and conferences and has written many publications. Conte was the principal investigator on a study that examined the effects of childhood sexual experiences on both child and adult survivors. For a project funded by the National Institute of Mental Health, he studied ways of educating children in the prevention of sexual abuse. Other areas of interest include the etiology of sexual violence and the effects of prevention education. He is the founding editor of the *Journal of Interpersonal Violence* and is past president of the American Professional Society on the Abuse of Children. He has also appeared on many local and national radio and television programs, including *Good Morning America, Donahue,* and a PBS special titled "What Your Child Should Know about Sexual Abuse." He has worked with John Briere in attempting to prove the existence of repressed memories.

As an expert on memory, in 2005 he appeared as a witness for the plaintiffs in the case against the Catholic Diocese of Spokane, Washington. He has evaluated the allegations of 300 to 400 people who claim to have been abused by members of the clergy and has developed personal injury evaluations to determine the damages that result from sexual abuse.

Christine Courtois

A psychologist in independent practice in Washington, D.C., Christine Courtois is co-founder of the CENTER: Posttraumatic Disorders Program at the Psychiatric Institute of Washington, where she is also a clinical and training consultant. She received her Ph.D. in psychology from the University of Maryland in 1979. Working in the area of post-traumatic stress, she is the author of three books: *Recollections of Sexual Abuse: Treatment Principles and Guidelines* (1999), *Adult Survivors of Child Sexual Abuse: A Workshop Model* (1993), and *Healing the Incest Wound: Adult Survivors in Therapy* (1988), in addition to many articles concerning sexual abuse. A former member of the board of directors of the International Society for Traumatic Stress Studies, she continues to conduct professional training on topics relating to traumatic stress.

Thomas Doyle

The Reverend Thomas Doyle first warned Roman Catholic bishops of the growing sexual abuse scandal in the Catholic Church in 1984, following the widespread publicity of the case in Louisiana against Father Gilbert Gauthe. Doyle was ordained as a Catholic priest in the Dominican Order in 1970. He has been an aide to the Vatican representative in Washington, has served as an Air Force chaplain, and was at Ramstein Air Force Base in Germany from 2001 until he was transferred to Seymour Johnson Air Force Base in North Carolina. This recent reassignment is widely believed to have been in retaliation for his active and vocal involvement in helping children who have been abused by Catholic priests. In 1985, in response to the sexual abuse case against Father Gilbert Gauthe, Doyle, Ray Mouton, and Father Mike Peterson wrote a report titled "The Problem of Sexual

Molestation by Roman Catholic Clergy: Meeting the Problem in a Comprehensive and Responsible Manner." They analyzed the financial and legal liability of the Church and suggested policies and procedures that should be adopted in response to the problem. While the executive committee of the U.S. Conference of Catholic Bishops did not adopt their recommendations and did not present the report to the full conference, the report did influence the policies on dealing with sexual abuse that many dioceses later adopted.

David Finkelhor

David Finkelhor, a leading expert on child sexual abuse, received his B.A. in social relations in 1968 from Harvard University, his Ed.M. in sociology from the Harvard Graduate School of Education in 1971, and his Ph.D. in sociology from the University of New Hampshire in 1978. He specializes in the areas of mental health, social psychology, sexual behavior, family violence, victimology, and criminology. He is currently the codirector of the Family Research Laboratory at the University of New Hampshire and a professor of sociology.

Finkelhor has written extensively on child sexual abuse and family violence. With his associates at the Family Research Laboratory, he conducted a national study of sexual abuse in day care. Results indicated that day-care centers do not place children at a significantly higher risk of sexual abuse than other settings, but results did suggest to parents that one way of reducing the risk of sexual abuse to their children is to get more involved in the day-care center's activities. In 1986, Finkelhor and several of his colleagues reviewed ten years of research on child sexual abuse and published *A Sourcebook on Child Sexual Abuse,* which helps others working in the field of sexual abuse as well as the general public to understand many of the current statistics on child sexual abuse.

Finkelhor has received many research grants from the National Institute of Mental Health, the National Center on Child Abuse and Neglect, the Office of Juvenile Justice and Delinquency Prevention, the Boy Scouts of America, and the National Institute on Aging. He has conducted research on incest and family sexual abuse, parental attitudes and reactions to sexual abuse, family violence, the development and dissemination of knowledge of child sexual abuse, sexual abuse in day care, the characteristics of incest offenders, the incidence of missing children, paternal characteristics and risk of sexual abuse in U.S. Navy families, and youth victimization prevention. He has made professional presentations on incest and sexually abused children to the Conference on Sexually Abused Children, the Vermont Planned Parenthood Association, the New Hampshire Nurses Association, the Sixth Annual Workshop on Child Abuse and Neglect, the National Center for the Prevention and Control of Rape, and Harvard Medical School. He is on the editorial boards of the *International Journal of Child Abuse and Neglect* and the *Journal of Interpersonal Violence* and is an associate editor of the journal *Violence and Victims.*

Gilbert Gauthe

Gilbert Gauthe was the first Catholic priest brought to trial for sexually abusing children. In 1984, he was indicted on thirty-four counts of various sex crimes against children. For ten years his superiors knew about his abuse but told him only to confess his sins, hoping that would solve the problem. He was moved from parish to parish and appeared to garner complaints at every parish. While he was pastor at two churches in Louisiana, he had slumber parties with the young altar boys, after scheduling altar boy practice for early in the morning and telling the parents that the boys might as well stay overnight so the parents did not have to make the long drive to the church early in the morning. One of the boys complained to his father, who called the bishop's office, and soon all of the parents were aware of the abuse. The parents sued the Church, which quickly settled the case, and Church officials believed that their troubles were over. However, in 1986 an eleven-year-old boy testified in court about how Gauthe had sexually abused him, hospitalizing him as a result of the severe abuse. The jury convicted Gauthe, and the court sentenced him to twenty years in prison. After serving ten years, he was released but not deemed "cured." Ten months after being released, however, he was arrested in Texas for molesting a three-year-old boy. He was sentenced to seven years' probation, and the Church was ordered to pay the boy $1 million.

Henry Giarretto

Henry Giarretto founded the Child Sexual Abuse Treatment Program (CSATP) in Santa Clara, California, in 1971, and organized several self-help groups associated with the program, including Parents United, Daughters and Sons United, and Adults Molested as Children United. Giarretto held a B.A., an M.A., and a Ph.D. in psychology. He published articles in several professional journals and in fifteen anthologies on child abuse, and he wrote a book on child sexual abuse treatment, *Integrated Treatment of Child Sexual Abuse: A Treatment and Training Manual* in 1982. He presented papers at major national and international conferences on child abuse.

Giarretto formed CSATP in response to the need for coordinated services for sexually abused children and their families. The Santa Clara Juvenile Probation Department (JPD) was the reporting agency for all cases of child sexual abuse; the help they provided to families was often fragmented, creating further trauma to the child and the family. Members of the JPD asked Giarretto, then a marriage and family counselor, to help establish a pilot project to provide counseling to the children and their families. At the end of the eight-week project, everyone who participated in the program recognized its benefits and decided to expand it to include the coordination of services required by the family, such as financial advice and legal assistance, and to help facilitate the reunification of the family. This reunification could take place only after individual counseling sessions were held to help each family member cope with the abuse and other dysfunctional aspects that may have contributed to it. The program's focus is on healing and resocializing the family through the use of humanistic psychology.

Giarretto believed that compassion and caring are the two critical qualities that affect the ability to treat families successfully. He saw his role as a family advocate, listening to the problems within the family with compassion and helping family members work out their difficulties. All families, indeed all individuals, are doing the best they can under the circumstances in which they find themselves. The role of the counselors at CSATP is to give these families, first as individuals, the help, support, and tools they need to understand why they do what they do and to understand their feelings and emotions about themselves and each other. Once they can help the individuals to grow, they can help the families reunite.

In the 1980s, Giarretto developed a model to distinguish pedophiles from abusers who commit incest. He first described the model in California and persuaded many people that individuals who commit incest should receive preferential treatment, because he believed that people who molest their own children should not be treated as pedophiles. Although not everyone agreed, this so-called Giarretto model grew in popularity throughout the United States during the 1980s and served as a model for family reunification: the Parents United organization modeled itself on this belief. Parents United became a popular treatment program used by social workers, child and family service workers, and mandated reporters. Unfortunately, many of the graduates of such programs were able to escape incarceration by participating in group counseling programs that claimed to have a high success rate but also had a high number of repeat, recidivist offenders.

Gail Goodman

In her positions as professor of psychology at the University of California, Davis, a consultant to the Sacramento County Child Protective Services, professor of forensic psychology at the University of Oslo (Norway), and director of the Center of Social Sciences and Law, Gail Goodman is prominent in the field of child sexual abuse. She has conducted research and published many articles about children's testimony in cases of child sexual abuse, children's memory, and children's perceived credibility as witnesses, specifically in testifying about events they have experienced or witnessed. She has conducted studies exploring the relationship between questions asked during hearings to determine whether children are competent witnesses and the children's accuracy in testifying, and another study on the susceptibility of children to leading questions asked by prosecutors or defense attorneys.

Goodman has also conducted a survey for the National Center on Child Abuse and Neglect that investigated more than 12,000 accusations of ritual sexual abuse committed by satanic cults. The researchers could not find one case with convincing evidence of the existence of a well-organized satanic cult that sexually molested children.

She has received many awards for her work. She received her academic degrees (B.A., M.A., and Ph.D.) from the University of California at Los Angeles.

Judith Herman

A leading expert on trauma and abuse, Judith Herman is a clinical professor of psychiatry at Harvard Medical School and is director of training at the Victims of Violence Program at Cambridge Hospital. She received her M.D. from Harvard Medical School and trained in general and community psychiatry at Boston University Medical Center. She has written several books on sexual and domestic violence, including child sexual abuse. In *Father-Daughter Incest,* first published in 1981, Herman reported on an extensive clinical study of forty incest victims and interviews of professionals in the field, including mental health, child protection, and law enforcement professionals. An updated edition of the book, published in 2000, provides an overview of the research and findings of studies conducted following its initial publication. In *Trauma and Recovery,* she explores various trauma experienced as a result of domestic violence, combat, and political terrorism and explores those experiences and options for recovery. In another study, with Emily Schatzow, Herman worked with fifty-three women in group therapy sessions and encouraged them to try to find evidence that their memories of abuse were accurate. Three-quarters of the women were able to corroborate their memories with information from other sources.

Michael Jackson

An American pop star, Michael Jackson began his career in music when he was four years old, singing with his brothers Tito, Jackie, Jermaine, and Marlon. They formed the Jackson Five, with Michael as lead singer, and had a successful music career. Michael made a solo album, *Got to Be There,* in 1972, while still a member of the Jackson Five, and he became an international star in 1983 following the release of his music video *Thriller.*

Beginning to be considered eccentric by many in the late 1980s, his appearance changed, and there were reports that he often slept in a hyperbaric chamber and that he had made an attempt to purchase the bones of the Elephant Man. Many people believed that he was simply a harmless eccentric and continued to enjoy his music. However, in 1993 a thirteen-year-old boy accused Jackson of sexually abusing him. Although no charges were ever filed, Jackson settled with the boy's family for an unknown amount, reported to be in the millions of dollars. Jackson again was accused in 2003 of molesting a child, conspiracy, and providing alcohol to minors. He was acquitted by the jury on all counts, and the verdict stunned many observers. After he was cleared, Jackson vowed that he would never again share his bed—or bedroom—with a child.

C. Henry Kempe

Charles Henry Kempe received his M.D. from the University of California in 1945 and interned in pediatrics in 1945 and 1946. At the University of Colorado Medical Center in Denver, he was a professor of pediatrics and microbiology and chairman of the Department of Pediatrics from 1956 through 1973. During that time, he also headed the battered children's team. He was founder and director of the C. Henry Kempe National Center for the Prevention and Treatment of Child Abuse and Neglect. He was a consultant to the U.S. attorney general, the U.S. Department of Defense, and the World Health Organization, and he was a member of the American Pediatric Society, the American Society for Pediatric Research, the American Public Health Association, and the American Association of Immunology. In 1984, he was nominated for the Nobel Peace Prize. Kempe played a key role in defining the "battered child syndrome," a means of helping doctors to identify children who have been abused. His wife, Ruth Kempe, was also well known in the field of child abuse and was instrumental in much of the initial work done to draw widespread attention to the problem in the 1960s.

Ruth S. Kempe

Ruth Svibergson Kempe received her B.A. in 1943 from Radcliffe College and her M.D. from Yale School of Medicine in 1946. She completed her internship and residency in pediatrics at New Haven Hospital and completed a residency in child psychiatry at the University of Colorado School of Medicine in 1961. From 1961 to 1973 she was an assistant clinical professor of pediatrics at the University of Colorado School of Medicine, and from 1973 through 1978 she was an assistant professor of psychiatry and pediatrics there. She became a staff psychiatrist at the C. Henry Kempe National Center for the Prevention and Treatment of Child Abuse and Neglect. With her husband, C. Henry Kempe, she wrote *Healthy Babies, Happy Parents* in 1958, *Child Abuse* in 1978, and *The Common Secret: Sexual Abuse of Children and Adolescents* in 1984. Ruth Kempe has written and lectured widely on child abuse, and she and her husband played an important role in bringing the problem of child abuse to national attention and in promoting prevention and treatment programs.

Kenneth V. Lanning

Prior to becoming a private consultant on crimes against children, Kenneth Lanning was the supervisory special agent assigned to the Behavioral Science Unit at the FBI Academy in Quantico, Virginia, which helps law enforcement agencies and prosecutors throughout the United States by developing practical applications of the behavioral sciences to the field of law enforcement and criminal justice.

Lanning is a well-known expert in the area of child sex rings and child sexual abuse in satanic cults. He has identified two major types of sex rings: historical child sex rings and multidimensional child sex rings. He has spent years researching, publishing, lecturing, and consulting on the sexual victimization of children, as well as the characteristics of those who sexually abuse children. He has written about child sex rings and the behavior of child molesters, and he provides a law enforcement perspective on those issues. He is a member of the advisory board of the Association for the Treatment of Sexual Abusers (ATSA) and a former member of the Boy Scouts of America Youth Protection Expert Advisory Panel. In addition, he has testified before the President's Task Force on Victims of Crime, the U.S. Attorney General's Task Force on Family Violence, and the U.S. Attorney General's Commission on Pornography. Lanning has also testified on several occasions before the U.S. Senate and House of Representatives and has appeared frequently as an expert witness in state and federal courts.

Bernard Law

Bernard Law became archbishop of Boston in 1984 and years later became embroiled in the child sexual abuse scandal that hit the Church. In 1998, Father John Geoghan of Boston was removed from the priesthood after his conviction of child sexual abuse and after many other victims came forward as a result of the resultant publicity. More than 600 people have claimed to be abused by priests in Boston, and more than 400 plaintiffs have sued or are suing the archdiocese. On April 29, 2006, the Roman Catholic Archdiocese of Boston revealed that the archdiocese has paid out more than $150 million in legal settlements to alleged victims of sexual abuse perpetrated by priests and was, at that time, running a deficit of $46 million.

Bernard Law, however, appeared uncaring to the victims of the abuse and more than willing to protect accused priests. Cardinal Law appeared to survive the crisis, even though many called for his resignation, until a court in 1998 ordered the archdiocese to release additional personnel files as part of one case against the Church and many people again began calling for his resignation. A 2003 report issued by the Massachusetts attorney general found that Cardinal Law and others in the archdiocese had not violated any laws, but the report did indicate that there had been institutional acceptance of the abuse. Finally, in 2002, he resigned as archbishop, although he still remains a cardinal. In 2004 he was named as the archpriest of St. Mary Basilica in Rome.

Mary Kay Letourneau

Mary Kay Letourneau is a former schoolteacher in Washington State who spent seven years in prison after being convicted of statutory rape for having had a sexual relationship with a thirteen-year-old student, Vili Fualaau. The relationship was discovered by her husband, who told other family members about it; one of her cousins reported the relationship to local child protection services professionals. In 1997 she was arrested and pleaded guilty to two counts of second-degree statutory rape. The court suspended the prison sentence and required that she serve six months in county jail and enroll in a sexual deviancy treatment program for three years. Released from jail early, Letourneau, as a condition of the early release, was not allowed to see Fualaau. However, she was again found with Fualaau, and her seven-year prison sentence was reimposed. Her husband divorced her while she was in prison. Following her release in 2004 she married Fualaau in 2005, and is helping to raise their two children.

This case received national attention, in part because it involved an adult woman and a boy. Some critics of her sentencing believed that boys are not as emotionally affected by sexual relations with an adult as girls, and that the abuse is less criminal than that between an adult man and a girl. In fact, Fualaau often claimed that he was not a victim.

Elizabeth Loftus

Elizabeth Loftus is one of the country's foremost experts on memory. She received her B.A. in mathematics and psychology from UCLA in 1966, her M.A. in psychology from Stanford University in 1967, and her Ph.D. in psychology from Stanford in 1970. She is currently a distinguished professor in the departments of Psychology and Social Behavior; Criminology, Law, and Society; and Cognitive Sciences. Previously, she was a professor of psychology at the University of Washington in Seattle.

Loftus has spent more than twenty-five years conducting laboratory studies on memory, supervising graduate students, and writing eighteen books and more than 250 scientific articles. Her books include *Eyewitness Testimony: Psychological Perspective, The Myth of Repressed Memory* (with Katherine Ketcham), and *Witness for the Defense: The Accused, the Eyewitness, and the Expert Who Puts Memory on Trial* (with Katherine Ketcham). Much of her work concerns the malleability of memory, the ways in which our memories of events can be distorted, confused, and incorrect. When testifying in court as an expert on memory, she tried to clarify for the judge and the jury the process of memory: "Think of your mind as a bowl filled with clear water. Now imagine each memory as a teaspoon of milk stirred into the water. Every adult mind holds thousands of these murky memories. . . . Who among us would dare to disentangle the water from the milk?" (Loftus and Ketcham 1994, 3). She believes that memories have a spiritual quality more than a physical reality.

Recently, Loftus has found herself in the center of a major controversy on the validity of recovered memories (see Chapter

2). As a result of her research, she believes that for the most part repressed memories do not exist. However, she is quick to point out her concern that if people do not believe in the possibility of these memories, we may be returning "to those days, not so very long ago, when a victim's cries for help went unheard and accusations of sexual abuse were automatically dismissed as fantasy or wish-fulfillment" (ibid., 32). She has seen both sides, including the families destroyed by allegations of sexual abuse that could not be substantiated at all except for the recovered memories and the pain of the alleged victim. She acknowledges that memory is not a black and white entity: it is difficult to understand, and no one knows for certain whether or not repressed memories are true.

Virginia McMartin

Virginia McMartin operated the McMartin Preschool in Manhattan Beach, California, when, in 1983, she and her grandson, Raymond Buckey, along with five other child-care staff members, were charged with molesting more than 350 children over a ten-year period. The investigation started with some mothers' suspicions that Raymond Buckey might have abused their children. When the mothers went to talk with Virginia McMartin's daughter and Raymond's mother, Peggy Buckey, she did not take their concerns seriously. However, a few weeks later when one child came home from the preschool with blood on his anus, his mother became concerned and took him to the Manhattan Beach Police Department and then to a local hospital. The doctors told her that her son had been sodomized, and a full-scale investigation of the McMartin Preschool began. During the ensuing investigation, investigators found that many of the children said that they had seen other children being sexually abused and that they had been sexually abused themselves. Some of the allegations included fondling, exposure to vaginal, oral, and anal sex, and ritualistic and satanic acts of abuse. After seven years of legal proceedings and a great deal of news media attention, no one was convicted.

Prior to these allegations, Virginia McMartin had been considered an upstanding member of the community. She was a member of an established Manhattan Beach family, she had received many awards from the city for her civic service, and her preschool had received great praise from child-care inspectors, who described it as well run, well staffed, and well equipped. Most parents were impressed with the way she operated her school, including the planning and organization of birthday parties, field trips, and educational projects.

Kelly Michaels

Working at the Wee Care Day Nursery in New Jersey, Kelly Michaels was accused by one of the children of taking his temperature by inserting a thermometer into his rectum. Investigators interviewed the three- and four-year-old children, who provided graphic details of sexual abuse as a result of intense and repeated questioning. In the end, Michaels was charged with 131 counts of sexual abuse against twenty children. None of the other teachers or care workers ever saw any of this abuse occurring. However, Michaels was convicted of 115 counts of abuse and was sentenced in 1988 to forty-seven years in prison. Some of the other teachers admitted that they did not come to her aid because they believed that prosecutors might have charged them as well. Michaels spent seven years in prison before her conviction was overturned.

Alice Miller

With a Ph.D. in psychology and sociology, Alice Miller has been a practicing psychoanalyst and instructor in psychoanalysis for more than twenty years. When *Thou Shalt Not Be Aware* was first published in Germany in 1981, Miller was virtually the only person in Europe to write about the sexual abuse of children. She visited the United States in 1982 and was delighted to see that the topic was written about openly in this country. She believes that children are "used and misused for adults' needs, including sexual needs, to a much greater extent than we realize" (Miller 1986, 309). She wrote that emotions that are blocked because of this abuse inevitably lead to emotional and physical problems. While attempting to integrate her theories into the mainstream of psychoanalytic theory, she realized that this was an impossible task. She believes that psychoanalysts tend to ignore the prevalence of sexual abuse of children and to deny the serious effects of this abuse. She argues that therapists must start listening to the children and identify with them in order to understand them. Therapists must become advocates for their clients instead of representing current societal theories and values. They must not spare the parents at any cost, but must understand the ways in which sexuality can be used to control or have power over those weaker in society.

Richard Ofshe

Richard Ofshe is a professor of sociology at the University of California, Berkeley. An expert on mind control and cults, he is well known for his research into extreme techniques of influence and social control. Ofshe is quick to admit that no one knows for certain that cults that kill babies and sexually abuse children and adults even exist, because no one has found any concrete proof of their existence. He is quite aware of all the rumors of satanic ritual abuse, and of the people who believe in or claim to have participated, usually against their will, in such rituals. He doubts that multiple personality disorder exists as a separate and readily identifiable disorder, and he tends to believe that these are highly suggestible people and that therapists suggest, unwittingly, symptoms that these patients will start manifesting. However, he is not willing to rule out the possibility that satanic cults exist. Ofshe shared a Pulitzer Prize in 1979 for his research into the Synanon cult in southern California. Other subjects he has written about include the thought-control techniques developed in Communist China, North Korea, and the Soviet Union, and how those techniques have been used by religious cults in the United States.

Ofshe testified for the prosecution in the trial of Paul Ingram, one of the better-known cases involving repressed memories of childhood sexual abuse. While Ofshe did not discount the possibility of the existence of a satanic cult, he still had not seen any conclusive evidence of one. The Ingram case was no exception. Ofshe believed that Ingram was visualizing events that had not occurred; nonetheless, those visualizations were real to him. Ofshe continues to search for verifiable evidence that satanic cults exist.

In 1994, he and Ethan Watters wrote *Making Monsters: False Memories, Psychotherapy, and Sexual Hysteria,* which explained the ways in which the false memories of Elaine Franklin led to the conviction of her father for sexual abuse. Franklin's father eventually won his appeal for a new trial, based in part on sections in the book concerning Elaine's therapy sessions.

Florence Rush

As a social worker at a residence for neglected and dependent girls, an activist in the Congress of Racial Equality, and a member of Older Women's Liberation, Florence Rush was no newcomer to social issues during the 1960s. However, after attending a speak-out on rape in New York City in which women had an open forum to tell their stories and share their emotions concerning rape, she realized the impact of sexual assault on women. Drawing on her experience as a social worker, she spoke during a subsequent conference on rape about her theories concerning the sexual abuse of children. Much of the information she shared that day was later developed into her book, *The Best Kept Secret: Sexual Abuse of Children.* This book, which quickly became a classic in the field, was one of the first to counter the common beliefs about the sexual abuse of children that were held prior to the 1980s. She exposed the historical abuse of children and argued against the common beliefs that children usually were not seriously harmed by sexual abuse and that they were often the instigators of the abuse. According to many professionals in the field, she was the first theorist to believe absolutely that the child is innocent in cases of sexual abuse.

Diana Russell

Born in Cape Town, South Africa, Diana Russell is a naturalized U.S. citizen. She received her B.A. from the University of Cape Town in 1958, a postgraduate diploma from the London School of Economics and Political Science in 1961, and her M.A. and Ph.D. in sociology from Harvard University. She was a professor of sociology at Mills College in Oakland, California, and currently is a researcher, writer, and consultant. She has been a member of the coordinating committee of the International Tribunal on Crimes against Women, a research consultant for the California Commission on Crime Control and Violence Prevention, and a founding member of Women against Violence in Pornography and Media.

Much of her early research was on women and rape. In *The Politics of Rape: The Victim's Perspective,* she presented a comprehensive study on sexual assault against women, dispelling many of the myths that surrounded rape. Her interviews with rape victims revealed that rapes could be perpetrated by men the victims knew, including friends and lovers, not just by strangers, as had been widely believed. In *Rape in Marriage,* she wrote about the sexual abuse of women by their husbands, presenting information gathered from almost 1,000 women.

The Secret Trauma: Incest in the Lives of Girls and Women detailed her findings in a study of women who had been sexually abused as children. Many of her findings were important to the study of incest. She found that 73 percent of those women whose abuse lasted for more than five years considered the experience extremely or considerably traumatic, compared with 62 percent of those whose abuse lasted from one week to five years, and 46 percent of those who were abused only once. No relationship was evident between the occurrence of sexual abuse and the father's level of education or his occupation. Girls who lived with their natural mother but without their natural father were more likely to be sexually abused. Similar rates of abuse occurred for African Americans and for Caucasians, and if a mother worked outside the home, the children were at higher risk of sexual abuse. Russell found that women who had experienced incest as children were more likely to experience problems later in life than women who had not been sexually abused as children. Her study was one of the first to combine stringent scholarship with an empathetic understanding of the incest victim.

In *Sexual Exploitation: Rape, Child Sexual Abuse, and Workplace Harassment,* Russell examines the relationship between sexual exploitation and patriarchal attitudes in our society. In *The Epidemic of Rape and Child Sexual Abuse in the United States* (see Chapter 8), she examines the findings of various incidence and prevalence studies and discusses the wide variations in those studies.

Suzanne Sgroi

Suzanne Sgroi received her B.A. from Syracuse University in 1964 and her M.D. at the State University of New York in 1968. She was assistant project director and then health director for the Connecticut Child Welfare Association Children's Advocacy Center in Hartford, and she was a member of the advisory board and steering committee of the Sex Crimes Analysis Unit of the Connecticut State Police. She currently is executive director of New England Clinical Associates, a private office devoted to the treatment of child sexual abuse, and director of the Saint Joseph College Institute for Child Sexual Abuse Intervention, both in West Hartford, Connecticut.

Sgroi is well known in the field of child sexual abuse and has written extensively on the subject. In assessing the sexually abused child and determining the appropriate treatment, she believes that ten impact issues should be kept in mind. These include the "damaged goods" syndrome, guilt, fear, depression, low self-esteem and poor social skills, repressed anger and hostility, inability to trust, blurred role boundaries and role confusion, pseudomaturity, and self-mastery and control (Sgroi 1988).

Paul Shanley

Paul Shanley was ordained as a priest in 1960 in West Roxbury, Massachusetts. Allegations of sexual abuse of children against him surfaced fairly quickly—he allegedly abused an altar boy beginning in 1960; the first complaint against him occurred in 1961. Working with alienated youth, Shanley had many opportunities to abuse young boys, who were unlikely to complain to anyone about the abuse. He had a cabin in the woods where the abuse allegedly took place. He was moved from one parish to another by Church officials, never having to account for his actions, even though Church officials began receiving allegations of abuse committed by Shanley in 1967. The Boston archdiocese paid $40,000 to one alleged victim of his abuse. Shanley was arrested in 2002 on charges of child rape, defrocked in 2004, and convicted on two counts of child rape and two counts of indecent assault and battery on a child in 2005; he was sentenced to twelve to fifteen years in prison.

Both Archbishop Humberto Medeiros and Bernard Law, who succeeded Medeiros as archbishop of the Boston archdiocese in 1984, were well aware of the many allegations against him, his unusual opinions on sexuality and homosexuality, and on statements he made endorsing man-boy sexuality. Both Medeiros and Law were slow to recognize the extent of Shanley's abuse of young boys. In fact, Shanley moved to Palm Springs, California, around 1990 and, according to a report submitted to the U.S. Conference of Catholic Bishops, "was provided with a letter of introduction to the Bishop of San Bernardino stating that he was a priest 'in good standing'" (National Review Board for the Protection of Children and Young People 2004, 42).

Roland C. Summit

The "believe the children" idea was popularized by Dr. Roland Summit in an influential article in the journal *Child Abuse and Neglect* in 1983. Summit wrote that "children never fabricate the kinds of explicit sexual manipulations they divulge in complaints or interrogations." Summit, who developed his theories without the benefit of any kind of scientific evidence, also claimed that denial of abuse is itself frequently a sign of abuse. If a person suspects that a child is being abused, but the child is unable to volunteer information, then the professional must attempt to elicit the information with specific and potentially leading questions.

But victims are worthless without perpetrators. So to tie the two together, Summit offers this observation: "Unless there is a special support for the child and immediate intervention to force responsibility on the father, the girl will follow the 'normal' course and retract her complaint" (Summit 1983, 187).

Developed around 1983 by Summit as a diagnostic tool, the Child Sexual Abuse Accommodation Syndrome (CSAAS) is at the center of a dispute: whether CSAAS can be used to distinguish between abused and nonabused children if the cluster of defined symptoms is presented. Summit has noted that since his original identification and description of CSAAS, which he referred to as "a clinical observation," it "has become both elevated as gospel and denounced as dangerous pseudoscience." In fact, Florida overturned two convictions for retrial on the grounds that it was error to admit CSAAS as evidence. (See Chapter 6 for a summary of these and other cases.)

Prior to the McMartin case, Summit was already well known in the mental health field for his theories on child sexual abuse. He had written and lectured extensively on the subject since 1975 and had served since 1979 as a consultant on child sex abuse to law enforcement officials, including the Los Angeles district attorney. Summit's deep involvement in the McMartin case came about while he served as a prosecution witness during the trial and in his role as the Los Angeles County Department of Mental Health liaison to Manhattan Beach during the early stages of the McMartin case.

Summit praised the hysteria-induced news media hype and community gossip as a public service. Without that type and extent of press coverage, the researchers and other professionals would not be able to gather this information and would be trapped by old myths about child sexual abuse. Summit complained that investigators were limiting the ability of parents to cope by discouraging them from meeting and discussing the case. The community's priority, he explained, should be to support the children. Hundreds of children had escaped sexual assault, he claimed, because of the publicity about the McMartin case.

Hollida Wakefield

As a forensic psychologist, Hollida Wakefield found herself in the middle of the day-care and recovered memories controversy in the late 1980s, when the first cases of children in day-care centers telling their parents about all types of bizarre behavior allegedly perpetrated by day-care workers began surfacing. By the early 1990s, she had been involved in several cases. Since 1988 her primary research interests in the area of child abuse have included the use of anatomically detailed dolls, evaluation of child witnesses in abuse cases, and allegations of abuse in day-care settings. She is currently a codirector of the Institute for Psychological Therapies in Northfield, Minnesota.

She is coauthor (with Ralph Underwager) of *Accusations of Child Sexual Abuse, The Real World of Child Interrogations,* and *Return of the Furies: An Investigation into Recovered Memory Therapy.* Wakefield and Underwager are founders of the False Memory Syndrome Foundation, and in their book *Return of the Furies,* they investigate the validity of repressed or false memory, noting that thousands have been falsely accused. They provide possible reasons for the initial popularity of this theory.

References

Armstrong, Louise. 1978. *Kiss Daddy Goodnight*. New York: Simon and Schuster.

Armstrong, Louise. 1994. *Rocking the Cradle of Sexual Politics: What Happened When Women Said Incest*. Reading, MA: Addison-Wesley.

Briere, John. 1992. *Child Abuse Trauma: Theory and Treatment of the Lasting Effects*. Thousand Oaks, CA: Sage.

Courtois, Christine. 1993. *Adult Survivors of Child Sexual Abuse: A Workshop Model*. Lewiston, NY: Manticore.

Courtois, Christine. 1996. *Healing the Incest Wound: Adult Survivors in Therapy*. Rev. ed. New York: W. W. Norton.

Courtois, Christine. 1999. *Recollections of Sexual Abuse: Treatment Principles and Guidelines*. New York: W. W. Norton.

Finkelhor, David. 1986. *A Sourcebook on Child Sexual Abuse*. Beverly Hills, CA: Sage.

Giarretto, Henry. 1982. *Integrated Treatment of Child Sexual Abuse: A Treatment and Training Manual*. Palo Alto, CA: Science and Behavior.

Hechler, David. 1988. *The Battle and the Backlash: The Child Sexual Abuse War*. Lexington, MA: Lexington.

Herman, Judith. 1997. *Trauma and Recovery: The Aftermath of Violence from Domestic Abuse to Political Terror*. New York: Basic.

Herman, Judith. 2000. *Father-Daughter Incest*. Cambridge: Harvard University Press.

Kempe, C. Henry, and Ruth S. Kempe. 1958. *Healthy Babies, Happy Parents*. New York: McGraw-Hill.

Kempe, Ruth S., and C. Henry Kempe. 1978. *Child Abuse*. Cambridge: Harvard University Press.

Kempe, Ruth S., and C. Henry Kempe. 1984. *The Common Secret: Sexual Abuse of Children and Adolescents*. New York: W. H. Freeman.

Loftus, Elizabeth. 1996. *Eyewitness Testimony: Psychological Perspective*. Cambridge: Harvard University Press.

Loftus, Elizabeth, and Katherine Ketcham. 1991. *Witness for the Defense: The Accused, the Eyewitness, and the Expert Who Puts Memory on Trial*. New York: St. Martin's.

Loftus, Elizabeth, and Katherine Ketcham. 1994. *The Myth of Repressed Memory: False Memories and Allegations of Sexual Abuse*. New York: St. Martin's.

Miller, Alice. 1986. *Thou Shalt Not Be Aware: Society's Betrayal of the Child.* Trans. Hildegarde and Hunter Hannum. New York: Meridian.

National Review Board for the Protection of Children and Young People. 2004. *A Report on the Crisis in the Catholic Church in the United States.* Washington, DC: U.S. Conference of Catholic Bishops.

Ofshe, Richard, and Ethan Watters. 1994. *Making Monsters: False Memories, Psychotherapy, and Sexual Hysteria.* New York: Simon and Schuster.

Rush, Florence. 1980. *The Best Kept Secret: Sexual Abuse of Children.* New York: McGraw-Hill.

Russell, Diana E. H. 1975. *The Politics of Rape: The Victim's Perspective.* New York: Stein and Day.

Russell, Diana E. H. 1984. *Sexual Exploitation: Rape, Child Sexual Abuse, and Workplace Harassment.* Beverly Hills, CA: Sage.

Russell, Diana E. H. 1990. *Rape in Marriage.* Rev. ed. Bloomington: Indiana University Press.

Russell, Diana E. H. 1999. *The Secret Trauma: Incest in the Lives of Girls and Women.* New York: Basic.

Russell, Diana E. H., and Rebecca M. Bolen. 2000. *The Epidemic of Rape and Child Sexual Abuse in the United States.* Newbury Park, CA: Sage.

Sgroi, Suzanne. 1988. *Vulnerable Populations: Evaluation and Treatment of Sexually Abused Children and Adult Survivors.* Lexington, MA: Lexington.

Summit, Roland. 1983. "The Child Sexual Abuse Accommodation Syndrome." *Child Abuse and Neglect* 7: 177, 181–188.

Underwager, Ralph, and Hollida Wakefield. 1989. *The Real World of Child Interrogations.* Springfield, IL: C. C. Thomas.

Wakefield, Hollida, and Ralph Underwager. 1988. *Accusations of Child Sexual Abuse.* Springfield, IL: C. C. Thomas.

Wakefield, Hollida, and Ralph Underwager. 1994. *Return of the Furies: An Investigation into Recovered Memory Therapy.* Chicago: Open Court.

6

Facts and Statistics

This chapter presents general facts and statistics on the prevalence and incidence of childhood sexual abuse, children who may be most at risk for abuse, and signs and symptoms of sexual abuse. State statutes providing definitions of child sexual abuse are provided, along with state sex offender registry websites and summaries of federal laws and international conventions. The final section summarizes selected U.S. Supreme Court and lower court decisions that pertain to a variety of issues that have come before the courts concerning child sexual abuse.

Prevalence and Incidence

Studies to determine the prevalence of child sexual abuse focus on estimating the proportion of the population who will be sexually abused as children, while studies to determine the incidence of child sexual abuse focus on determining the number of new cases arising during a given time period, usually a year.

Experts and researchers often differ in their estimates of the extent of child sexual abuse. Many reasons for these differences exist, but most experts will agree that the reporting of child sexual abuse probably underestimates the extent of the abuse, based upon our assumptions about incest and the incest taboo, on research conducted on adults who were sexually abused as children but did not report the abuse, and on societal factors such as differing expectations of male and female sexual behavior. Most estimates come from three sources: research studies conducted on adults who were sexually abused as children, annual reports of sexual abuse made to child protection agencies, and the National Incidence Studies, two federally funded studies.

Prevalence

Most prevalence studies start with the assumption that the majority of cases of child sexual abuse are never reported to authorities and that the most reliable method of estimating the prevalence is to gather information from victim or perpetrator self-reports. Many factors influence the reporting of child sexual abuse, however. Parents, family members, and some professionals may hesitate to report incidents to the authorities because of the stigma and the resulting trauma to the family; they may also fear breaking up the family, or they may believe that they can deal with the problem themselves. Our society traditionally and legally supports the integrity and sanctity of the family, offering many families protection from the public eye and public censure. Children often will keep their abuse to themselves, not even telling parents or other close family members; they may, however, reveal the abuse later in life, either while in therapy or when trying to overcome the trauma it inflicted on their lives. Studies of the prevalence of child sexual abuse often discover that adults admit that they never reported the abuse when it was happening to them.

For the purposes of determining the prevalence of the problem, researchers have defined child sexual abuse in various ways. Some include acts such as exhibitionism, while others limit their definitions to actual physical contact. Some include only adults as perpetrators, while others include peers as well as adults, believing that children are capable of sexually abusing other children. These definitions usually exclude sexual exploration between teenagers.

Finkelhor and his colleagues conducted a national survey of a random sample of respondents in 1985 to determine the prevalence of child sexual abuse. They found that 27 percent of the women (out of 1,481 women) and 16 percent of the men (out of 1,145 men) disclosed some form of sexual abuse while they were children; the median age for boys was 9.9 years, and the median age for girls was 9.6 years (Finkelhor et al. 1990). Diana Russell studied prevalence using a random sample of more than 900 households in San Francisco. She found that 54 percent reported at least one instance of incestuous or extrafamilial sexual abuse before the age of fourteen (Russell 1986). Wyatt sampled 248 women in Los Angeles County and found that 62 percent reported at least one instance of sexual abuse before the age of eighteen (Wyatt 1985).

The Committee for Children estimates that "at least one in four girls and one in ten boys will be sexually abused before reaching the age of 18. The actual incidence is probably much greater, especially for boys" (Committee for Children 1993, 8).

Christine Courtois believes that "a very substantial percentage of the female population, possibly as high as twenty percent, has had an experience of incestuous abuse at some time in their lives, twelve percent before the age of fourteen, sixteen percent before the age of eighteen. Possibly five percent of all women have been abused by their fathers. Boys are also sexually victimized within the family, but in smaller numbers" (Courtois 1988, 5).

In his landmark study of sexual behavior, Alfred Kinsey and his colleagues found that one in four women interviewed for his research study had reported experiencing as a child some sort of undesired sexual contact or other sexual experience initiated by an adult male. Kinsey was surprised that most of the women reported that they were frightened by this contact:

> It is difficult to understand why a child, except for its cultural conditioning, should be disturbed by having its genitalia touched, or disturbed by seeing the genitalia of another person. . . . Some of the more experienced students of juvenile problems have come to believe that the emotional reactions of the parents, police and other adults . . . may disturb the child more seriously than the contacts themselves. The current hysteria over sex offenders may well have serious effects on the ability of many of these children to work out sexual adjustments some years later in their marriages. (Kinsey et al. 1953, 121).

Kinsey also believed that males were in danger of being persecuted by females intent on protecting the children and themselves. He claimed that the law, by prosecuting offenders, did more harm than

> was ever done by the individual in his illicit sexual activity. The histories which we have accumulated contain

many such instances. The intoxicated male who accidentally exposes his genitalia before a child may receive a prison sentence which leaves his family destitute for some period of years, breaks up his marriage, and leaves three or four children wards of the state and without the sort of guidance which the parents might well have supplied. . . . The child who has been raised in fear of all strangers and all physical manifestations of affection may ruin the lives of the married couple who had lived as useful and honorable citizens through half or more of a century, by giving her parents and the police a distorted version of the old man's attempt to bestow grandfatherly affection upon her. (Ibid., 20–21)

Sandra Butler, in her research for her book *Conspiracy of Silence: The Trauma of Incest,* began to understand the reasons why incest was kept a secret but was appalled at the level of denial and lack of services provided by the professional community to incest victims and their families. She says:

Priests, ministers and rabbis insisted "that" [incest] did not happen among their parishioners. Although there were a few men who did admit "that" was mentioned in the sanctity of the confessional or in private conversation, they felt untrained and unskilled in ways to deal with incestuous assault and seldom attempted counseling or intervention with the members of such troubled families. Pediatricians, other doctors and nurses did not see "that" in their practices, and one young resident in a Midwestern city assured me that contrary to all the medical literature I had read, "Seven-year-olds can catch gonorrhea from dirty sheets." Occasionally I found a clinical report of "that" published in a medical journal or a paper presented to a group of psychiatrists by a peer who was working with a sexually abused client. But overwhelmingly I encountered silence. (Butler 1985, 8–9)

Butler goes on to say that

[as] long as we continue to believe that incestuous assault can happen only in other families, we can avoid examining our own lives. As long as we insist upon imagining the incestuous aggressor to be an easily identifiable, skulking, lascivious male who ravishes his luscious and

budding daughter across town, we can keep a safe distance. This distance protects us from sexual feelings we may have experienced for older family members and any possible interplay that may have occurred in our own childhood as well as feelings we may have toward our children as we watch them developing to young men and women. While most of us do not act upon these feelings, it is our refusal to acknowledge to ourselves that we have ever had such feelings that creates our silence, aversion and unwillingness to openly discuss the issues involved in incestuous abuse. (Ibid., 11)

Incidence

The National Center on Child Abuse and Neglect (NCCAN) in 1976 supported the first comprehensive incidence study of child abuse and neglect. Known as the National Incidence Study, it estimated that 44,700 cases of child sexual abuse, or 0.7 per 1,000 children, were known to professionals during the period from April 1979 to March 1980 (National Center on Child Abuse and Neglect 1981). Repeated in 1986, the study revealed a threefold increase, estimating that 138,000, or 2.2 per 1,000 children, were known to authorities during that year. When they expanded the definition of child sexual abuse to include those acts committed by caretakers, the researchers found that the number jumped to 155,000, or 2.5 per 1,000 children (Sedlak 1987).

Since 1989, the National Committee for Prevention of Child Abuse has conducted an annual survey of all fifty states to examine the trends in reports of child abuse and neglect. In 1993 the researchers estimated that 2,989,000 children had been reported to child protective services as alleged victims of abuse or neglect, and of those, 15 percent, or approximately 450,000, were cases of child sexual abuse (McCurdy and Daro 1994).

Bahroo (2003) reports that between 100,000 to 500,000 children are sexually abused in the United States annually. Between 15 and 25 percent of children will be sexually abused by the time they reach their eighteenth birthday; analyzed by sex, between 30 and 40 percent of girls, and 10 and 15 percent of boys, will be sexually abused (Bahroo 2003).

According to the FBI, 109,062 females were forcibly raped in 1992. The U.S. Bureau of Justice Statistics survey of the states and the District of Columbia examined forcible rape by the age of the victim. While thirty-six states reported that they did not analyze their statistics by age, the remaining fourteen states and the District of Columbia provided information on 26,427 cases of forcible rape. According to their findings, approximately one-third of all rape victims were under the age of thirteen in Delaware, Michigan, and North Dakota; under the age of sixteen in Nebraska, Pennsylvania, and Wisconsin; under the age of seventeen in Alabama; and under the age of eighteen in the District of Columbia and Idaho (Langan and Harlow 1994).

Many of these studies do not include the incidence of sexual abuse of children while in day care or by nonparental caretakers, such as teachers, priests, or babysitters. David Finkelhor and his colleagues examined all cases of sexual abuse of children while in day care reported from 1983 through 1985. They identified 270 cases and estimated the incidence of child sexual abuse in day-care settings to be 5.5 per 10,000 children enrolled. They concluded that children attending day care are not at a disproportionately higher risk of child sexual abuse than are other children in other settings. The high number of abuse reports from day-care settings, they believe, is a reflection of the large number of children placed in day care in this country, rather than an indication that those children are at a higher risk of abuse (Finkelhor et al. 1989).

In a study of the national statistics for 2004, the most recent year available, based on data voluntarily submitted to the Children's Bureau of the U.S. Department of Health and Human Services, the National Center on Child Abuse and Neglect examined numbers of reports of child abuse and neglect, rates of abuse and neglect, and other information concerning victims and perpetrators. The results, shown in Table 6.1, indicate that the number of children who were sexually abused in the United States stayed relatively stable for the years 2000 through 2004. The rate of children sexually abused also stayed the same for the years 2000 through 2004: 1.2 percent of all children in the United States are sexually abused each year.

More than one-half of the perpetrators of the sexual abuse were parents (29.1 percent) or other relatives (27.7 percent). Table 6.2 provides the breakdown by perpetrator.

The majority of child sexual abuse victims are between the ages of four and eleven years (73.2 percent). The age distribution of child victims of sexual abuse is indicated in Table 6.3.

TABLE 6.1
Number of Children Reported to Be Sexually Abused, by Year

Year	Number of Children
2000	87,770
2001	86,857
2002	88,688
2003	87,078
2004	84,398

Source: Adapted from NCANDS data for 2004 (U.S. Dept. of Health and Human Services 2006).

TABLE 6.2
Type of Perpetrator of Sexual Abuse of Children

Perpetrator	Number	Percent
Parent	13,957	29.1
Other relative	13,271	27.7
Foster parent	191	0.4
Residential facility staff	131	0.3
Child day-care provider	1,115	2.3
Unmarried partner of parent	3,150	6.6
Legal guardian	34	<0.1
Other professional	264	0.6
Friends or neighbors	1,302	2.7
Other	11,022	23.0
Unknown or missing data	3,459	7.2
Total	47,896	100.0

Source: Adapted from NCANDS data for 2004 (U.S. Dept. of Health and Human Services 2006).

As reported by state agencies, most of the children sexually abused are white, with African American and Hispanic children ranking second and third, respectively. See Table 6.4 for the distribution of child sexual abuse victims by race.

TABLE 6.3
Sexually Abused Children by Age Group

Age Range of Child	Number	Percent
<1–3	5,145	10.7
4–7	17,018	35.3
8–11	18,294	37.9
12–15	7,480	15.5
Unknown	278	0.6
Total	48,215	100.0

Source: Adapted from NCANDS data for 2004 (U.S. Dept. of Health and Human Services 2006).

TABLE 6.4
Sexually Abused Children by Race

Race of Child Victim	Number	Percent
White	29,716	56.8
African American	9,350	17.9
Hispanic	8,905	17.0
Multiple race	465	0.9
Asian	322	0.6
American Indian or Alaska Native	307	0.6
Pacific Islander	99	0.2
Unknown	3,183	6.0
Total	52,347	100.0

Source: Adapted from NCANDS data for 2004 (U.S. Dept. of Health and Human Services 2006).

The distribution of child sexual abuse cases by state is shown in Table 6.5. Table 6.5 displays some interesting numbers. Many of the states with large populations, such as California, New York, Florida, Ohio, and Texas, also show relatively high numbers of children who have been sexually abused. However, there are

TABLE 6.5
Sexually Abused Children by State

State	Number	State	Number
Alabama	2,263	Montana	152
Alaska	no report	Nebraska	384
Arizona	426	Nevada	169
Arkansas	2,021	New Hampshire	176
California	7,932	New Jersey	662
Colorado	1,024	New Mexico	340
Connecticut	631	New York	2,867
Delaware	208	North Carolina	1,178
District of Columbia	109	North Dakota	156
Florida	5,384	Ohio	7,541
Georgia	2,447	Oklahoma	867
Hawaii	196	Oregon	1,150
Idaho	117	Pennsylvania	2,822
Illinois	5,912	Rhode Island	163
Indiana	3,922	South Carolina	849
Iowa	849	South Dakota	76
Kansas	813	Tennessee	3,579
Kentucky	927	Texas	6,822
Louisiana	776	Utah	2,552
Maine	521	Vermont	520
Maryland	1,885	Virginia	1,100
Massachusetts	1,67	Washington	464
Michigan	1,451	West Virginia	451
Minnesota	847	Wisconsin	4,034
Mississippi	905	Wyoming	72
Missouri	2,619	**Total**	**84,398**

Source: Adapted from NCANDS data for 2004 (U.S. Dept. of Health and Human Services 2006).

other states, such as Utah, Missouri, and Tennessee, that also show relatively high rates of sexual abuse of children, especially when compared with their total populations. One reason for this anomaly may be that states vary on how they define child sexual abuse and whom they designate as mandatory reporters; another may be that some states are more aggressive in their tracking and reporting of child sexual abuse.

Signs and Symptoms of Sexual Abuse

Most professionals agree on the symptoms that children typically display when they have been sexually abused, although they readily agree that a child displaying any of these symptoms has not necessarily been sexually abused. These symptoms may also be caused by other conditions or situations. The following list of signs of possible sexual abuse (by age group) is excerpted from material issued by the Victim Services Agency (1991, 61–63) in New York.

Children Eighteen Months and Under:

- urinary and bowel problems
- fretful behavior
- flat affect
- lacerations of sex organs
- bleeding, discharge, or odors from sex organs
- inappropriate fear of adults
- fear of being abandoned
- excessive clinging behavior or the opposite
- failure to thrive
- excessive crying
- extreme behavior change
- sleep disturbances

Toddlers and Preschoolers:

- fear of a particular adult or specific places
- sex play with toys
- poor peer relationships
- lacerations of sex organs
- bleeding, discharge, or odors from sex organs

- depersonalization
- fear, guilt, or anxiety
- regressive or non–age appropriate behavior
- increase in genital play
- toileting issues
- fear of refusal
- new problems in bowel or bladder control
- sexual acting out that is age inappropriate
- advanced knowledge of detailed adult sexual activity

School Age Children:

- sleep disturbances
- school problems
- poor peer relationships (feel older than peers)
- depersonalization
- school phobias
- anorexia
- role confusion
- self-blame
- fear
- low self-esteem
- wish for normal family
- responsible for family
- running away

Adolescents:

- school problems
- drug or alcohol use
- clinical depression
- promiscuity
- prostitution
- suicide attempts
- overly compliant behavior
- poor body image
- eating disorders

Adults (Effects from Being Sexually Abused as a Child):

- problems with intimacy
- confusion in sexual identity

- lack of trust
- poor body image
- sexual dysfunction

State Definitions of Child Sexual Abuse

All states include a definition of sexual abuse in their statutes. Some states refer in general terms to sexual abuse, while others are quite specific in their definitions. Sexual exploitation, including allowing the child to engage in prostitution or in the production of child pornography, is an element of the definition of sexual abuse in most jurisdictions.

Alabama

Sexual Abuse § 26–14–1(1)-(3). Sexual abuse includes:

- The employment, use, persuasion, inducement, enticement, or coercion of any child to engage in, or having a child assist any other person to engage in, any sexually explicit conduct
- Any simulation of the conduct for the purpose of producing any visual depiction of the conduct
- The rape, molestation, prostitution, or other form of sexual exploitation of children
- Incest with children

Sexual exploitation includes:

- Allowing, permitting, or encouraging a child to engage in prostitution
- Allowing, permitting, encouraging, or engaging in the obscene or pornographic photographing, filming, or depicting of a child for commercial purposes

Alaska

Sexual Abuse § 47.17.290.

- Child abuse or neglect includes sexual abuse or sexual exploitation
- Sexual exploitation includes the following conduct by a person responsible for the child's welfare:
  - Allowing, permitting, or encouraging a child to engage in prostitution
  - Allowing, permitting, or encouraging a child to engage in actual or simulated activities of a sexual nature that are prohibited by criminal statute

Arizona

Sexual Abuse § 8–201. Abuse shall include:

- Inflicting or allowing sexual abuse
- Sexual conduct with a minor
- Sexual assault
- Molestation of a child
- Commercial sexual exploitation of a minor
- Sexual exploitation of a minor
- Incest
- Child prostitution

Arkansas

Sexual Abuse § 12–12–503. Sexual abuse means:

- Sexual intercourse, deviate sexual activity, or sexual contact by forcible compulsion
- Attempted sexual intercourse, deviate sexual activity, or sexual contact
- Indecent exposure
- Forcing, permitting, or encouraging the watching of pornography or live sexual activity

Sexual exploitation means allowing, permitting, or encouraging participation or depiction of the juvenile in prostitution, obscene photographing, filming, or obscenely depicting a juvenile for any use or purpose.

California

Sexual Abuse Penal Code § 11165.1.

- Sexual abuse means sexual assault or sexual exploitation as defined below:
  - Sexual assault includes rape, statutory rape, rape in concert, incest, sodomy, lewd or lascivious acts upon a child, oral copulation, sexual penetration, or child molestation.
- Sexual exploitation refers to any of the following:
  - Depicting a minor engaged in obscene acts; preparing, selling, or distributing obscene matter that depicts minors; employing a minor to perform obscene acts
  - Knowingly permitting or encouraging a child to engage in, or assisting others to engage in, prostitution or a live performance involving obscene sexual conduct, or to either pose or model alone or with others for purposes of preparing a film, photograph, negative, slide, drawing, painting, or other pictorial depiction, involving obscene sexual conduct
  - Depicting a child in, or knowingly developing, duplicating, printing, or exchanging any film, photograph, video tape, negative, or slide in which a child is engaged in an act of obscene sexual conduct

Colorado

Sexual Abuse § 19–1–103.

- Abuse or child abuse or neglect means any case in which a child is subjected to sexual assault or molestation, sexual exploitation, or prostitution
- Sexual conduct means any of the following:
  - Sexual intercourse, including genital-genital, oral-genital, anal-genital, or oral-anal, whether between persons of the same or opposite sex or between humans and animals

- Penetration of the vagina or rectum by any object
- Masturbation
- Sexual sadomasochistic abuse

Exceptions §§ 19–1–103; 19–3–103:

- Those investigating cases of child abuse shall take into account child-rearing practices of the culture in which the child participates
- The reasonable exercise of parental discipline is not considered abuse
- No child who, in lieu of medical treatment, is under treatment solely by spiritual means through prayer in accordance with a recognized method of religious healing shall, for that reason only, be considered neglected
- The religious rights of the parent shall not limit the access of a child to medical care in a life-threatening situation

Connecticut

Sexual Abuse § 46b–120. Abuse includes sexual molestation or exploitation.

Delaware

Sexual Abuse Tit. 16, § 902. Abuse includes sexual abuse and exploitation.

District of Columbia

Sexual Abuse § 16–2301. Sexual abuse means:

- Engaging in, or attempting to engage in, a sexual act or sexual contact with a child
- Causing or attempting to cause a child to engage in sexually explicit conduct
- Exposing the child to sexually explicit conduct

Sexual exploitation means a parent, guardian, or other custodian allows a child to engage in prostitution, or engages a child or allows a child to engage in obscene or pornographic photography, filming, or other forms of illustrating or promoting sexual conduct.

Florida

Sexual Abuse § 39.01. Sexual abuse of a child means one or more of the following acts:

- Any penetration, however slight, of the vagina or anal opening of one person by the penis of another person, whether or not there is the emission of semen
- Any sexual contact or intentional touching between the genitals or anal opening of one person and the mouth or tongue of another person
- The intentional masturbation of the perpetrator's genitals in the presence of a child
- The intentional exposure of the perpetrator's genitals in the presence of a child, or any other sexual act intentionally perpetrated in the presence of a child, if such exposure or sexual act is for the purpose of sexual arousal or gratification, aggression, degradation, or other similar purpose
- The sexual exploitation of a child, that includes allowing, encouraging, or forcing a child to solicit for or engage in prostitution, or engage in a sexual performance

Georgia

Sexual Abuse § 19–7–5(b). Sexual abuse means a person's employing, using, persuading, inducing, enticing, or coercing any minor who is not that person's spouse to engage in any act that involves:

- Sexual intercourse, including genital-genital, oral-genital, anal-genital, or oral-anal, whether between persons of the same or opposite sex
- Bestiality or masturbation

- Lewd exhibition of the genitals or pubic area of any person
- Flagellation or torture by or upon a person who is nude
- Condition of being fettered, bound, or otherwise physically restrained on the part of a person who is nude
- Physical contact in an act of apparent sexual stimulation or gratification with any person's clothed or unclothed genitals, pubic area, or buttocks or with a female's clothed or unclothed breasts
- Defecation or urination for the purpose of sexual stimulation
- Penetration of the vagina or rectum by any object except when done as part of a recognized medical procedure

Sexual exploitation means conduct by a child's parent or caretaker who allows, permits, encourages, or requires that child to engage in prostitution or sexually explicit conduct for the purpose of producing any visual or print medium depicting such conduct.

Exceptions § 19–7–5(b):

- Physical forms of discipline may be used as long as there is no physical injury to the child
- No child who in good faith is being treated solely by spiritual means through prayer in accordance with the tenets and practices of a recognized church or religious denomination by a duly accredited practitioner thereof shall, for that reason alone, be considered to be an abused child
- Sexual abuse does not include consensual sex acts between persons of the opposite sex who are minors or a minor and adult who is no more than 5 years older

Hawaii

Sexual Abuse § 350–1. Child abuse or neglect means when the child has been the victim of:

- Sexual contact or conduct including, but not limited to, sexual assault
- Molestation or sexual fondling

- Incest
- Prostitution
- Obscene or pornographic photographing, filming, or depiction, or other similar forms of sexual exploitation

Idaho

Sexual Abuse § 16–1602. Abused means any case in which a child has been the victim of sexual conduct, including rape, molestation, incest, prostitution, obscene or pornographic photographing, filming or depiction for commercial purposes, or other similar forms of sexual exploitation harming or threatening the child's health, welfare, or mental injury to the child.

Illinois

Sexual Abuse Ch. 325, § 5/3. Abused child means a child whose parent, immediate family member, any person responsible for the child's welfare, any individual residing in the same home as the child, or a paramour of the child's parent commits or allows to be committed any sex offense against the child.

Indiana

Sexual Abuse §§ 31–34–1–3; 31–34–1–4; 31–34–1–5. A child is a child in need of services if before the child becomes 18 years of age the child is the victim, lives in the same household as another child who was the victim, or lives in the same household as the adult who was convicted of a sex offense as defined in the criminal statutes pertaining to:

- Rape
- Criminal deviate conduct
- Child molesting
- Child exploitation or possession of child pornography
- Child seduction
- Sexual misconduct with a minor
- Indecent exposure
- Prostitution
- Incest

A child is a child in need of services if before the child becomes 18 years of age the child's parent, guardian, or custodian allows the child:

- To participate in an obscene **performance**
- To commit a sex offense prohibited by criminal statute

Iowa

Sexual Abuse § 232.68. Child abuse or abuse means:

- The commission of a sexual offense with or to a child
- Allowing, permitting, or encouraging the child to engage in prostitution
- The commission of bestiality in the presence of a minor by a person who resides in a home with a child, as a result of the acts or omissions of a person responsible for the care of the child

Kansas

Sexual Abuse § 38–1502. Sexual abuse means any act listed below, committed with a child, regardless of the age of the child:

- Unlawful sexual act
- Rape
- Indecent liberties with a child or aggravated indecent liberties with a child
- Indecent solicitation of a child or aggravated indecent solicitation of a child
- Sexual exploitation of a child
- Aggravated incest

Kentucky

Sexual Abuse § 600.020. Abused or neglected child means a child whose health or welfare is harmed or threatened with harm when his parent, guardian, or other person exercising custodial control or supervision of the child:

- Commits or allows to be committed an act of sexual abuse, sexual exploitation, or prostitution upon the child
- Creates or allows to be created a risk that an act of sexual abuse, sexual exploitation, or prostitution will be committed upon the child

Sexual abuse includes, but is not necessarily limited to, any contacts or interactions in which the parent or guardian uses or allows, permits, or encourages the use of the child for the purposes of sexual stimulation of the perpetrator or another person.

Sexual exploitation includes, but is not limited to, allowing, permitting, or encouraging the child to engage in prostitution, or an act of obscene or pornographic photographing, filming, or depicting of a child.

Louisiana

Sexual Abuse Ch. Code art. 603. Abuse includes any one of the following acts that seriously endanger the physical, mental, or emotional health of the child:

- The involvement of the child in any sexual act with a parent or any other person
- The aiding or toleration by the parent or caretaker of the child's sexual involvement with any other person
- The aiding or toleration by the parent of the child's involvement in pornographic displays
- Any other involvement of a child in sexual activity constituting a crime under the laws of the State

Child pornography means visual depiction of a child engaged in actual or simulated sexual intercourse, deviate sexual intercourse, sexual bestiality, masturbation, sadomasochistic abuse, or lewd exhibition of the genitals.

Crime against a child includes rape, sexual battery, incest, carnal knowledge of a juvenile, indecent behavior with a juvenile, pornography involving juveniles, or molestation of a juvenile.

Maine

Sexual Abuse Tit. 22, § 4002.

- Abuse or neglect means a threat to a child's health or welfare by sexual abuse or exploitation by a person responsible for the child
- Serious harm includes sexual abuse or exploitation

Maryland

Sexual Abuse Fam. Law § 5–701.

- Sexual abuse means any act that involves sexual molestation or exploitation of a child by a parent or other person who has permanent or temporary care, custody, or responsibility for supervision of a child, or by any household or family member
- Sexual abuse includes incest, rape, sexual offense in any degree, sodomy, and unnatural or perverted sexual practices

Massachusetts

Sexual Abuse Ch. 119, § 51A. Injured, abused, or neglected child includes sexual abuse.

Michigan

Sexual Abuse § 722.622.

- Sexual abuse means engaging in sexual contact or sexual penetration with a child, as those terms are defined in the penal code
- Sexual exploitation includes allowing, permitting, or encouraging a child to engage in prostitution, or allowing, permitting, encouraging, or engaging in

the photographing, filming, or depicting of a child engaged in a sexual act.

Minnesota

Sexual Abuse § 626.556. Sexual abuse means the subjection of a child by a person responsible for the child's care, a person who has a significant relationship to the child, or a person in a position of authority to any act that constitutes criminal sexual conduct. Sexual abuse includes any act that involves a minor that constitutes a violation of prostitution offenses. Sexual abuse also includes threatened sexual abuse.

Mississippi

Sexual Abuse § 43–21–105.

- Abused child includes sexual abuse or sexual exploitation
- Sexual abuse means obscene or pornographic photographing, filming, or depiction of children for commercial purposes, or the rape, molestation, incest, prostitution, or other such forms of sexual exploitation of children under circumstances that indicate that the child's health or welfare is harmed or threatened

Missouri

Sexual Abuse § 210.110. Abuse includes sexual abuse.

Montana

Sexual Abuse § 41–3–102.

- Sexual abuse means the commission of sexual assault, sexual intercourse without consent, indecent exposure, deviate sexual conduct, ritual abuse, or incest
- Sexual exploitation means allowing, permitting, or encouraging a child to engage in a prostitution offense, or allowing, permitting, or encouraging sexual abuse of children

- Physical or psychological harm to a child means the harm that occurs whenever the parent or other person responsible for the child's welfare commits or allows sexual abuse or exploitation of the child

Nebraska

Sexual Abuse § 28–710. Abuse or neglect means knowingly, intentionally, or negligently causing or permitting a minor child to be:

- Sexually abused
- Sexually exploited by allowing, encouraging, or forcing such person to solicit for or engage in prostitution, debauchery, public indecency, or obscene or pornographic photography, films, or depictions

Nevada

Sexual Abuse §§ 432B.100; 432B.110 Sexual abuse includes acts upon a child constituting:

- Incest
- Lewdness with a child
- Sadomasochistic abuse
- Sexual assault
- Statutory sexual seduction
- Mutilation of the genitalia of a female child, aiding, abetting, encouraging, or participating in the mutilation of the genitalia of a female child, or removal of a female child from this State for the purpose of mutilating the genitalia of the child

Sexual exploitation includes forcing, allowing, or encouraging a child:

- To solicit for or engage in prostitution
- To view a pornographic film or literature
- To engage in filming, photographing, or recording on videotape, or posing, modeling, depicting, or a live

performance before an audience that involves the exhibition of a child's genitals or any sexual conduct with a child

New Hampshire

Sexual Abuse § 169-C:3. Sexual abuse means the following activities under circumstances that indicate that the child's health or welfare is harmed or threatened with harm:

- The employment, use, persuasion, inducement, enticement, or coercion of any child to engage in, or having a child assist any other person to engage in, any sexually explicit conduct or any simulation of such conduct for the purpose of producing any visual depiction of such conduct
- The rape, molestation, prostitution, or other form of sexual exploitation of children, or incest with children

New Jersey

Sexual Abuse §§ 9:6–8.9; 9:6–8.21. Abused child means a child under the age of 18 years whose parent, guardian, or other person having his custody and control commits or allows to be committed an act of sexual abuse against the child.

New Mexico

Sexual Abuse § 32A-4–2.

- Abused child means a child who has suffered sexual abuse or sexual exploitation inflicted by the child's parent, guardian, or custodian
- Sexual abuse includes, but is not limited to, criminal sexual contact, incest, or criminal sexual penetration, as those acts are defined by State law
- Sexual exploitation includes, but is not limited to:
  - Allowing, permitting, or encouraging a child to engage in prostitution

- Allowing, permitting, encouraging, or engaging a
  child in obscene or pornographic photographing
- Filming or depicting a child for obscene or
  pornographic commercial purposes

New York

Sexual Abuse Soc. Serv. Law § 371. Abused child means a child
less than 18 years of age whose parent or other person legally responsible for his or her care commits, or allows to be committed,
an act of sexual abuse against such child, as defined in title H, article 130 of the penal law.

North Carolina

Sexual Abuse § 7B-101. Abused juvenile means any juvenile less
than 18 years of age whose parent, guardian, custodian, or caretaker commits, permits, or encourages the commission of a violation of the following laws regarding sexual offenses by, with, or
upon the juvenile:

- First and second degree rape or sexual offense
- Sexual act by a custodian
- Crime against nature or incest
- Preparation of obscene photographs, slides, or
  motion pictures of the juvenile
- Employing or permitting the juvenile to assist in a
  violation of the obscenity laws
- Dissemination of obscene material to the juvenile
- Displaying or disseminating material harmful to
  the juvenile
- First and second degree sexual exploitation of the
  juvenile
- Promoting the prostitution of the juvenile
- Taking indecent liberties with the juvenile,
  regardless of the age of the parties

North Dakota

Sexual Abuse § 50–25.1–02.

- Abused child means an individual under the age of 18 years who is suffering from or was subjected to any sex offenses against a child
- Harm means negative changes in a child's health that occur when a person responsible for the child's welfare commits, allows to be committed, or conspires to commit against the child a sex offense as defined in chapter 12.1–20

Ohio

Sexual Abuse §§ 2151.031; 2907.01; 2919.22.

- Abused child includes any child who is the victim of sexual activity where such activity would constitute an offense, except that the court need not find that any person has been convicted of the offense in order to find that the child is an abused child
- Sexual conduct means vaginal intercourse between a male and female; anal intercourse, fellatio and cunnilingus between persons regardless of sex; and, without privilege to do so, the insertion, however slight, of any part of the body or any instrument, apparatus, or other object into the vaginal or anal cavity of another. Penetration, however slight, is sufficient to complete vaginal or anal intercourse
- Sexual contact means any touching of an erogenous zone of another, including without limitation, the thigh, genitals, buttocks, pubic region, or if the person is a female, a breast, for the purpose of sexually arousing or gratifying either person
- A person commits the crime of endangering children when the person does any of the following to a child: Entice, coerce, permit, encourage, compel, hire, employ, use, or allow the child to act, model, or in any other way participate in, or be photographed for, the production, presentation, dissemination, or advertisement of any material or performance that the offender knows or reasonably should know is obscene, sexually oriented, or nudity-oriented matter

Oklahoma

Sexual Abuse Tit. 10, § 7102.

- Harm or threatened harm to a child's health or safety includes, but is not limited to, sexual abuse or sexual exploitation
- Sexual abuse includes, but is not limited to, rape, incest, and lewd or indecent acts or proposals, as defined by law, by a person responsible for the child's health, safety, or welfare
- Sexual exploitation includes, but is not limited to:
  - Allowing, permitting, or encouraging a child to engage in prostitution, as defined by law, by a person responsible for the child's health, safety, or welfare
  - Allowing, permitting, encouraging, or engaging in the lewd, obscene, or pornographic photographing, filming, or depicting of a child by a person responsible for the child's health, safety, or welfare

Oregon

Sexual Abuse § 419B.005. Abuse means:

- Rape of a child, that includes but is not limited to, rape, sodomy, unlawful sexual penetration, and incest
- Sexual abuse
- Sexual exploitation, including but not limited to:
  - Contributing to the sexual delinquency of a minor
  - Any other conduct that allows, employs, authorizes, permits, induces, or encourages a child to engage in the performing for people to observe, or the photographing, filming, tape recording, or other exhibition that, in whole or in part, depicts sexual conduct or contact, sexual abuse involving a child, or rape of a child

- Allowing, permitting, encouraging, or hiring a child to engage in prostitution

Pennsylvania

Sexual Abuse Tit. 23, § 6303. Child abuse shall mean any of the following:

- An act or failure to act by a perpetrator that causes sexual abuse or sexual exploitation of a child under 18 years of age
- Any recent act, failure to act, or series of such acts or failures to act by a perpetrator that creates an imminent risk of sexual abuse or sexual exploitation of a child under 18 years of age
- Sexual abuse or exploitation means the employment, use, persuasion, inducement, enticement, or coercion of any child to engage in or assist any other person to engage in any sexually explicit conduct or any simulation of any sexually explicit conduct for the purpose of producing:
  - Any visual depiction, including photographing, videotaping, computer depicting, or filming of any sexually explicit conduct
  - The rape, sexual assault, involuntary deviate sexual intercourse, aggravated indecent assault, molestation, incest, indecent exposure, prostitution, statutory sexual assault, or other form of sexual exploitation of children

Rhode Island

Sexual Abuse § 40–11–2. Abused and/or neglected child means a child whose physical or mental health or welfare is harmed or threatened with harm when his or her parent or other person responsible for his or her welfare:

- Commits or allows to be committed against the child an act of sexual abuse
- Sexually exploits the child in that the person allows, permits, or encourages the child to engage in prostitution

- Sexually exploits the child in that the person allows, permits, encourages, or engages in the obscene or pornographic photographing, filming, or depiction of the child in a setting that taken as a whole suggests to the average person that the child is about to engage in or has engaged in any sexual act, or that depicts any such child under 18 years of age performing sodomy, oral copulation, sexual intercourse, masturbation, or bestiality
- Commits or allows to be committed any sexual offense against the child
- Commits or allows to be committed against any child an act involving sexual penetration or sexual contact if the child is under 15 years of age; or if the child is 15 years or older, and (1) force or coercion is used by the perpetrator, or (2) the perpetrator knows or has reason to know that the victim is a severely impaired person, or physically helpless

South Carolina

Sexual Abuse § 20–7–490. Child abuse or neglect or harm occurs when the parent, guardian, or other person responsible for the child's welfare commits or allows to be committed against the child a sexual offense or engages in acts or omissions that present a substantial risk that a sexual offense would be committed against the child.

South Dakota

Sexual Abuse § 26–8A-2. Abused or neglected child means a child who is subject to sexual abuse, sexual molestation, or sexual exploitation by the child's parent, guardian, custodian, or any other person responsible for the child's care.

Tennessee

Sexual Abuse § 37–1–602. Child sexual abuse means the commission of any act involving the unlawful sexual abuse, molestation, fondling, or carnal knowledge of a child under 13 years of age that on or after November 1, 1989, constituted the criminal offense of:

- Aggravated rape, sexual battery, or sexual exploitation of a minor
- Criminal attempt for any of the offenses listed above
- Especially aggravated sexual exploitation of a minor
- Incest
- Rape, sexual battery, or sexual exploitation of a minor

Child sexual abuse also means one or more of the following acts:

- Any penetration, however slight, of the vagina or anal opening of one person by the penis of another person, whether or not there is the emission of semen
- Any contact between the genitals or anal opening of one person and the mouth or tongue of another person
- Any intrusion by one person into the genitals or anal opening of another person, including the use of any object for this purpose
- The intentional touching of the genitals or intimate parts, including the breasts, genital area, groin, inner thighs, and buttocks, or the clothing covering them, of either the child or the perpetrator
- The intentional exposure of the perpetrator's genitals in the presence of a child, or any other sexual act intentionally perpetrated in the presence of a child, if such exposure or sexual act is for the purpose of sexual arousal or gratification, aggression, degradation, or other similar purpose
- The sexual exploitation of a child, which includes allowing, encouraging, or forcing a child to solicit for or engage in prostitution, or engage in sexual exploitation of a minor

Exceptions § 37–1–602: Child sexual abuse does not include acts intended for a valid medical purpose, or acts that may reasonably be construed to be normal caretaker responsibilities, interactions with, or affection for a child.

Texas

Sexual Abuse Fam. Code § 261.001. Abuse includes the following acts or omissions by a person:

- Sexual conduct harmful to a child's mental, emotional, or physical welfare, including conduct that constitutes the offense of indecency with a child, sexual assault, or aggravated sexual assault
- Failure to make a reasonable effort to prevent sexual conduct harmful to a child
- Compelling or encouraging the child to engage in sexual conduct
- Causing, permitting, encouraging, engaging in, or allowing the photographing, filming, or depicting of the child if the person knew or should have known that the resulting photograph, film, or depiction of the child is obscene or pornographic
- Causing, permitting, encouraging, engaging in, or allowing a sexual performance by a child

Utah

Sexual Abuse § 62A-4a–402.

- Harm or threatened harm means damage or threatened damage to the physical or emotional health and welfare of a child through neglect or abuse, and includes but is not limited to incest, sexual abuse, sexual exploitation, or molestation
- Sexual abuse means acts or attempted acts of sexual intercourse, sodomy, or molestation directed towards a child
- Sexual exploitation of minors means knowingly employing, using, persuading, inducing, enticing, or coercing any minor to pose in the nude for the purpose of sexual arousal of any person or for profit, or to engage in any sexual or simulated sexual conduct for the purpose of photographing, filming, recording, or displaying in any way sexual or simulated sexual conduct, and includes displaying, distributing, possessing for the purpose of distribution, or selling material depicting minors in the nude, or engaging in sexual or simulated sexual conduct

Vermont

Sexual Abuse Tit. 33, § 4912.

- An abused or neglected child also means a child who is sexually abused or at substantial risk of sexual abuse by any person
- Sexual abuse consists of any act or acts by any person involving sexual molestation or exploitation of a child including, but not limited to, incest, prostitution, rape, sodomy, or any lewd and lascivious conduct involving a child
- Sexual abuse also includes the aiding, abetting, counseling, hiring, or procuring of a child to perform or participate in any photograph, motion picture, exhibition, show, representation, or other presentation which, in whole or in part, depicts sexual conduct, sexual excitement, or sadomasochistic abuse involving a child

Virginia

Sexual Abuse § 63.2–100. Abused or neglected child means any child less than 18 years of age whose parents or other person responsible for his or her care commits or allows to be committed any act of sexual exploitation or any sexual act upon a child in violation of the law.

Washington

Sexual Abuse § 26.44.020.

- Abuse or neglect means the sexual abuse or sexual exploitation of a child by any person under circumstances that indicate that the child's health, welfare, and safety are harmed
- Sexual exploitation includes:
  - Allowing, permitting, or encouraging a child to engage in prostitution by any person
  - Allowing, permitting, encouraging, or engaging in the obscene or pornographic photographing, filming, or depicting of a child by any person

West Virginia

Sexual Abuse § 49–1–3. Child abuse and neglect or child abuse or neglect means sexual abuse or sexual exploitation of a child by a parent, guardian, or custodian who is responsible for the child's welfare, under circumstances that harm or threaten the health and welfare of the child.

Sexual abuse means the acts of sexual intercourse, sexual intrusion, or sexual contact, when they occur under the following circumstances:

- As to a child who is less than 16 years of age, those acts that a parent, guardian, or custodian shall engage in, attempt to engage in, or knowingly procure another person to engage in with the child, notwithstanding the fact that the child may have willingly participated in such conduct or the fact that the child may have suffered no apparent physical, mental, or emotional injury as a result of such conduct
- As to a child who is 16 years of age or older, those acts that a parent, guardian, or custodian shall engage in, attempt to engage in, or knowingly procure another person to engage in with the child, notwithstanding the fact that the child may have consented to such conduct or the fact that the child may have suffered no apparent physical, mental, or emotional injury as a result of such conduct

Sexual abuse also means any conduct whereby a parent, guardian, or custodian displays his or her sex organs to a child, or procures another person to display his or her sex organs to a child, for the purpose of gratifying the sexual desire of the person making such display, or of the child, or for the purpose of affronting or alarming the child.

Sexual exploitation means an act whereby:

- A parent, custodian, or guardian, whether for financial gain or not, persuades, induces, entices, or coerces a child to engage in sexually explicit conduct
- A parent, guardian, or custodian persuades, induces, entices, or coerces a child to display his or her sex organs for the sexual gratification of the parent, guardian,

custodian, or a third person, or to display his or her sex organs under circumstances in which the parent, guardian, or custodian knows such display is likely to be observed by others who would be affronted or alarmed

Wisconsin

Sexual Abuse § 48.02. Abuse means any of the following:

- Sexual intercourse or sexual contact
- A violation of the statute regarding the sexual exploitation of a child
- Permitting, allowing, or encouraging a child to engage in prostitution
- A violation of the statute that prohibits causing a child to view or listen to sexual activity
- A violation of the statute that prohibits the exposure of the genitals to a child

Wyoming

Sexual Abuse § 14–3–202. Abuse with respect to a child means the commission or allowing the commission of a sexual offense against a child, as defined by law.

State Sex Offender Registries

Each state is required by federal law to maintain a sex offender registry. Table 6.6 provides the website addresses for each state's sex offender registry.

Federal (U.S.) Laws

Summaries of several laws, at the federal level, are included in this section. Beginning with the Child Abuse Prevention and Treatment Act, initially passed in 1974, the U.S. government has enacted several laws to protect children and their families and provide services to those families. Some of these laws focus specifically on child sexual abuse, while others have broader coverage that includes children who are exposed to all types of abuse and neglect.

TABLE 6.6
Website Addresses for State Sex Offender Registries, by State

State	Web Address
Alabama	http://www.dps.state.al.us/public/abi/system/so
Alaska	http://www.dps.state.ak.us/nSorcr/asp/
Arizona	http://www.azsexoffender.org/
Arkansas	http://www.acic.org
California	http://meganslaw.ca.gov/disclaimer.htm
Colorado	http://sor.state.co.us/
Connecticut	http://www.state.ct.us/dps/Sor.htm
Delaware	http://www.state.de.us/dsp/sexoff/index.htm
District of Columbia	http://mpdc.dc.gov/serv/sor/sor.shtm
Florida	http://www3.fdle.state.fl.us/sexual_predators
Georgia	http://www.ganet.org/gbi/sorsch.cgi
Hawaii	http://pahoehoe.ehawaii.gov/sexoff/
Idaho	http://www.isp.state.id.us/identification/sex_offender/index.html
Illinois	http://www.isp.state.il.us/sor/frames.htm
Indiana	http://www.ai.org/cji/html/sexoffender.html
Iowa	http://www.state.ia.us/government/dps/dci/isor/
Kansas	http://www.accesskansas.org/kbi/ro.shtml
Kentucky	http://kspsor.state.ky.us
Louisiana	http://www.lasocpr.lsp.org/socpr/
Maine	http://www.informe.org/sor/
Maryland	http:www.dpscs.state.md.us/sor/
Massachusetts	http://www.mass.gov/sorb/community.htm
Michigan	http://www.mipsor.state.mi.us/
Minnesota	http://www.dps.state.mn.us/bca/Invest/Documents/Page-07.html
Mississippi	http://SOR.MDPS.STATE.MS.US
Missouri	http://mshp.dps.Missouri.gov/MSHPWeb/PatrolDivisions/CRID/SOR/SORPage.html
Montana	http://svor.doj.state.mt.us/
Nebraska	http://www.nsp.state.ne.us/sor/
Nevada	http://www.nvrepository.state.nv.us/SexOffender.htm
New Hampshire	http://www.oit.nh.gov/nsor/search.asp
New Jersey	http://www.njsp.org/info/reg_sexoffend.html

(continues)

TABLE 6.6 *(continued)*
Website Addresses for State Sex Offender Registries, by State

State	Web Address
New Mexico	http://www.nmsexoffender.dps.state.nm.us/servlet/hit_serv.class
New York	http://www.criminaljustice.state.ny.us/nsor/
North Carolina	http://sbi.jus.state.nc.us/DOJHAHT/SOR/Default.htm
North Dakota	http://www.ndsexoffender.com
Ohio	http://www.esorn.ag.state.oh.us
Oklahoma	http://dpcapp8.doc.state.ok.us/servlet/page?_pageid=190&_dad=portal30 &_schema=PORTAL30
Oregon	http://egov.oregon.gov/OSP
Pennsylvania	http://www.pameganslaw.state.pa.us/
Rhode Island	http://www.paroleboard.ri.gov/L3_offenders/listings.htm
South Carolina	http://www.scattorneygeneral.org/
South Dakota	http://www.dci.sd.gov/administration/id/sexoffender/index.asp
Tennessee	http://www.ticic.state.tn.us//SEX_ofndr/search_short.asp
Texas	http://records.txdps.state.tx.us/
Utah	http://www.udc.state.ut.us/asp-bin/sexoffendersearchform.asp
Vermont	http://170.222.24.9/cjs/s_registry.htm
Virginia	http://www.vsp.state.va.us/vsp.html
Washington	http://ml.waspc.org/Accept.aspx?ReturnUrl=/index.aspx
West Virginia	http://www.wvstatepolice.com/sexoff/
Wisconsin	http:widocoffenders.org
Wyoming	http://attorneygeneral.state.wy.us/dci/so/so_registration.html

The Child Abuse Prevention and Treatment Act (CAPTA) of 1974, P.L. 93–247
Amended 1978, 1984, 1988, 1992, 1996, 2003

Following C. Henry Kempe's identification of the battered child syndrome in 1961, doctors and other medical personnel began to take notice of child abuse, including child sexual abuse. In the next several years, the general public became more aware of abused children. While several states had established laws regarding the reporting of child abuse and neglect, these laws were not uniform, and not every state had such a law. Public interest encouraged the federal government to examine the issue of child abuse and neglect and establish uniform state guidelines for the reporting of child abuse and neglect.

The purpose of the act was to protect children from abuse and neglect by increasing the identification, reporting, and investigation of child abuse and neglect as well as to monitor and encourage research, and compile research results and provide them to the public. States were provided with assistance in developing child abuse and neglect programs, and intervention was encouraged to actively protect children. The National Center on Child Abuse and Neglect (see Chapter 7) was established, administering grant programs, identifying issues for further research, and serving as the primary source of information on various aspects of child abuse and neglect. The National Clearinghouse on Child Abuse and Neglect Information was also established to gather and disseminate information on child abuse and neglect.

Keeping Children and Families Safe Act of 2003, P.L. 108–36, amended the Child Abuse and Prevention Treatment Act

The Keeping Children and Families Safe Act reauthorized CAPTA, the Adoption Opportunities, Abandoned Infants Assistance, and Family Violence Prevention and Services acts. One reason it was enacted was general concern among legislators and their constituents that many children and their families were not receiving adequate protection or treatment. The act encourages enhanced links between child protective service agencies and public health, mental health, and developmental disabilities agencies and focuses increased attention on children who are infected with HIV or have a life-threatening illness and children placed in adoptive families.

Indian Child Welfare Act (ICWA) of 1978, P.L. 95–608

State courts were removing a high proportion of Indian children from their families and placing them off the reservations in non-Indian environments; there was growing concern that the courts were not aware of the cultural and social aspects of Indian society and that these children were losing their heritage. The appropriateness of this removal was questioned, and this act was passed to protect the best interests of American Indian children and their families. Among other benefits, this act established minimum standards for removal of children, provided assistance to the tribes to operate child and family service programs, and provided funds to the tribes to improve child welfare services.

Family Preservation and Support Services Program, enacted as part of the Omnibus Budget Reconciliation Act of 1993, P.L. 103–66
Title XIII, Chapter 2, Subchapter C, Part 1
Amended Title IV-B of the Social Security Act

This program was enacted out of concern that the number of reported cases of child abuse and neglect was increasing; the focus of services appeared to be on treatment rather than on prevention; and child welfare services were not coordinated with other services needed by many families. The program provided funding to states to establish a continuum of family-focused services for at-risk children and their families; required states to develop a comprehensive planning process to help provide family support and preservation activities; and provided funding to encourage states to incorporate prevention strategies into their treatment programs.

Adoption and Safe Families Act (ASFA) of 1997, P.L. 105–89, amended Title IV-E of the Social Security Act

Supporters of this act wanted to promote permanency in foster care, ensure that abused and neglected children were in safe environments, accelerate permanent placements of children, and make the child welfare system increasingly accountable for the welfare of these children. The act reauthorized the Family Preservation and Support Services Program, renaming it the Safe and Stable Families Program. It ensured the safety of abused and neglected children by ensuring that health and safety concerns are addressed as states place children in foster/permanent care. It also required the U.S. Department of Health and Human Services to report on the scope of substance abuse in the child welfare system, added "safety of the child" to all case plan and review process steps, and required criminal background checks for foster and adoptive parents who receive federal funds for care of a child.

Child Abuse Prevention and Enforcement Act of 2000, P.L. 106–177

The Child Abuse Prevention and Enforcement Act of 2000 was enacted in response to concerns that responses to reports of child abuse and neglect were inadequate. The act addressed these concerns about the level and quality of responses by allowing states to use federal law enforcement funds to provide timely and accurate criminal history background information to child welfare agencies, organizations, and programs that provide services to protect abused and neglected children, including children who have been sexually abused.

The act allows law enforcement agencies to use federal funds to enforce child abuse and neglect laws, including laws to protect children from sexual abuse, to promote prevention programs, and to establish cooperative programs between law enforcement agencies and news media organizations to collect and disseminate information concerning suspected criminal offenders.

The Victims of Child Abuse Act of 1990, P.L. 101–647

This act was enacted to address problems faced by abused children during investigations into the validity of the abuse. It encourages the development of model technical assistance and training programs to improve the way in which courts handle child abuse and neglect cases, and it facilitates adoption of laws to protect children against a second assault on them in the courtroom. Children are provided with the right to have an adult accompany them into court during testimony and to assist them during other procedures and processes. Criminal justice personnel are to be provided with training on current innovative techniques for investigating and prosecuting cases of child abuse, including cases of child sexual abuse. Communities are encouraged to develop Children's Advocacy Centers as a multidisciplinary approach to investigating, prosecuting, and treating child abuse cases. The National Court Appointed Special Advocate (CASA) Association provides technical assistance, information, and other support to local CASA programs and assists in developing new programs in communities.

Protection of Children against Sexual Exploitation Act of 1977

This act was the first attempt by the federal government to regulate child pornography. It focused on the commercial production and dissemination of visual and print images of minors engaged in any sexually explicit activity.

Communications Decency Act (CDA) of 1996, P.L. 104–104, part of the Telecommunications Act

This act was enacted by Congress to criminalize the "knowing transmission of obscene or indecent messages" to minors along with sending or displaying clearly offensive materials to minors. It was challenged in *Reno v. ACLU* (521 U.S. 844 [1997]), and the Supreme Court found that the statute was overbroad according to the First Amendment. The justices held that provisions of the CDA prohibiting transmission of obscene or indecent communications by means of telecommunications devices to persons under age eighteen, or sending patently offensive communications through use of interactive computer service to persons under age eighteen, was content-based blanket restrictions on speech.

The Child Pornography Prevention Act of 1996 (CPPA), P.L. 104–208

This act added virtual child pornography, images that appear to be of minors, to the definition of child pornography. However, the statute was struck down by the Supreme Court (see *Ashcroft v. Free Speech Coalition* (535 U.S. 234 [2002]), noting that speech "within rights of adults to hear may not be silenced completely in an attempt to shield children from it."

Protection of Children from Sexual Predators Act of 1998, P.L. 105–314

The purpose of this act is to protect children from sexual predators and from child pornography, and to prevent sexual abuse. It prohibits the transfer of obscene materials to minors and increases the penalties for sexual offenses against children and for repeat offenders. Online service providers are required to report evidence of child pornography offenses to law enforcement agencies.

Other Federal Laws and Codes to Protect Children

Several other means exist to protect children against sexual abuse and sexual exploitation, and they are found primarily in the Federal Criminal Code under Title 18 of the U.S. Code (USC), which defines a "minor" as a child under the age of eighteen unless specified otherwise. Excerpts from the relevant sections are provided below.

Section 1466A. Obscene Visual Representations of the Sexual Abuse of Children

Any person who knowingly produces, distributes, receives, or possesses with intent to distribute, a visual depiction of any kind that depicts a minor engaging in sexually explicit behavior, or that is obscene, or depicts an image that appears to be that of a minor shall be fined and imprisoned not less than 5 years and not more than 20 years; persons with prior convictions shall be fined and imprisoned for not less than 15 years nor more than 40 years.

Section 1470. Transfer of Obscene Material to Minors

Whoever, using the mail or any facility or means of interstate or foreign commerce, knowingly transfers obscene matter to another individual who has not attained the age of 16 years knowing that such other individual has not attained the age of 16 years, or attempts to do so, shall be fined under this title, imprisoned not more than 10 years, or both.

Section 2241(a)(c). Aggravated Sexual Abuse

Whoever, in the special maritime and territorial jurisdiction of the United States or in a federal prison, knowingly causes or attempts to cause another person to engage in a sexual act by using force against that other person, threatening or placing them in fear that another person will be subjected to death, serious bodily injury, or kidnapping, or attempts to do so, shall be fined and imprisoned for any term of years or life, or both.

Whoever knowingly crosses a state line with intent to engage in a sexual act with a person who has not attained the age of 12 years; or in the territorial jurisdiction of the United States or in a federal prison engages in a sexual act with a person who has not attained the age of 12 years; or whoever engages in a sexual activity by using force, threat, or other means described above, with an individual who has attained 12 years but has not attained 16 years of age shall be fined, imprisoned for any term of years or life, or both.

Section 2243. Sexual Abuse of a Minor or Ward

Whoever, in the territorial jurisdiction of the United States or in a federal prison knowingly engages in a sexual act (or attempts to do so) with another person who has attained the age of 12 years but not 16 years and is at least four years younger than the person so engaging shall be fined, imprisoned not more than fifteen years, or both.

Section 2251(a)(b)(c). Sexual Exploitation of Children

Any person who employs, uses, persuades, induces, entices, or coerces any minor to engage in; or who has a minor assist any other person to engage in; or who transports any minor in interstate or foreign commerce with the intent that such minor engage in, any sexually explicit conduct for the purpose of producing any visual depiction of such conduct. This statute applies when the person knows that such visual depiction will be, or has actually been, transported in interstate or foreign commerce or mailed.

Any parent, legal guardian, person, or organization having custody or control of a minor who knowingly permits such minor to engage in or assists any person to engage in sexually explicit conduct for the purpose of producing any visual depiction of such conduct. This statute also applies if such visual depiction will be or has actually been transported in interstate or foreign commerce, mailed, and/or such depiction was produced with materials that have been mailed, shipped, or transported in interstate or foreign commerce by any means, including by computer.

Any person, who knowingly prints, publishes, or causes to be made, any notice or advertisement seeking or offering to receive, exchange, buy, produce, display, distribute, or reproduce any visual depiction involving the use of a minor engaging in sexually explicit conduct. This statute also applies when such person knows that such notice or advertisement will be, or has been, transported in interstate or foreign commerce by any means, including by computer.

Penalties under this section shall include a fine, imprisonment for not less than fifteen nor more than 30 years unless the person has a prior conviction, in which case they shall be fined and imprisoned for not less than twenty-five years nor more than fifty years. If the person has two or more convictions, they shall be fined and imprisoned not less than thirty-five years nor more than life.

Section 2251A(a)(b). Selling or Buying of Children

Any parent, legal guardian, or other person having custody or control of a minor who sells, offers to sell, or otherwise transfers custody or control of such minor with knowledge that, as a consequence of the sale or transfer, the minor will be portrayed in a visual depiction engaging in, or assisting another person to engage in sexually explicit conduct, shall be punished by imprisonment for not less than thirty years or for life and by a fine.

Any person who purchases, offers to purchase, or otherwise obtains custody or control of a minor with knowledge that, as a consequence of the sale or transfer, the minor will be portrayed in a visual depiction engaging in, or assisting another person to engage in sexually explicit conduct shall be punished by imprisonment for not less than 30 years or for life and by a fine.

Section 2252. Certain Activities Relating to Material Involving the Sexual Exploitation of Minors

Any person who knowingly possesses in the territorial jurisdiction of the United States one or more images, books, magazines, periodicals, films, videotapes, or other matter which contain any visual depiction of a minor engaged in sexually explicit conduct.

Any person who knowingly transports or ships in interstate or foreign commerce, by any means including by computer or mail, any visual depiction of a minor engaged in sexually explicit conduct.

Any person who knowingly receives, reproduces, or distributes any visual depiction of a minor engaged in sexually explicit conduct that has been mailed, or has been shipped or transported in interstate or foreign commerce.

Any person who knowingly sells, or possesses with intent to sell, any visual depiction of a minor engaged in sexually explicit conduct that has been mailed, or has been shipped or transported in interstate or foreign commerce. Punishment in this section includes a fine, and imprisonment for not less than five years and not more than twenty years, unless the person has a prior conviction, in which case they shall be fined and imprisoned for not less than fifteen years nor more than forty years.

Section 2252A. Certain Activities Relating to Material Constituting or Containing Child Pornography

Any person who knowingly mails, transports, or ships in interstate or foreign commerce child pornography by any means, including by computer.

Any person who knowingly receives or distributes any child pornography or any book, magazine, film, videotape, computer disk, or any other material containing child pornography that has been mailed, transported, or shipped in interstate or foreign commerce by any means, including by computer.

Any person who knowingly reproduces any child pornography for distribution through the mail, or in interstate or foreign commerce by any means, including by computer.

Any person who knowingly sells or possesses with the intent to sell any child pornography. Punishment in this section includes a fine, and imprisonment for not less than five years and not more than twenty years, unless the person has a prior conviction, in which case they will be fined and imprisoned for not less than fifteen years nor more than forty years.

At times, portions of this Section may not apply when the individual is in possession of less than three child pornography images and in good faith promptly took reasonable steps to destroy each image, report the matter to a law enforcement agency, and/or afford that agency access to the image.

Section 2253. Criminal Forfeiture; and Section 2254. Civil Forfeiture

A person who is convicted of an offense under Sections 2251, 2251A, 2252, 2252A, 2260 or Sections 2421, 2422, 2423 shall forfeit any visual depiction described in Sections 2251, 2251A, 2252; any property constituting gross profits or other proceeds obtained from such offense; and any property used or intended to be used to commit or to promote the commission of the above offenses.

Section 2260(a)(b). Production of Sexually Explicit Depictions of a Minor for Importation into the United States

A person outside the U.S. who employs, uses, persuades, induces, entices, or coerces any minor to engage in, or who has a minor assist any other person to engage in, or who transports any minor with the intent that such minor engage in any sexually explicit conduct for the purpose of producing any visual depiction of such conduct, intending that the visual depiction will be imported into the U.S. or waters within 12 miles of a U.S. coast.

A person outside the U.S. who knowingly receives, transports, ships, distributes, or possesses with intent to transport, ship, sell or distribute any visual depiction of a minor engaged in sexually explicit conduct, intending that the visual depiction will be imported into the U.S. or waters within 12 miles of a U.S. coast. Punishment for anyone in this section includes a fine, imprisonment of not more than ten years, or both. If the person has a prior conviction, they shall be fined, imprisoned for not more than twenty years, or both.

Section 2421. Transportation Generally

Whoever knowingly transports any individual in interstate or foreign commerce, or in any Territory or Possession of the United States, with intent that such individual engage in prostitution or in any sexual activity for which any person can be charged with a criminal offense shall be fined or imprisoned not more than ten years or both.

Section 2422. Coercion and Enticement

Whoever knowingly persuades, induces, entices, or coerces any individual to travel in interstate or foreign commerce, or in any Territory or Possession of the United States, to engage in prostitution or in any sexual activity for which any person can be charged with a criminal offense shall be fined under this title and imprisoned not less than five years and not more than thirty years.

Section 2423(a). Transportation of Minors with Intent to Engage in Criminal Sexual Activity

Whoever knowingly transports or attempts to transport any individual under the age of 18 years in interstate or foreign commerce, or in any Territory or Possession of the United States, with intent that the individual engage in prostitution or in any sexual activity for which any person can be charged with a criminal offense shall be fined and imprisoned not less than 5 years and not more than thirty years.

Section 2423(b). Interstate or Foreign Travel with Intent to Engage in a Sexual Act with a Juvenile

Whoever knowingly travels or conspires to do so in interstate or foreign commerce, or in any Territory or Possession of the United States, with the intent to engage in any sexual activity with a person under 18 years of age for which any person can be charged with a criminal offense shall be fined, imprisoned not more than 30 years, or both.

Section 2425. Use of Interstate Facilities to Transmit Information about a Minor

Whoever, using the mail or any facility or means of interstate or foreign commerce, knowingly initiates or attempts to initiate the transmission of the name, address, telephone number, social security number, or electronic mail address of any individual who has not attained the age of 16 years with the intent to entice, encourage, offer, or solicit that minor to engage in any sexual activity that can be charged as a criminal offense shall be fined, imprisoned not more than five years or both.

Title 42 of the U.S. Code (USC) concerns public health and welfare. The following are summaries from the Federal Criminal Code and Rules under Title 42 that relate to child sexual abuse.

Section 13032. Reporting of Child Pornography by Electronic Communication Service Providers

Creates a mandatory reporting requirement for electronic communication service providers, Internet Service Providers, and remote computing service providers to report violations of federal child pornography laws to any law enforcement agency and/or the National Center for Missing and Exploited Children.

Section 14072. Pam Lychner Sexual Offender Tracking and Identification Act of 1996

A registered sex offender must notify and register with both the FBI and state authorities within ten days of moving to a new state. Registration includes providing a current address, fingerprints, and photograph for inclusion in the FBI's National Sex Offender Registry (NSOR).

International Conventions

Convention on the Rights of the Child, G.A. res. 44/25, annex, 44 U.N. GAOR Supp. (No. 49) at 167, U.N. Doc. A/44/49 (1989), entered into force September 2, 1990

The Convention on the Rights of the Child defines a child as "every human being below the age of eighteen years unless under the law applicable to the child, majority is attained earlier" (Article 1). All parties to the convention must take appropriate measures to protect the child from discrimination or punishment (Article 2). Article 11 requires all parties to "combat the illicit transfer and non-return of children abroad." All parties are required to protect children from all forms of physical and mental violence, including sexual abuse and exploitation (Articles 19 and 34).

A Committee on the Rights of the Child is established to examine the progress of reaching the goals of the convention, and all parties should submit reports to the committee providing information on the measures they have taken to support the convention (Article 43).

Protocol to Prevent, Suppress and Punish Trafficking in Persons, Especially Women and Children, Supplementing the UN Convention against Transnational Organized Crime (United Nations 2003)

This protocol was established to prevent and combat trafficking and sexual exploitation in persons, focusing on women and children, and to promote cooperation among all parties to the convention in preventing trafficking and sexual exploitation. It is a supplement to the UN Convention against Transnational Organized Crime. A child is defined as a person under the age of 18 years. All parties are required to adopt legislative and other measures creating criminal consequences for trafficking and exploitation. Prevention policies and programs must be established by all parties to combat these activities, and they are required to share information.

Optional Protocol to the Convention on the Rights of the Child on the Sale of Children, Child Prostitution and Child Pornography

This protocol grew out of concern over the increasing international traffic in children, including the sale of children, child prostitution, and child pornography; the growing ease of obtaining child pornography on the Internet; and the fact that female children are at greater risk of sexual exploitation. Parties to the protocol agree to prohibit child prostitution and child pornography and establish criminal penalties for sexually exploiting a child through sale, child prostitution, or child pornography, and producing or distributing child pornography, among other activities. Also required are the provision of services to child victims, protection of children and their families during the legal process, training of service providers, and adoption of laws, policies, and programs to prevent the sale and exploitation of children.

Within two years of the entry into force of the protocol, each party is required to submit a report to the Committee on the Rights of the Child that describes in detail the steps it has taken to meet the requirements of the protocol.

Summary of Significant Court Cases in U.S. Courts

In this section, several important Supreme Court cases are provided, along with a sample of lower court cases that show the variety of cases that have been brought in the courts.

New York v. Ferber, 458 U.S. 747 (1982)

A New York statute prohibits individuals from knowingly promoting a sexual performance by a child under the age of sixteen by distributing material that depicts a sexual performance. The statute defines sexual performance as "any performance or part thereof which includes sexual conduct by a child less than sixteen years of age."

Paul Ferber, the proprietor of a bookstore in Manhattan that specializes in sexually oriented products, sold two films to an undercover police officer. The films depicted young boys masturbating. Ferber was indicted on two counts of violating the two New York statutes that control dissemination of child pornography. A jury acquitted Ferber on the two counts of promoting an obscene sexual performance but found him guilty on two counts under §263.15, which did not require proof that the films were obscene. The Appellate Division of the New York Supreme Court affirmed, and the verdict was appealed. The New York Court of Appeals reversed, holding that §263.15 violated the First Amendment.

The U.S. Supreme Court was asked to decide whether the law violated the First Amendment. This was the Court's first examination of a statute that specifically targeted child pornography, and it found that the state's interest in preventing child sexual exploitation was a compelling "government objective of surpassing importance." The law was carefully crafted to protect children from the mental, physical, and sexual abuse associated with pornography and did not violate the First Amendment. The Court found that, in respect to child pornography, a "trier of fact need not find that the material appeals to the prurient interest of the average person; it is not required that sexual conduct portrayed be done so in a patently offensive manner; and the material at issue need not be considered as a whole" (764).

Osborne v. Ohio, 495 U.S. 103 (1990)

Osborne was convicted of possession of four photographs of a nude male adolescent in sexually explicit poses. He appealed, challenging the state statute that prohibited any person from possessing or viewing any materials showing a minor who is not his child in a state of nudity, unless the material is presented for a bona fide purpose or if the possessor knows that the minor's parents or guardians have consented to the photographing of the child. Osborne challenged Ohio's right to proscribe his possession of the pornography. An intermediate appellate court and the Ohio State Supreme Court affirmed his conviction.

The U.S. Supreme Court ruled that Ohio could indeed constitutionally forbid the possession of child pornography. Children are harmed physiologically, emotionally, and mentally when they are the subject in the production of child pornography. The statute, by penalizing individuals for possessing child pornography, would provide an opportunity to "destroy a market for the exploitative use of children." The Court also determined that, because child pornography is a permanent record of the abuse of children who are used in its production, its "continued existence causes the child victims continuing harm by haunting the children in years to come." The Court relied on the justifications in *Ferber* of preventing exploitation of children and destroying the market for child pornography.

Idaho v. Wright, 497 U.S. 805 (1990)

Wright was charged under Idaho law with two counts of lewd conduct with a minor, specifically her 5.5- and 2.5-year-old daughters. At the trial, while it was agreed that the younger daughter was not "capable of communicating to the jury," the court admitted, under Idaho's residual hearsay exception, certain statements she had made to a pediatrician having extensive experience in child abuse cases. The doctor testified that she had reluctantly answered questions about her own abuse, but had spontaneously volunteered information about her sister's abuse. Wright was convicted on both counts, but appealed only from the conviction involving the younger child.

The State Supreme Court reversed, finding that the admission of the doctor's testimony under the residual hearsay exception violated Wright's rights under the Confrontation Clause. The court noted that the child's statements did not fall within a traditional hearsay exception and lacked "particularized guarantees of trustworthiness" because the doctor had conducted the interview without procedural safeguards: he failed to videotape the interview, asked leading questions, and had a preconceived idea of what the child should be disclosing. This error, the court found, was not harmless beyond a reasonable doubt. The court held that the admission of the child's hearsay statements violated Wright's Confrontation Clause rights.

Reno v. American Civil Liberties Union, 521 U.S. 844 (1997)

At issue in this case was whether the provisions of the Communications Decency Act (CDA) of 1996 that prohibit the transmission of indecent and patently offensive materials to minors over the Internet violate the First Amendment. The CDA was the government's first attempt to make the Internet safe for minors. Finding that the governmental interest in protecting children from harmful materials does not justify an unnecessarily broad suppression of speech addressed to adults, the Supreme Court upheld the lower court ruling that, while the state had an interest in protecting children, the CDA was overbroad in attempting to accomplish this purpose.

Ashcroft v. Free Speech Coalition, 535 U.S. 234 (2002)

The Free Speech Coalition, a trade association involved in the adult entertainment industry, and other parties—including Bold Type, Inc., the publisher of a book dedicated to the ideals and philosophy associated with nudism, Jim Gingerich, a painter of nudes, and Ron Raffaelli, a photographer that specializes in nude and erotic photographs—sought injunctive relief by a pre-enforcement challenge to the "appears to be" and "conveys the impression" provisions of the Child Pornography Protection Act of 1996. At issue was whether the Child Pornography Prevention Act (CPPA) of 1996 abridges freedom of speech where it proscribes a significant universe of speech that is neither obscene under *Miller v. California* nor child pornography under *New York v. Ferber.*

The district court granted the government's motion for summary judgment and upheld the CPPA. The court found that the interests advanced by the government were sufficiently compelling to satisfy the intermediate level of scrutiny that it thought should be applied. However, the Ninth Circuit reversed, finding that the CPPA was unconstitutionally vague and overbroad. The U.S. Supreme Court found that the CPPA cannot be read as prohibiting obscenity; a ban on virtual child pornography abridges the freedom to engage in a substantial amount of lawful speech and thus is overbroad and unconstitutional under the First Amendment. The ruling suggested "that the Government's interest in enforcing prohibitions against real child pornography cannot justify prohibitions on virtual child pornography" (259).

Stogner v. California, 539 U.S. 607 (2003)

The law at issue in Stogner was enacted by the California legislature in 1993. It provided that a defendant accused of sex-related child abuse crimes could be prosecuted—even though the statute of limitations had expired—if the victim reported an allegation to the police, if there was independent evidence to corroborate the victim's allegations, and if the prosecution began within one year of the victim's report (Cal. Penal Code § 803[g], amended by 2003 Cal. Legis. Serv. 73).

Marion Stogner was indicted in 1998 for sex-related child abuse committed between 1955 and 1973. Without the law enacted in 1993, the state could not have brought charges against Stogner. Stogner moved to dismiss the complaint against him on the grounds that the Ex Post Facto Clause forbids revival of a previously barred prosecution. The trial court agreed and dismissed the complaint; however, the California Court of Appeals reversed the lower court's ruling. The U.S. Supreme Court held that a law enacted after a previously applicable limitations period expires violates the Ex Post Facto Clause when it is applied to revive a previously time-barred prosecution.

The Stogner decision is important because it clearly establishes that the government may not retroactively void the statute of limitations for criminal prosecutions, even though the Court's decision should have no effect on laws pertaining to civil liability.

Ashcroft v. American Civil Liberties Union, 542 U.S. 656 (2004)

The U.S. Congress attempted to narrow the focus of the Communications Decency Act (CDA) following the Supreme Court's decision in *Reno v. American Civil Liberties Union*. The Child Online Protection Act (COPA) was the result. COPA imposes criminal penalties of a $50,000 fine and six months in prison for the knowing posting, for "commercial purposes," of World Wide Web content that is "harmful to minors." At issue in this case was whether COPA's use of "community standards" to identify "material that is harmful to minors" violates the First Amendment. The Supreme Court held that the Court of Appeals was correct to affirm a ruling by the District Court that enforcement of COPA should be enjoined because the statute likely violates the First Amendment.

Smith et al. v. Doe et al., 538 U.S. 84 (2002)

Two convicted sex offenders and the wife of one of them brought an action that challenged the constitutionality of Alaska's Sex Offender Registration Act as a violation of the Ex Post Facto Clause, which forbids retroactive punishment. The Alaska Sex Offender Registration Act requires that convicted sex offenders register with law enforcement authorities, and some of the information provided is made public. The two sex offenders pleaded nolo contendere to sexual abuse of a child. Following their release from prison in 1990 and completion of a rehabilitative program, they were required to register as sex offenders. They contended that, since the Alaska law was enacted in 1994, it constituted retroactive punishment. The U.S. Supreme Court held that the Alaska act was nonpunitive and that its retroactive application did not violate the Ex Post Facto Clause.

United States v. American Library Association, 539 U.S. 194 (2003)

At issue in this case was whether the Children's Internet Protection Act (CIPA) induces public libraries to violate the First Amendment, by requiring them to install Internet filtering software on their computers in order to qualify for federal spending. The American Library Association and others challenged the law, claiming that it improperly required them to restrict the First Amendment rights of their patrons. The U.S. Supreme Court held that, because the use of Internet filtering software by public libraries does not violate their patron's First Amendment rights, CIPA does not induce libraries to violate the Constitution and is a valid exercise of Congress's spending power.

United States v. Hilton, 363 F. 3d 58 (1st Cir. 2004)

Hilton appealed his conviction in the U.S. District Court for the District of Maine on one count of violating the Child Pornography Prevention Act (CPPA), by possessing child pornography. Following the U.S. Supreme Court's decision in *Ashcroft v. Free Speech Coalition*, holding that the government may not criminalize possession of nonobscene sexually explicit images that appear to, but do not in fact, depict actual children, Hilton sought and was granted postconviction relief. The government appealed. The First Circuit Court of Appeals affirmed the grant of relief vacating Hilton's conviction, holding that a doctor's testimony that an image looks as though it depicts an actual child based on the physical characteristics of the child in the image is not sufficient evidence that the image depicts an actual child.

Cummings v. State of Arkansas, 353 Ark. 618 (Ark. Sup. Ct. 2003)

James and Donna Cummings were convicted in Circuit Court, Logan County, Arkansas, of producing, directing, or promoting a sexual performance, and allowing a child to engage in sexually explicit conduct for use in visual or print media. James Cummings had taken pictures of his thirteen-year-old stepdaughter in various stages of undress and loaded them onto his computer. At some point, they were posted to a website. His stepdaughter testified that James had videotaped her posing nude with her mother, Donna. On appeal, the court ruled that the evidence was sufficient to support a finding that James and Donna Cummings knowingly engaged a minor victim in sexually explicit or lewd conduct, as required to support convictions for producing, directing, or promoting sexual performance by a child and permitting a child to engage in sexually explicit conduct for use in visual or print media. The thirteen-year-old victim testified that she posed for photographs that James took for a website; photographs depicted the victim in various states of undress that exposed her breasts and pubic area. The victim testified that James videotaped her posing nude with Donna Cummings, and that the male voice on the videotape directing her to pose was that of James Cummings. The Supreme Court of Arkansas upheld the convictions.

Doe v. Chamberlin, 299 F. 3d 192 (3rd Cir. 2002)

Kathryn Lesoine is the wife of William Lawson Chamberlin; his daughter is Lesoine's stepdaughter. In August 1995, Lesoine took photographs of her stepdaughter and three friends at the beach near their home on Martha's Vineyard. One friend was Jane Doe (1), then fifteen years old, and another was Jane Doe (2), then sixteen years old. In March 1996, she took photos of the same two plaintiffs in her studio at the Chamberlin home in Pennsylvania. In the beach photos the girls were naked, taking a shower. In the studio photos, they were partially clothed. Another amateur photographer saw the photos that Lesoine had taken and informed the mother of Jane Doe (2), who informed her husband and the parents of Jane Doe (1), of the photos' existence. The parents asked the Lackawanna County district attorney to investigate. The Lesoine house was searched and the photos found, but the district attorney determined that they did not justify prosecution.

The parents of Jane Doe (1) and Jane Doe (2) filed an amended complaint in the Middle District of Pennsylvania asking for damages for violation of the Protection of Children against Sexual Exploitation Act, as well as violation of state law. The district judge granted summary judgment for the defendants on the federal claim and declined to exercise jurisdiction on the state claims. The parents of the two Jane Does appealed, and the appellate court affirmed the lower court's ruling. Nude photos of minors, taken in a shower on the beach, were not lascivious and therefore did not qualify as sexually explicit conduct, as required for violation of the statute prohibiting knowing possession of films and other materials, showing sexual exploitation of minors. The photos depicted the natural activity of washing off sand; pubic areas of minors were not focal; the shower was not a place associated with sexual activity; and minors did not display any sexual coyness.

References

Bahroo, Bhagwan A. 2003. "Pedophilia Psychiatric Insights." *Family Court Review* 41: 497–507.

Butler, Sandra. 1985. *Conspiracy of Silence: The Trauma of Incest.* New York: Bantam.

Committee for Children. 1993. *Child Abuse and Neglect.* Seattle, WA: Committee for Children.

Courtois, Christine. 1988. *Healing the Incest Wound: Adult Survivors in Therapy.* New York: W. W. Norton.

Finkelhor, David, Gerald T. Hotaling, I. A. Lewis, and Christine Smith. 1990. "Sexual Abuse in a National Survey of Adult Men and Women: Prevalence, Characteristics, and Risk Factors." *Child Abuse and Neglect* 14: 19–28.

Finkelhor, David, Linda Williams, and Nanci Burns. 1989. *Nursery Crimes: Sexual Abuse in Day Care.* Newbury Park, CA: Sage.

Kinsey, Alfred C., Wardell B. Pomeroy, Clyde E. Martin, and Paul H. Gebhard. 1953. *Sexual Behavior in the Human Female.* Philadelphia: W. B. Saunders.

Langan, Patrick A., and Caroline Wolf Harlow. 1994. "Child Rape Victims, 1992." Crime Data Brief. Washington, DC: U.S. Department of Justice, Bureau of Justice Statistics.

McCurdy, Karen, and Deborah Daro. 1994. *Current Trends in Child Abuse Reporting and Fatalities: The Results of the 1993 Annual Fifty State Survey.* Chicago: National Committee for the Prevention of Child Abuse.

National Center on Child Abuse and Neglect (NCCAN). 1981. *Study Findings: National Study of the Incidence and Severity of Child Abuse and Neglect.* Washington, DC: U.S. Department of Health and Human Services.

Russell, Diana E. H. 1986. *The Secret Trauma: Incest in the Lives of Girls and Women.* New York: Basic.

Sedlak, A. J. 1987. *Study of National Incidence and Prevalence of Child Abuse and Neglect Final Report.* Prepared for the National Center on Child Abuse and Neglect. Washington, DC: Westat.

U.S. Department of Health and Human Services, Administration on Children, Youth and Families. 2006. *Child Maltreatment 2004.* Washington, DC: U.S. Government Printing Office.

Victim Services Agency. 1991. *Incest Treatment: A Curriculum for Training Mental Health Professionals.* New York: Victim Services Agency.

Wyatt, Gail E. 1985. "The Sexual Abuse of Afro-American and White American Women in Childhood." *Child Abuse and Neglect* 9: 507–519.

7

Directory of Organizations, Associations, and Agencies

This chapter describes organizations, listed alphabetically, that work in a variety of ways with children who have been sexually abused, or with the abusers themselves. They may be research oriented, prevention oriented, or service oriented. These organizations represent the types of services offered by programs throughout the country. This list is by no means inclusive of all organizations dealing with childhood sexual abuse.

Adults Molested as Children United
232 East Gish Road
San Jose, CA 95112
Telephone: 408-453-7616

As one component of the Parents United program (see separate entry) of the Giarretto Institute, this self-help program was founded in 1981 to help adults who were sexually abused as children. The program's goals include re-evaluating and developing values, confronting the perpetrator, stopping self-destructive behavior, showing members how to make choices in their lives, becoming active by living in the present, learning self-awareness and self-help skills, forming new kinds of relationships, and helping members to feel good about themselves. The emphasis in the open group meetings is on self-help and support by allowing members to tell their stories and receive feedback. Professionals at each meeting help to redirect negative feelings and behavior toward positive and constructive activities.

American Bar Association (ABA)
Center on Children and the Law
740 15th Street, NW
Washington, DC 20005
Telephone: 202-662-1720
Fax: 202-662-1775
Website: abanet.org/child/home2.html

The center was founded in 1978 by the ABA Young Lawyers Division to improve children's quality of life by improving laws, policies, and judicial procedures concerning children; conducting research and disseminating results; enhancing skills of legal professionals; educating and assisting nonattorneys in understanding child-related law; and increasing public awareness. Areas of expertise include child abuse and neglect, including child sexual abuse and exploitation, child welfare and child protective service system enhancement, foster care, termination of parental rights, parental substance abuse, child custody, and parental kidnapping. Working with child welfare agencies to develop curricula and training materials, the center offers training programs in advanced trial skills for child welfare agency attorneys, interstate child support enforcement, improving attorney/caseworker teamwork, reducing delays in termination of parental rights cases, legal training for child welfare caseworkers, and a judicial legal training curriculum on drugs, alcohol, and families. Statewide policy studies are conducted to help states update child welfare laws and procedures.

Publications: *Children's Legal Rights Journal*, a quarterly periodical that contains articles written for anyone interested in the protection of children under the law, updates on new cases, legislation, and news; *Sexual Relationships between Adult Males and Young Teen Girls: Exploring the Legal and Social Responses*, which reports on study findings concerning interventions in statutory rape cases; *Child Sexual Abuse Judicial Education Manual*, for judges and other professionals, providing training units on multidisciplinary issues, a bibliography, listings of experts in the fields of law, medicine, and social science, and major conferences and training programs related to multidisciplinary issues involving sexual abusers and victims, and reprints of materials; and *A Judicial Primer of Child Sexual Abuse Cases.*

American Humane Association
Children's Division

63 Inverness Drive E
Englewood, CO 80112-5117
Telephone: 303-792-9900; 800-227-5242
Fax: 303-792-5333
Website: http://www.americanhumane.org

The American Humane Association was founded in 1877 and is the only national organization working to protect both children and animals from abuse, neglect, cruelty, and exploitation. Their Children's Division works to break the cycle of abuse through training, risk assessment, research, and policy development programs initiated to provide effective child protective systems. Through their child advocacy efforts, they work to influence the development of better laws and public policy. They offer continuing education programs and set program standards and program evaluation methods that have improved the quality of care and services. They sponsor national conferences and regional workshops and offer a variety of publications.

They also operate the National Resource Center on Child Abuse and Neglect. This center provides current information about the causes and effects of child abuse and neglect, including child sexual abuse. They advocate for national standards, improved child welfare policies, and federal and state legislation important to the support of children and their families. The center provides resource materials for professionals, advocates, legislators, and the general public, as well as various programs enhancing community awareness.

Publications: *Protecting Children and Animals: Agenda for a Non-Violent Future;* and *Helping in Child Protective Services: A Competency-Based Casework Handbook.* Posters, informative brochures, and resource packets are also available.

American Professional Society on the Abuse of Children, Inc. (APSAC)
P.O. Box 30669
CHO 3B-3406
Charleston, SC 29417
Telephone: 843-764-2905; 877-402-7722
Fax: 803-753-9823
Website: http://www.apsac.org

The American Professional Society on the Abuse of Children is an interdisciplinary society of professionals working with abused and neglected children and their families. Their mission is to improve society's response to abused and neglected children through the promotion of effective interdisciplinary approaches to identifying, intervening in, treating, and preventing abuse and neglect. Members include psychologists, social workers, attorneys, physicians, nurses, law enforcement personnel, child protection workers, and administrators, researchers, and members of allied professions. Several task forces usually are working on guidelines for professionals in the field. Task forces currently are working on guidelines in the areas of medical evaluation of physical and sexual abuse, treatment of sexually abused children, and the use of anatomically correct dolls. APSAC works to encourage research in all areas of child abuse and neglect, to further interdisciplinary professional education, to develop national guidelines for professionals in the field, to improve coordination among professionals, and to provide guidance, support, and encouragement to professionals.

Association for Sexual Abuse Prevention (ASAP)
210 Pratt Avenue
Huntsville, AL 35801
Telephone: 256-533-KIDS (5437)
Fax: 256-534-6883
Website: http://www.nationalcac.org/ncac

Founded in 1986, the Association for Sexual Abuse Prevention emphasizes the importance of developing effective prevention strategies in dealing with child sexual abuse, promoting collaborative prevention activities at the national as well as local level, and, eventually, eliminating the sexual abuse of children. ASAP is working to develop a national movement and strategy for eliminating sexual abuse, encouraging individuals and organizations committed to preventing sexual abuse to communicate, educate, and network with each other. ASAP promotes excellence in the field of prevention through emphasizing comprehensive primary prevention approaches, creating new effective approaches, and supporting criteria for effective prevention programs and activities.

Association for the Treatment of Sexual Abusers (ATSA)
4900 Griffith Drive, Suite 274
Beaverton, OR 97005

Telephone: 503-643-1023
Fax: 503-643-5084
Website: http://www.atsa.com

The Association for the Treatment of Sexual Abusers offers an interdisciplinary approach to the treatment of sexual offenders, including those that prey on children. Its purpose is to foster research and the exchange of information concerning sexual offenders, encourage professional education, and promote the advancement of standards and practices in the area of evaluation and treatment of sex abusers. Conferences are held regarding research and treatment of sexual abusers. The association also awards research grants, develops state chapters and policy statements, and has established the Collaborative Outcome Project, which investigates effective treatment programs and practices.

Association of Sites Advocating Child Protection (ASACP)
5042 Wilshire Blvd., #540
Los Angeles, CA 90036
Telephone: 323-908-7864
Website: http://www.asacp.org

A nonprofit organization founded in 1996, the Association of Sites Advocating Child Protection focuses on eliminating child pornography from the Internet. It operates an online hotline for web users to report child pornography sites. Once a report is received, ASACP reviews the report and forwards the information to the appropriate governmental agencies, including the FBI, the National Center for Missing and Exploited Children, and appropriate European hotlines. Members are informed of current and pending laws and regulations relating to child pornography. ASACP also works to educate its members and other interested individuals, organizations, and governments about issues concerning child abuse and child pornography. The staff have also developed best practices guidelines for adult sites, search engines and directories, billing companies, TGPs, hosting companies, and adult dating sites.

Awareness Center
P.O. Box 65273
Baltimore, MD 21209
Telephone: 443-857-5560
Website: http://theawarenesscenter.org

Also known as the Jewish Coalition against Sexual Abuse/Assault (JCASA), the Awareness Center is an international Jewish organization that addresses sexual violence in Jewish communities throughout the world. It acts as a clearinghouse for information and resources on sexual assault, child sexual abuse, clergy abuse, and sex offenders. A speakers' bureau is available, and an international conference on sexual violence in Jewish communities is in the planning stages. A wide variety of articles concerning child sexual abuse is available from their website.

Blue Sky Bridge
P.O. Box 19122
Boulder, CO 80308
Telephone: 303-444-1388
Fax: 303-444-2045
Website: www.blueskybridge.org

Blue Sky Bridge is a nonprofit organization formed in 1996 to ensure that children who have been sexually abused and their families have access to a variety of services provided in a safe, compassionate, and culturally sensitive environment. Their Community Resource Program provides educational opportunities and resources to parents, professionals who work with children, and others interested in the prevention of child sexual abuse. Their Case Management Program ensures that a variety of direct services are provided to children and their families. Forensic interviews are conducted in their child-friendly facility, using state of the art video and audio taping. Support groups are offered to victims of child sexual abuse and their nonoffending parents. The Court School Program teaches children about the court system, the people who will be involved, and court procedures in a safe environment.

Center for Sex Offender Management (CSOM)
c/o Center for Effective Public Policy
8403 Colesville Road, Suite 720
Silver Spring, MD 20910
Telephone: 301-589-9383
Fax: 301-589-3505
Website: http://www.csom.org

The goal of the Center for Sex Offender Management is to improve public safety by improving the management of adult and juvenile sex offenders who are now out of prison. Established in 1997, CSOM is sponsored by the Office of Justice Programs, U.S. Department of Justice, in collaboration with the National Institute of Corrections, State Justice Institute, and the American Probation and Parole Association. It disseminates current information about managing sex offenders to those responsible for their management. Major activities include an information exchange, training and technical assistance programs, and resource sites.

Center on Child Abuse and Neglect (CCAN)
University of Oklahoma Health Sciences Center
P.O. Box 26901, CHO 3B 3406
Oklahoma City, OK 73190
Telephone: 405-271-8858
Fax: 405-271-2931
Website: http://www.ccan.ouhsc.edu/home.asp

The Center on Child Abuse and Neglect (CCAN) was established at the University of Oklahoma Health Sciences Center with its main purpose to coordinate the Health Sciences Center's efforts to treat and prevent child abuse and neglect, including child sexual abuse. The center conducts various training programs, including the Interdisciplinary Training Program in Child Abuse and Neglect and Child Abuse Medical Examiners Training. Conferences are conducted on child abuse and neglect and juvenile sex offender training to professionals who work with juvenile sex offenders.

Child and Family Advocacy Center (CFAC)
1000 W. Hively Avenue
Elkhart, IN 46515
Telephone: 574-295-2277
Fax: 574-295-7642
Website: http://www.capselkhart.org

The Child and Family Advocacy Center was formed to provide leadership and coordination of services to children who have allegedly been abused, both physically and sexually. The center's goal is to provide leadership and coordination services to agencies to create a multidisciplinary, standardized response to child abuse investigations, improve treatment of children and their families, and provide more effective primary and secondary prevention. Law enforcement or child protective service teams conduct integrated forensic interviews to gather evidence for criminal and civil proceedings. They have developed and implemented countywide standardized protocols regarding child abuse investigations, polygraph procedures, protective custody strategies, and the collection of physical evidence. A follow-up meeting with the family is conducted at intervals of one month, three months, and six months to ensure that the child and family are receiving all necessary services.

Child Lures Prevention
5166 Shelburne Road
Shelburne, VT 05482
Telephone: 802-985-8458
Fax: 802-985-8418
Website: http://childlures.com

The mission of Child Lures Prevention is to raise public awareness concerning the prevalence of childhood sexual abuse and exploitation and related crimes against children and to work to make prevention of those crimes a national priority.

Publications include the *Child Lures Prevention Parent Guide*, which offers specific prevention strategies for each of the sixteen lures described, tips for keeping children safe, and what to do if a child is sexually abused or goes missing. Other publications include *Internet Safety Tips; What to Do If Your Child Discloses Sexual Abuse;* and *Missing Child Early Response System.*

Child Molestation Research and Prevention Institute
1100 Piedmont Avenue, Suite 2
Atlanta, GA 30309
Telephone: 404-872-5152
Website: http://www.childmolestationprevention.org

This program is a national nonprofit organization dedicated to preventing child sexual abuse through research, education, and family support activities. Their goals include a drastic reduction in the number of children who are sexually abused, the education of professionals who work with children to help identify and treat children quickly and effectively, the education and support of families, the training of volunteers who can teach prevention of sexual abuse, and the implementation of research focusing on prevention.

Publications include *The Stop Child Molestation Book: What Or-dinary People Can Do in Their Everyday Lives to Save Three Million Children,* written by Gene Abel, M.D., and Nora Harlow, which offers specific strategies for preventing child sexual abuse.

Child Sexual Abuse Treatment Program (CSATP)
The Giarretto Institute
232 E. Gish Road
San Jose, CA 95112
Telephone: 408-379-3796
Website: http://www.emq.org/about/services/giarretto.html

Founded in 1971, the Child Sexual Abuse Treatment Program has provided in-depth professional treatment and guided self-help services to more than 20,000 sexually abused children and their families. It is the first program to have provided integrated pro-fessional and self-help services. Prior to Hank Giarretto's death in 2003, the Giarretto Institute, its parent organization, was a non-profit, licensed psychology clinic specializing in the treatment of child sexual abuse. EMQ Children and Family Services has taken over the program, which offers individual, family, and group therapy to children and their families as well as guided self-help support. The program's goals are to encourage positive changes within the family in order to ensure the safety and well-being of the child. Program personnel focus on stopping the abuse and preventing its reoccurrence, alleviating the child's feelings of guilt and anger, developing high self-esteem by encouraging the development of healthy family relationships, and teaching par-ents positive and effective parenting and communication skills. Intensive workshops and one-day basic and advanced seminars are offered to professionals who work in the field of child sexual abuse, including mental health professionals, child protective services workers, probation officers, attorneys, police, judges, medical professionals, and educators. Programs supported in-clude Adults Molested as Children United, Parents United, and Daughters and Sons United (see separate listings).

Child Watch
P.O. Box 691782
Orlando, FL 32869
Telephone: 407-290-5100 (business); 1-888-CHILDWATCH (hotline)
Website: http://wwwchildwatch.org

Child Watch was started in 1993 as a private, nonprofit organization. Their purpose is to help prevent child abduction, primarily through the use of their KIDGUARD safety program, which teaches parents and children how to recognize situations in which children might be in danger and how to react and prevent child abduction. If a child is abducted, Child Watch will assist the family in the search for the missing child by providing free investigative and search and rescue services.

Child Welfare League of America
440 First Street, NW, Third Floor
Washington, DC 20001
Telephone: 202-638-2952
Fax: 202-638-4004
Website: http://www.cwla.org

The Child Welfare League focuses on improving care and services for abused, neglected, or dependent children, youth, and their families. The league provides consultation services, conducts research, maintains a library and information services, develops standards for child welfare practice, and administers special projects.

Publications: *Children's Voice Magazine* and *Child Welfare Journal*, presenting articles for child welfare professionals; *In Their Own Words: A Sexual Abuse Workbook for Teenage Girls*, written by two therapists who tell of the experiences of young women who have been sexually abused; *What Only a Mother Can Tell You about Child Sexual Abuse*, providing tips to parents whose children have been sexually abused, as told by a mother whose own child was sexually abused; and *Treating the Aftermath of Sexual Abuse: A Handbook for Working with Children in Care. Confronting Child Sexual Abuse*, a video training series for professionals involved in providing services to children who have been sexually abused.

Childhelp USA
15757 N. 78th Street
Scottsdale, AZ 85260
Telephone: 480-922-8212
Fax: 480-922-7061
Website: http://www.childhelpusa.org

Childhelp USA is one of the largest nonprofit organizations focusing on the prevention and treatment of child abuse and neglect, including child sexual abuse. They have offices in Los Angeles; Rochester, Michigan; Fairfax and Culpeper, Virginia; and Knoxville, Tennessee; they also operate the Village of Childhelp in Beaumont, California, and the Alice C. Tyler Village of Childhelp East in Lignum, Virginia, as well as the Childhelp National Child Abuse Hotline (800-4-A-CHILD), which includes 62,000 local service organizations. Children at both Childhelp villages receive psychological therapy, speech therapy, recreational therapy, play therapy, and art therapy, and also participate in ranch activities, sports programs, and a chapel program. The villages offer parenting classes and family therapy for abusive parents. Community resources are encouraged and provided, including a speakers' bureau, parenting resources, and public information programs.

Childnet International
Studio 14 Brockley Cross Business Centre
96 Endwell Road
London SE4 2PD England
Telephone: +44 (0)20 7639 6967
http://www.childnet-int.org

A nonprofit organization, Childnet International's purpose is to help children benefit from the growing ease of use of international communications, specifically the Internet, while protecting them from the negative aspects of the Internet. Information is gathered from child welfare organizations, educational groups, governments, and international agencies and disseminated to a wide range of individuals and organizations on how to protect children from the negative aspects of the Internet. They focus on three primary areas: helping children to use the Internet constructively, helping them acquire safe skills for using the Internet, and working with other individuals and organizations to help protect children from exploitation.

Children of the Night
14530 Sylvan Street
Van Nuys, CA 91411
Telephone: 818-908-4474; toll free: 800-551-1300
Fax: 818-908-1468
Website: http://www.childrenofthenight.org

Children of the Night is a private, nonprofit organization begun in 1979 to assist child prostitutes between the ages of eleven and seventeen. Many of these children were first victimized by a parent or other caregiver, and then were kicked out or felt forced to run away from home to prevent further abuse. The program offers a residential program, where the children attend an on-site school. They formulate a "life plan" with the assistance of caseworkers, attend independent living classes, and participate in various recreational activities. Counselors and other staff members help these children to prepare to live normal lives in mainstream society.

Children's Advocacy and Treatment Center
322 NW F Street
Grants Pass, OR 97526
Telephone: 541-474-5437
Fax: 541-471-6254

The Children's Advocacy and Treatment Center offers a sanctuary and resource for children, promoting a homelike atmosphere to provide the sexually abused child with a feeling of safety and security. The center's goal is to prevent the child from being revictimized by coordinating the child's community, legal, and treatment needs, thus ensuring that the child's care and well-being are the first priority of all team members. Treatment facilities equipped with special therapy rooms and office space are provided to help make the child feel accepted, warm, and secure. All sexually abused children in the area are taken into the center. Investigative interviews are conducted by a trained team of law enforcement and social work personnel. Videotapes of interviews are made to minimize the need for multiple interviews. A court-appointed special advocate (CASA) program is offered that provides a specially trained volunteer appointed by a judge to represent the best interests of abused children in court, and to ensure continuity in all judicial proceedings. These volunteers are trained to help develop a plan to provide permanency for a child; they conduct a complete investigation of the case by interviewing all involved parties and then submit a report to the court that includes an independent recommendation as to what services are in the best interest of the child. They help to ensure that the case is kept active and that the child understands the court system. They also monitor the treatment plan set up by the court.

Children's Advocacy Center of Georgia
P.O. Box 1192
Decatur, GA 30031
Telephone: 404-377-6127
Fax: 303-377-1365
Website: http://wwwcacga.org

The Children's Advocacy Center of Georgia provides a variety of services to children who have been abused, including those who have been sexually abused. Services include videotaped interviews that are conducted in a safe, child-friendly environment, forensic medical examinations, crisis intervention and emotional support services, counseling and medical services, an interdisciplinary review of cases, and professional training and community education. They have several locations throughout the state.

Committee for Children
568 First Avenue South, Suite 600
Seattle, WA 98104
Telephone: 800-634-4449; Seattle area: 206-343-1223
Fax: 206-438-6765
Website: http://www.cfchildren.org

Founded in 1979, the Committee for Children is a nonprofit organization providing educational materials, original research, training, and community education for the prevention of child abuse and youth violence. They offer a client support line for people who are in the process of implementing their programs, a preview library which provides free preview copies of their curricula and videos, and research assistance; they also publish *Prevention Update*, a newsletter.

  Publications: *Talking about Touching*™, a curriculum to help children from preschool through high school avoid becoming victims of sexual abuse; *Yes You Can Say No*, a video that teaches assertiveness and reporting skills; and *What Do I Say Now?*, a video packet that assists educators in leading parent-education meetings on prevention of child abuse.

Corner House
Interagency Child Abuse Evaluation Center
2502 10th Avenue South

Minneapolis, MN 55404
Telephone: 612-813-8300
Fax: 612-813-8330
Website: http://www.cornerhousemn.org

Corner House is a partnership of public and private agencies
providing a safe and welcoming environment to children who
have been sexually abused. Agencies involved in providing
services include Hennepin County Children and Family Service,
the Hennepin County attorney, the Minneapolis Police Department, the Minneapolis Children's Medical Center, suburban police jurisdictions in Hennepin County, and the Hennepin
County Medical Center. Their purpose is to improve the assessment and investigation of child sexual abuse by emphasizing
the needs of sexually abused children, facilitating coordination
of services, and sharing the knowledge, skills, and expertise of
all professionals involved in child sexual abuse prevention and
treatment. Videotaped interviews are conducted by professionals sensitive to the dynamics of child sexual abuse. A medical
team conducts nonemergency physical examinations in a
friendly homelike environment. A case team reviews cases and
makes recommendations for treatment. The interagency team
meets monthly to discuss issues of concern to the coordination
of services. The partnership's training and resource center offers
an interviewer training course for police officers, child protection workers, and assistant county attorneys. Additional training courses include advanced forensic interview training, pre-
assessment training, videotaped interview assessment, and
on-site interview training.

Publications: A workbook, *Interviewing Children Reliably and
Credibly*, contains information on the art and science of an interview, dynamics of sexual abuse, the "child first" doctrine, the interview process, essential skills and tools, cultural competency,
and making a determination.

Crimes against Children Research Center (CCRC)
University of New Hampshire
No. 126 Horton Social Science Center
20 College Road
Durham, NH 03824
Telephone: 603-862-1888
Fax: 603-862-1122
Website: http://www.unh.edu/ccrc

The Research Center, created in 1998 at the University of New Hampshire and currently directed by David Finkelhor, focuses on reducing crimes against children, including child abduction, rape, assault, and physical and sexual abuse, through research into the impact of those crimes. The CCRC has four primary goals: to encourage greater recognition of the extent to which children are victimized, to provide protection of child victims, to provide services and programs to help rehabilitate child victims, and to encourage greater public accountability through an evaluation of the justice system and its effects on children. It provides research and statistics to the general public, law enforcement personnel, policy-makers, and child welfare and therapy professionals.

Darkness to Light
7 Radcliffe Street, Suite 200
Charlestown, SC 29403
Telephone: 843-965-5444; toll free: 1-866-FOR-LIGHT (1-866-367-5444)
Fax: 843-965-5449
Website: http://www.darkness2light.org

This program focuses specifically on the prevention of child sexual abuse by encouraging adults to help prevent such abuse. They work to reduce the incidence through educational and public awareness activities, and provide adults with the means of identifying children who have been abused. The organization's newest program, Stewards of Children, is a sexual abuse prevention training program that offers training for organizations that serve children and youth.

Publications: 7 *Steps to Protecting Our Children from Child Sexual Abuse: A Guide for Responsible Adults.*

Daughters and Sons United
232 East Gish Road
San Jose, CA 95112
Telephone: 408-453-7616

Daughters and Sons United is the children's component of Parents United (see separate entry). This program closely coordinates their activities with the Child Sexual Abuse Treatment Program of the Giarretto Institute and is available at approximately ninety local Parents United chapters across the nation. Local programs can help to alleviate the trauma each sexually abused child experiences by providing intensive emotional support during the initial crisis, helping the children understand their feelings, and assuring the children that they are not alone (that is, that other children have also been sexually abused). Chapters aim to promote personal growth and communications skills, to help alleviate any guilt the child may feel, to prevent self-abusive behavior, to prevent future dysfunctional patterns in relationships, and to break the multigenerational pattern of abuse. Members meet regularly under the guidance of professionals who lead discussions on topics relevant to members' physical and emotional well-being. They may also participate in community education programs.

FaithTrust Institute
2400 N. 45th Street, #10
Seattle, WA 98103
Telephone: 206-634-1903
Fax: 206-634-0115
Website: http://wwwfaithtrustinstitute.org

The FaithTrust Institute, an international and multifaith organization, provides a wide range of resources and services, including training, consultation, and educational materials to end sexual and domestic violence. The institute was formed in 1977 by the Rev. Dr. Marie M. Fortune after she discovered that many of her clergy colleagues were silent on the issue of domestic violence and did not know how to minister to women and children who were sexually abused or the victims of other types of domestic violence. In addition, public and other social service agencies were unable to assist these individuals with religious questions. The institute has developed training and other educational materials to address various religious and cultural issues relating to sexual abuse and other forms of domestic violence.

False Memory Syndrome Foundation
1955 Locust St.
Philadelphia, PA 19103
Telephone: 215-940-1040
Fax: 215-940-1042
Website: http://www.fmsfonline.org

The purpose of the False Memory Syndrome Foundation is to examine the reasons why and how this syndrome occurs, to prevent new cases, to help the victims, and to help reconcile and reunite family members. In order to achieve those goals, the foundation works with professionals to publicize the nature and prevalence of this syndrome, to provide access to counseling, to promote and sponsor scientific and medical research into the causes of this syndrome, and to help determine reliable methods of distinguishing between true cases of sexual abuse and those created by false memories. Information on causes, current research, and legal rights also is provided.

Four Corners Child Advocacy Center
140 N. Linden
Cortez, CO 81321
Telephone: 970-565-8155

The Four Corners Child Advocacy Center is a private, nonprofit program dedicated to the well-being of sexually and physically abused children. It is a grassroots community and professional response to the more than 300 cases of physical and sexual abuse reported locally each year. The center's goal is to minimize the emotional trauma to children and their families during the investigation and prosecution of child abuse. They operate a home in which the goal is to create a safe, nurturing, and child-friendly atmosphere. A trained volunteer victim advocate provides emotional support as well as information and guidance. Agencies, professionals, and therapists come to see the child at the center for investigative interviews, medical exams, pretrial preparation, and therapy. Services can be coordinated to provide the best, most effective treatment possible. The center also offers community education and prevention programs, an information clearinghouse, and training programs for professionals and lay persons. Improvement of the regional response to abuse is achieved through coordination of federal, tribal, state, and local efforts.

Garth House
Mickey Mehaffy Children's Advocacy Center
1895 McFadden
Beaumont, TX 77701
Telephone: 409-838-9084

Fax: 409-838-9106
Website: http://www.centerforchildprotection.org
/Regional_Centers.htm

The Garth House, a nonprofit program begun in 1991, attempts to provide an environment that reflects the physical and emotional atmosphere of a home, rather than the atmosphere of a clinic or institution. Children who have been sexually or physically abused are referred to Garth House by law enforcement officials and child protective services personnel. Professionals provide their services to the children in one location, preventing the child from being shuttled around from police headquarters to Child Protective Services offices to physicians and then to mental health professionals. Each interview is videotaped and made available to all agencies involved in the provision of services. The videotape can be used by law enforcement personnel and the district attorney's office in criminal or civil proceedings. Weekly meetings are held, and all agencies involved participate in reviewing cases. Staff members also maintain a data file in order to provide comprehensive statistical information about sexual and physical abuse.

Generation Five
2 Massasoit Street
San Francisco, CA 94110
Telephone: 415-285-6658
Fax: 415-861-6659
Website: http://generationfive.org/index.html

The purpose of this program is to work to end sexual abuse of children within five generations. Generation Five is a nonprofit organization that provides leadership training to activists, professionals working in the field of child sexual abuse, and members of the community. They work with service providers to ensure that support is available to survivors, offenders, and affected families. Their Community Response Project is a model program designed to encourage individuals, communities, and existing agencies to take a leadership role in working to end child sexual abuse.

Healing Alliance
P.O. Box 429
Pewee Valley, KY 40056

Telephone: 502-241-5544
Fax: 502-241-0031
Website: http://www/healingall.org

The Healing Alliance was organized by individuals who were victims of clergy abuse. The program offers positive options to individuals who have been sexually abused by clergy members. They reach out to individuals through meetings and conferences throughout the United States, and they provide information about sexual abuse. They operate the Farm, a place where victims of sexual abuse can gather to relax and talk with others who have had similar experiences. It is not considered a treatment center, but rather a safe place in which to gather, socialize, and exchange information. They offer guided exercises and workshops on a variety of topics. Their programs are developed as a supplement to any therapy that survivors may be receiving at home.

Incest Survivors Anonymous
P.O. Box 17245
Long Beach, CA 90807-7245
Telephone: 562-428-5599
Website: http://www.lafn.org/medical/isa/home.html

Founded in 1980 by an incest survivor, Incest Survivors Anonymous is a twelve-step program that aims to help incest survivors and their family members, spouses, and friends recover from their experiences. They have adapted the Twelve Steps and Twelve Traditions from Alcoholics Anonymous to help people who have experienced incest. While the format of their group meetings may vary, they often choose a topic relating to incest and talk freely about their feelings, experiences, and memories. In their meetings, members seek understanding, acceptance, forgiveness, and serenity. The goals of the program are to recognize the negative behavior patterns and programming that many people who have been sexually abused have developed in childhood, often in response to fear, and to develop a new way of life, with peace of mind and understanding.

Incest Survivors Resource Network International (ISRNI)
P.O. Box 7375
Las Cruces, NM 88006-7375
Telephone: 505-521-4260
Fax: 505-521-3723

In 1983 at the New York City Friends Meeting House, the Incest Survivors Resource Network International was founded as an educational resource for both national and international community and professional organizations. It is operated as a religious group focusing on world peace witness by survivors of incest interested in the relationship between unresolved traumatic stress and violence in the world. ISRNI encourages communication and cooperation between professionals and self-help organizations. It operates the first national helpline answered by survivors of incest. It cosponsors several conferences, including the National Forum on Victim Rights, with the National Organization for Victim Assistance.

International Society for Prevention of Child Abuse and Neglect (ISPCAN)
245 W. Roosevelt Road
Building 6, Suite 39
West Chicago, IL 60185
Telephone: 630-876-6913
Fax: 630-876-6917
Website: http://www.ispcan.org

One of the few multidisciplinary international organizations that works to prevent child abuse, neglect, and exploitation, ISPCAN encourages the cooperation of participants throughout the world. They work to prevent all forms of abuse, including physical and sexual abuse, neglect, emotional abuse, child fatalities, child prostitution, the use of children in war, and child labor.

Kempe Center
1825 Marion Street
Denver, CO 80218
Telephone: 303-864-5300
Website: http://www.kempecenter.org

The Kempe Center was opened in 1972 to provide a clinically based resource for training, consultation, program development and education, and research into all forms of child abuse and neglect. The center is committed to multidisciplinary approaches to improving the recognition, treatment, and prevention of all forms of abuse and neglect. Several programs have been instituted to help children and their families, including Therapeutic Preschool, the Family Evaluation Team, the Child Advocacy and Protection

Team, the Community Caring Project, the Perpetration Prevention Project, the National Child Abuse and Neglect Clinical Resource Center, and the Prevention Research Center for Family and Child Health.

Kids First, Inc.
110 South Pool Street
P.O. Box 23
Elizabeth City, NC 27909
Telephone: 252-331-1653

Kids First, established in 1992, offers advocacy and support services to child victims of sexual and physical abuse, including child and family counseling, forensic medical examinations, a Kids in Court school to help prepare child witnesses for their upcoming court appearances, community education programs, and training programs for professionals who work with sexually and physically abused children and their families. The program offers a multidisciplinary team approach: team members include representatives from departments of social services, law enforcement, sheriff's departments, the district attorney's office, and the medical community; also included are adult probation personnel, court counselors, public school system personnel, guardian ad litem program members and representatives from local and state governments, juvenile services divisions, child abuse hotlines, and mental health services. Once a case is reported to the center, the director assigns a primary team that is responsible for coordinating a comprehensive plan to help the child and the child's family.

King County Sexual Assault Resource Center
P.O. Box 300
Renton, WA 98057
Telephone: 425-226-5062
Fax: 425-271-6332
Website: http://www/kcsarc.org

Originally founded as King County Rape Relief, this resource center is a nonprofit organization providing services to women, children, and men who have been sexually victimized. The staff's goal is to help all clients make the transition from victim to survivor. Individual counseling is provided for children who have been sexually abused, and the families of these children receive family therapy and support. The center's philosophy is that education is the key to preventing and eventually eliminating sexual assault, and it offers a wide variety of educational and training programs to educators, service providers, professionals, and the community. Their advocacy staff offer crisis intervention and confidential support and information twenty-four hours a day, medical information, legal information, advocacy, court accompaniment, and forensic medical examinations for children that are coordinated through the County Health Department. Training workshops are provided on topics such as ending sexual violence, striving for empowerment (an education support group model for teenage girls), chemical dependency and sexual assault (based on the premise that many children who are sexually abused grow up to have problems with alcohol and drugs), and related risks, including child abuse, family violence, and chemical dependency.

Publications: *He Told Me Not to Tell,* a booklet on how to talk with children about sexual abuse. Other publications available on their website include *Talking to Your Children about Sexual Assaults; Sex Offender Grooming Techniques;* and *Tips for Internet Safety and Information about Internet Victimization.*

La Rabida Joli Burrell Children's Advocacy Center
202 Lakewood Boulevard
Park Forest, IL 60466
Telephone: 708-481-9799
Fax: 708-481-9951
Website: http://www.larabida.org

The La Rabida Joli Burrell Children's Advocacy Center provides a safe and child-friendly environment for children who have been sexually abused or those who have experienced other psychological trauma. Investigative, therapeutic, and other support services are provided to children and their families. Investigative services include child-friendly interviews, conducted by individuals trained in child mental health and forensic interviewing techniques. These interviews are observed by law enforcement, child protective services, and the state attorney's office to minimize the number of times a child must be interviewed. Therapeutic services include psychotherapy provided by staff who have expertise in child abuse and trauma. The program also runs support groups for parents and other caregivers of sexually abused children, individual parent/caregiver support, case management and referral services, and legal advocacy.

Lake County Children's Advocacy Center
323 N. West Street
Waukegan, IL 60085
Telephone: 708-360-6870

The Lake County Children's Advocacy Center was founded as a result of a 1985 task force on child sexual abuse. The center is a co-operative effort between the Illinois Department of Children and Family Services, the Lake County Sheriff's Police, the Waukegan Police Department, the state's attorney's office, and local law enforcement agencies; it employs a multidisciplinary treatment concept to help victims of child sexual abuse. The center's multidisciplinary and single-interview approach is designed to reduce the trauma that children often face when being subjected to multiple, independent interviews. The goal is to implement a strong social and legal support structure to minimize trauma and stress to the child, using a highly trained staff to conduct sensitive and thorough investigations. Crisis intervention and court advocacy for children and their families are provided by a social worker. A speakers' bureau is available to interested organizations and groups.

LaPorte County Child Abuse Prevention Council
7451 W. Johnson Rd.
Michigan City, IN 46360
Telephone: 219-874-0007

The LaPorte County Child Abuse Prevention Council was founded in 1989 as a nonprofit organization dedicated to increasing community awareness of child abuse and neglect and coordinating services for children and their families. They provide community education through a speakers' bureau as well as information and referral services. Family programs include a parent education program, a school body-safety program, and parent support groups. The council plans to meet family needs through survivors' groups, people against child abuse groups, and an annual survivors'-days workshop. Professionals in the field of child abuse receive training, consultation services through a child abuse advisory team, and legislative advocacy. The council also operates Dunebrook, a multidisciplinary child abuse prevention care center designed to offer a warm, safe place in which children can be interviewed and other services can be coordinated.

Making Daughters Safe Again (MDSA)
Telephone: 877-735-5603
Website: http://mdsa-online.org

This online program provides support and advocacy for survivors of sexual abuse committed by their mothers. The organization, founded in 2000, offers support to survivors as well as programs that focus on the lack of knowledge and publicity about mother-daughter sexual abuse. It provides a unique online support program for survivors, and their website contains additional information on the topic.

Midwest Regional Children's Advocacy Center
345 N. Smith Ave.
St. Paul, MN 55102
Telephone: 651-220-6000
Website: http://www.childrensmn.org

The Midwest Regional Children's Advocacy Center is a regional resource center for children, professionals, and programs in diagnosing, treating, and preventing child abuse. The center provides diagnosis, treatment, and consultation services for sexually, physically, and emotionally abused children. It is the only site in Minnesota for comprehensive multidisciplinary training in the area of child abuse; more than 1,000 law enforcement personnel, child protection workers, county attorneys, medical professionals, and mental health professionals are trained each year.

Mothers against Sexual Abuse (MASA)
P.O. Box 371
Huntersville, NC 28070
Website: http://www.againstsexualabuse.org

Mothers against Sexual Abuse focuses on protecting children from sexual abuse. It offers educational programs to teachers, caregivers, and professionals in the area of detection and prevention of child sexual abuse and provides educational materials to families of children who have been sexually abused. A resource referral network that can assist in the recovery of children and adults who have been sexually abused is provided. Educational conferences are organized for professionals in the field, survivors, and anyone else concerned about sexual abuse. MASA also initiates and supports legislation that protects children from sexual abuse.

National Center for Assault Prevention (NCAP)
606 Delsea Drive
Sewell, NJ 08080
Telephone: 908-369-8972; toll free: 800-258-3189
Website: http://www.ncap.org

The purpose of the National Center for Assault Prevention is to protect children and improve their quality of life by reducing instances of interpersonal violence through training in assault prevention. The program is the host agency for the Child Assault Prevention (CAP) program, which holds educational seminars that address child abuse and neglect.

National Center for Missing and Exploited Children
Charles B. Wang International Children's Building
699 Prince Street
Alexandria, VA 22314
Telephone: 703-274-3900
Hotline: 800-THE-LOST [(800) 843-5678]
Fax: 703-274-2200
Website: http://www.missingkids.com

The National Center for Missing and Exploited Children was mandated by the U.S. Congress in 1984 and in 1990 merged with the Adam Walsh Child Resource Center. Since 1984 it has handled almost 700,000 calls through its toll-free hotline for reporting information on missing or exploited children. The center offers a staff of case managers who are former law enforcement and social service professionals. Services provided include instructions on how to conduct an investigation into the whereabouts of the missing or exploited child, national distribution of the child's photo, and legal and technical assistance. The case enhancement and information analysis unit helps local law enforcement agencies by providing useful, up-to-date information about the child. Project ALERT (America's Law Enforcement Retiree Team) offers free, on-site support to state and local police in missing or exploited child cases. The center also receives tips on people who participate in child pornography. The CyberTipLine provides online reporting of sexual abuse or exploitation of children. It offers educational programs to children, teachers, parents, health care professionals, and law enforcement personnel. The legal staff offers information to attorneys, families, and legislators.

Publications: *Child Molesters: A Behavioral Analysis; Child Molesters Who Abduct: Summary of the Case in Point Series; Child Pornography: The Criminal Justice System Response; Internet Sex Crimes against Minors: The Response of Law Enforcement;* and *Family Abduction.* Brochures include topics such as child protection, tips to help prevent sexual exploitation of children, rules for safety, and the *Just in Case . . . Series,* which offers advice on finding professional help for children who have been sexually assaulted, advice on choosing day care and preventing the exploitation or sexual abuse of children, on what to do if your child is sexually abused or exploited, and on other related topics.

National Center for Prosecution of Child Abuse
99 Canal Center Plaza, Suite 510
Alexandria, VA 22314
Telephone: 703-549-4253
Fax: 703-836-3195
Website: http://www.ndaa.org/apri/programs/ncpca

The purpose of the National Center for Prosecution of Child Abuse is to improve the handling of child abuse cases by providing expert training and technical assistance, research, a clearinghouse on case law, and information on statutory initiatives, court reforms, and other legal matters. The center conducts national conferences on a variety of topics, including online crimes against children, multidisciplinary investigation and prosecution of computer-facilitated child sexual exploitation, and interviewing and preparing children for court. Their attorneys conduct state and local training on all aspects of child abuse prosecution.

National Center on Child Abuse and Neglect (NCCAN)
National Clearinghouse on Child Abuse and Neglect
Information
Children's Bureau/ACYF
1250 Maryland Avenue, SW, Eighth Floor
Washington, DC 20024
Telephone: 703-385-7565; 800-394-3366

Fax: 703-385-3206
Website: http://www.childwelfare.gov

The National Center on Child Abuse and Neglect was established in 1974 by the Child Abuse Prevention and Treatment Act (Public Law 93-247) as the primary federal agency charged with helping states and communities address the problems of child maltreatment. NCCAN oversees all federal child abuse and neglect efforts and allocates child maltreatment funds appropriated by Congress. They are responsible for conducting research on the causes, prevention, and treatment of child abuse and neglect; collecting, analyzing, and disseminating information to professionals concerned with child abuse and neglect; increasing public awareness of the problems of child maltreatment; and assisting states and communities in developing programs relating to the prevention, identification, and treatment of child abuse and neglect.

NCCAN operates a clearinghouse that collects, stores, organizes, and disseminates information on all aspects of child maltreatment. They provide services and products in a variety of areas to organizations, researchers, and the general public. Manuals, reports, directories, catalogs, literature reviews, annotated bibliographies, and fact sheets are available through the clearinghouse. For a fee, clearinghouse information specialists provide custom searches of the child abuse and neglect database.

Publications: *Child Sexual Abuse: Intervention and Treatment Issues,* a manual designed for all professionals working in the field of child sexual abuse; *Child Sexual Abuse,* a review of the current literature on child sexual abuse; and annotated bibliographies on interviewing techniques used with sexual abuse victims, male victims of sexual abuse, prevention, treatment for victims, and treatment for perpetrators.

National Child Abuse Defense and Resource Center (NCADRC)
P.O. Box 638
Holland, OH 43528
Telephone: 419-865-0513
Fax: 419-865-0526
Website: http://www.falseallegation.org

A nonprofit organization, the National Child Abuse Defense and Resource Center was founded to offer help to people who have been falsely accused of some form of child abuse, including sexual abuse. The program's goals are to provide information to professionals, organizations, and government units; to ensure that due process, constitutional rights, human rights, and family concerns are considered when people are reported for abuse; to reduce public hysteria over child sexual abuse; to ensure that those implementing child abuse law and policy are properly trained and qualified; to help formulate laws and policies that define child abuse and specify investigative procedures; and to provide information and emotional support to all people falsely accused of sexual abuse. They operate an extensive library of research materials, legal case law, and articles. All of the staff members are volunteers; they provide general information and may offer limited advice on steps people can take when falsely accused. They can also recommend attorneys and other experts in the field.

Publications: *Guilty until Proven Innocent: A Manual for Surviving False Allegations of Child Abuse,* by Kimberly Hart, the current executive director of NCADRC; and *Making Monsters,* by Richard Ofshe and Ethan Waters, which discusses false memories, psychotherapy, and sexual hysteria. These are samples of available publications.

National Children's Advocacy Center
210 Pratt Avenue
Huntsville, AL 35801
Telephone: 205-533-5437
Website: http://www.nationalcac.org

The National Children's Advocacy Center is a nonprofit organization composed of members and affiliates whose mission is to provide technical assistance, training, and networking opportunities to help communities establish and maintain children's advocacy centers. The goals of the centers are to provide quality services for victims of child abuse, particularly child sexual abuse. There are four regional child advocacy centers in the United States—located in the Midwest, the Northeast, the South, and the West—and, in addition, each state has child advocacy centers affiliated with the national center. The regional centers have been established through the U.S. Department of Justice's Office of Juvenile Justice and Delinquency Prevention to provide information, consulting services, training, and technical assistance in the development of new programs and in the improvement of current programs. As of this writing, there are almost 500 programs throughout the country.

National Committee to Prevent Child Abuse
332 South Michigan Avenue
Suite 1600
Chicago, IL 60604
Telephone: 312-663-3520
Fax: 312-939-8962

This volunteer organization is dedicated to involving all concerned citizens in actions to prevent child abuse in all of its forms, including physical abuse, emotional maltreatment, neglect, and sexual abuse. Activities include prevention programs, public awareness, education and training, research, and advocacy.

Publications: *A Look at Child Sexual Abuse*, by Jon Conte, which reviews current information; *Sexual Victimization of Children*, which explains the various forms of sexual exploitation of children, characteristics of molesters, and behavioral characteristics of children who have been molested; *Basic Facts about Child Sexual Abuse; Talking about Sexual Abuse*, a guide for parents; *What Every Kid Should Know about Sexual Abuse*; and *You Don't Have to Molest That Child*, which speaks directly to molesters and potential molesters.

National Council of Juvenile and Family Court Judges
P.O. Box 8970
Reno, NV 89507
Telephone: 775-784-6012
Facsimile: 775-784-6628
Website: http://www.ncjfcj.org

The National Council of Juvenile and Family Court Judges provides direction on juvenile and family law to the nation's juvenile and family jurists. It offers continuing education to judges, referees, probation officers, social workers, law enforcement personnel, and other juvenile justice professionals. It stays abreast of the changing areas of the law in such areas as child abuse and neglect, crack babies, foster care, custody issues, school violence, gangs, and serious juvenile crime, and it offers programs addressing current topics in those areas.

National Organization against Male Sexual Victimization
PMB 103
5505 Connecticut Avenue, N.W.
Washington, DC 20015
Telephone: 800-738-4181
Website: http://www.malesurvivor.org

Founded in 1995, this organization helps to bring together professionals and other individuals interested in a better understanding of, and treatment for, men who were sexually abused as children. The program organizes annual conferences on male sexual victimization, provides information on male victimization, and offers referrals to victims. They also provide an online bulletin board and chat room.

North American Man/Boy Love Association (NAMBLA)
P.O. Box 174 Midtown Station
New York, NY 10018
Telephone: 212-631-1194 (voice mail)
Website: http://216.220.97.17/

Founded in 1978, the North American Man/Boy Love Association (NAMBLA) is a political, civil rights, and educational organization that works to end the oppression of men and boys in mutual relationships to which both consent, by building support and understanding of those relationships; by providing information and education to the general public on the positive aspects of man/boy love, by cooperation with lesbian, gay, feminist, and other liberation movements, and by support of the effort to free all people from sexual oppression. They make it clear on their website that they "condemn sexual abuse and all forms of coercion." However, they believe that young people can make informed decisions as to their sexual activities and should not be prohibited by law from engaging in sexual activities with adults. They strongly oppose all legislation concerning age of consent and any other laws that would deny boys the "full enjoyment of their bodies and control over their own lives." NAMBLA does not act as a clearinghouse to match individuals together.

Publications include the *NAMBLA Journal; A Call for Justice* by Fri Beslut, which advocates a boy's right to decide what he wants to do with his body; and *Liberation: Participation, Not Passivity.*

Northeast Regional Children's Advocacy Center
4 Terry Drive, Suite 16
Newtown, PA 18940
Telephone: 800-662-4124
Fax: 215-860-3112
Website: http://www.nrcac.org

The Northeast Regional Children's Advocacy Center is a non-profit organization composed of members and affiliates whose mission is to provide technical assistance, training, and networking opportunities to help communities establish and maintain children's advocacy centers. The centers' goals are to provide quality services for helping victims of child abuse, particularly child sexual abuse. General information packets contain a description of CACs, including membership criteria, literature concerning the benefits of interagency coordination, and sample interagency agreements. The centers have also produced the publication *Developing a Children's Advocacy Center Four-Step Methodology*, which explains the steps to take to develop a children's advocacy center. In addition, they offer an on-site training/technical assistance program and a mentoring program.

Northern Kentucky Children's Advocacy Center
103 Landmark Drive, Suite 360
Bellevue, KY 41073
Telephone: 859-261-3441
Fax: 859-261-9788

The Northern Kentucky Children's Advocacy Center of the St. Luke's Hospitals is dedicated to providing a child-friendly environment for the prevention, evaluation, and treatment of child sexual abuse. Services offered include interviewing services, multidisciplinary case reviews, counseling and support groups for children and their families, a comprehensive tracking system, community education, training programs for professionals, and medical examinations. The center coordinates the community's response to child sexual abuse under one roof, with the goal of preventing the revictimization of children by eliminating the need for multiple interviews and visits to several agencies.

Parents Anonymous (PA)
The National Organization
675 West Foothill Boulevard, Suite 220
Claremont, CA 91711
Telephone: 909-621-6184
Fax: 909-625-6304
Website: http://www.parentsanonymous.org

Parents Anonymous was founded in 1970 as a national parent self-help program to prevent child abuse and neglect, with specialized groups for children. The national organization provides leadership and support to state and local organizations, which offer more than 2,100 groups for parents and children; these groups are offered free of charge to families. Their programs include parent support groups, parent education workshops, home visitation services, stressline (stress hotline) services, advocacy, and public awareness activities. All of these programs are based on seven guiding principles: mutual assistance, empowerment, support, ownership, caring, nonviolence, and anonymity and confidentiality. PA designs and helps to implement new programs, develops curricula and materials, conducts workshops and conferences, provides professional consultation services, encourages public awareness activities, conducts and encourages research, and provides information and referral services to parents, professionals, and the general public.

Parents United International, Inc.
615 15th Street
Modesto, CA 95354
Telephone: 209-572-3446
Fax: 209-524-7780
Website: http://members.tripod.com/~Parents_United
/Chapters/PUI.htm

Parents United is a self-help organization dedicated to assisting parents, children, and others concerned with child sexual abuse. It began under the direction of Hank Giarretto and is one of the best-known national organizations representing the interests of sexually abused children and their families. It has two associated programs: Daughters and Sons United, and Adults Molested as Children United (see separate entries). Members may include offenders, spouses of offenders, children who have been sexually abused, adults molested as children, and others, including siblings, step-parents, parents, and spouses. The organization works closely with law enforcement, social services, the judicial system, and other professional agencies. The goal is to help individuals who have been sexually abused to explore the factors that might have contributed to the abuse and work through the damage the abuse caused. Community education is also an important part of the program.

Pueblo Child Advocacy Center
301 West 15th Street
Pueblo, CO 81003
Telephone: 719-583-6332

The Pueblo Child Advocacy Center is a nonprofit organization established in 1986 to break the cycle of sexual and physical child abuse through intervention and prevention services. The center works closely with other local agencies to coordinate services provided to children and their families. These agencies include police and sheriff's departments, social services personnel, the district attorney's office, mental health professionals, health department personnel, and medical personnel. Children are interviewed at the center, medically examined, provided with therapy, and sometimes prepared for court proceedings. The program is one of the original six child advocacy centers developed in the country and is a nationally recognized model program. The center offers a setting designed to be warm and nurturing in which investigations, medical examinations, crisis intervention, victim assistance, and treatment services are provided. Interagency problem solving, open communications, and professional skills development are encouraged and facilitated by the program, which also encourages community commitment to preventing the physical and sexual abuse of children.

Safer Society Foundation, Inc.
P.O. Box 340
Brandon, VT 05733-0340
Telephone: 802-247-3132
Fax: 802-247-4233
Website: http://www.safersociety.org

A nonprofit organization, Safer Society offers research, advocacy, and referral services for the prevention and treatment of sexual abuse throughout the country. They maintain a computerized database of agencies, institutions, and individuals who provide specialized assessment and treatment services for juvenile and adult sex offenders; a computer file containing those programs that treat abused children is also maintained. Referrals are made for individuals and family members to programs, professionals, and specialized treatment programs throughout the country. The society conducts specialized training institutes, which are intensive three-day educational workshops, on issues of current importance in the field of sexual abuse prevention and treatment. Consultation services are provided to states and counties to help plan and set up comprehensive treatment programs.

Publications: *Shining Through: Pulling It Together after Sexual Abuse,* by Mindy Loiselle and Leslie Bailey Wright, a workbook for young women who have been sexually abused; *Female Adolescent Sexual Abusers,* by Marcia R. Turner and Tracey N. Turner, an exploratory study of mothers who molest their daughters; guided workbooks for adult sex offenders; *Women and Men Who Sexually Abuse Children,* by Craig Allen, a comparative study of female and male abusers; *Adults Molested as Children,* by Euan Bear, a manual for adults beginning to remember and face being abused as children; and "Mother-Son Incest: The Unthinkable Broken Taboo," a literature review of findings on this often ignored subject.

St. Clair Children's Advocacy Center
18200 Alabama Highway 174
Pell City, AL 35125
Telephone: 205-338-8847
Fax: 205-338-1979

The St. Clair Children's Advocacy Center offers programs to children who have been physically or sexually abused and to their families. It offers a forum for agency representatives and professionals who work with abused children to coordinate their work to assist the children and their families. Before the Advocacy Center was organized, child abuse victims would undergo multiple interviews to satisfy the needs of the Department of Human Resources, law enforcement officials, the district attorney, and providers of mental health counseling services. Their program, the Children's Place, replaces that system with a united approach, offering a nonthreatening environment in which children who are believed to have been sexually or severely physically abused and their nonoffending family members can go for interviews, evaluation, intervention, evidence gathering, and counseling. The center strives to provide children with a warm, nonthreatening environment and someone to talk to about their problems. The program also provides training and education for professionals.

St. Luke's Regional Medical Center
Children at Risk Evaluation Services (CARES) Program
190 E. Bannock Street
Boise, ID 83712
Telephone: 208-386-3063
Website: http://www.stlukesonline.org/SLCH/services
/CARES/index.html

The Children at Risk Evaluation Services Program was founded in 1989 in response to the need for a neutral, centralized service for the assessment and evaluation of children who are alleged victims of sexual abuse. It provides a comprehensive evaluation of the alleged abuse by using videotaped interviews conducted by specially trained registered nurses and audiotaped physical examinations, conducted by a physician or a pediatric nurse practitioner. The program seeks to minimize the trauma to which child victims of sexual abuse are exposed. It provides a sensitive, professional, and caring environment; expert and comprehensive evaluation; a cooperative effort with community agencies; a safe, controlled, and confidential setting for patients and their families; and a quick response to referrals made to help protect and meet the needs of children.

Salt Lake County Children's Justice Center
257 11th Avenue
Salt Lake City, UT 84103
Telephone: 801-355-0781
Fax: 801-355-3578
Website: http://www.cjcslc.org/

The Children's Justice Center offers a homelike facility in which to provide services to children who have been sexually or physically abused. It offers a child-friendly environment, designed to make children feel safe and comfortable. A multidisciplinary team coordinates the interview process, assesses the need for support services, and reviews police investigation results, child protection issues, medical concerns, treatment issues, and prosecution concerns. The program offers a comprehensive child and family interview process, audiotaped and videotaped interviews, counseling and treatment referrals, victim-witness support services, community education, professional training, support and information services for parents, case staffings, and assistance and coordination on difficult cases. They also screen cases for prosecution and monitor case progress.

Sexual Abuse Investigative Team (SAINT)
3444 East Bonanza Road
Las Vegas, NV 89101
Telephone: 702-455-5592
Website: http://www.caclasvegas.com/saint.htm

The SAINT program uses a multidisciplinary approach in dealing with sexual abuse of children to reduce the trauma to child victims. Members of the multidisciplinary team include law enforcement personnel, the district attorney, child protective services personnel, medical personnel, and mental health counselors. The program provides a nonthreatening, child-friendly location for interviews and medical examinations, reduces the number of interviewers who question the child, conducts forensically complete medical examinations, and provides crisis intervention, assessment, and referral for long-term therapy. They have a comfortable, nonthreatening interview room with a one-way mirror that allows for observation of the interviews by appropriate professionals; audio and videotaping equipment is also available. Forensic medical examinations are conducted in a brightly decorated room by specially trained medical practitioners, in an effort to reduce the trauma that sexually abused children experience when examined in a cold, institutional setting. Therapeutic assistance is provided to the children and their families.

Sexual Assault Recovery Anonymous Society (SARA)
P.O. Box 16
Surrey, BC V3T 4W4 Canada
Telephone: 604-584-2626; toll free: 1-866-SARA
Fax: 604-584-2636
Website: http://www.sarasociety.ca

The Sexual Assault Recovery Anonymous Society believes that every child who has been sexually abused can heal from the trauma of that abuse. The program helps those individuals by providing self-help literature, adult groups, and groups for teenage girls. They offer public education activities—including presentations at local high schools and service clubs and relevant publications to professionals—and work with other self-help groups.

Southern Regional Children's Advocacy Center
210 Pratt Avenue
Huntsville, AL 35801
Telephone: 256-533-KIDS
Fax: 256-327-3859
Website: http://www.nationalcac.org/professionals/srcac

Established through a grant from the U.S. Department of Justice's Office of Juvenile Justice and Delinquency Prevention, the Southern Regional Children's Advocacy Center provides a variety of resources to individuals and organizations hoping to develop their own children's advocacy center. Information, consulting services, training, and technical assistance are offered to help communities determine their capacity to provide services, establish facilities, prevent trauma to children by limiting the number of contacts children have with community professionals and the courts, increase community understanding of child abuse, identify and develop funding sources, and other activities necessary for establishing a children's advocacy center.

Stop Educator Sexual Abuse, Misconduct, and Exploitation (SESAME)
P.O. Box 94601
Las Vegas, NV 89193
Telephone: 702-371-1290
Website: http://www.sesamenet.org

The SESAME program believes that the imbalance of power between students and teachers can create an environment that can lead to a teacher sexually abusing a student. This national program works to prevent sexual exploitation, abuse, and harassment of students by teachers and other school administrators and staff. Activities include increasing public awareness; encouraging recovery of victims through support and newsletters; encouraging victims to report their abuse to the proper authorities; advocating for implementation of sexual harassment policies, regulations, and laws for the protection of students; and promoting adoption of professional standards and codes of ethics to which teachers and other school administrators and staff should subscribe.

Stop It Now!
351 Pleasant Street
Northampton, MA 01060
Telephone: 413-587-3500
Fax: 413-587-3505
Website: http://www.stopitnow.org

This program is concerned with ending the sexual abuse of children through the use of public advocacy. It was founded on the principle that our society has the ability to challenge unwanted human behaviors and to change them through intelligent use of mass media. While they believe that children should be warned and trained to prevent their own sexual abuse, this program's focus is to put the burden of stopping the sexual abuse of children on the shoulders of adults. They also believe that, because most experts agree that a large proportion of sexual abusers can and will stop their harmful behavior if they are reached and are provided with good treatment programs, society must hold them responsible for their criminal behavior and expect them to change. Their Reach Out program works to stop abuse by challenging offenders to stop their abuse and seek treatment, helping to identify potential abusers and encouraging them to seek help, empowering family and friends to confront the abuser, and creating a social climate in this country that will not tolerate the sexual abuse of children. They use op-ed articles, a speakers' bureau, talk shows, television and radio public service announcements, magazine articles, and slogans to educate the public about childhood sexual abuse.

Survivor Connections, Inc.
52 Lyndon Road
Cranston, RI 02905
Telephone: 401-941-2548
Fax: 401-941-2335
Website: http://members.cox.net/survivorconnections

Survivor Connections was started in 1993 by Frank Fitzpatrick for survivors of sexual abuse perpetrated by Catholic priest James Porter. Over time, Fitzpatrick and others realized the great need of all survivors of sexual abuse for information and support. The organization created the first database of reported sexual offenders in 1993.

Survivors Network of Those Abused by Priests (SNAP)
P.O. Box 6416
Chicago, IL 60680
Telephone: 877-762-7432
Website: http://www.snapnetwork.org

Survivors Network of Those Abused by Priests is the oldest, largest, and most active support group for individuals who have been abused by religious authority figures, including priests, ministers, bishops, deacons, and nuns. Founded in 1989 by Barbara Blaine, SNAP has helped thousands of survivors and offers support services over the phone, online through their website, and at national meetings held two times each year. Their website is full of helpful news and information concerning sexual abuse.

Survivors of Incest Anonymous
World Service Office
P.O. Box 190
Benson, MD 21018-9998
Telephone: 410-893-3322
Website: http://www.siawso.org

Survivors of Incest Anonymous is a twelve-step program organized to help incest survivors and their family members, spouses, and friends recover from their incest experiences. They have taken the Twelve Steps and Twelve Traditions from Alcoholics Anonymous and adapted them to incest. In their meetings they seek understanding, acceptance, forgiveness, and serenity. They strive to recognize the negative behavior patterns they developed in childhood in order to survive their experiences and develop a new, more positive way of life.

VOICES in Action
8041 Hosbrook Road, Suite 236
Cincinnati, OH 45236
Telephone: 800-7-VOICE-8 (800-786-4238)
Website: http://www.voices-action.org

VOICES (Victims of Incest Can Emerge Survivors) is a nonprofit organization founded in 1980 as a self-help group providing support for victims of incest and child sexual abuse. The program's goals are to help victims of incest and child sexual abuse become survivors and to educate the public in the area of child sexual abuse, its prevalence and impact, and ways to prevent it. VOICES serves as a clearinghouse for the gathering and disseminating of information regarding incest; it works to help victims find support in their efforts to move from victim to survivor, fosters programs that reflect the needs of incest victims, generates public-awareness activities and educational programs, facilitates research in the field of child sexual abuse, and offers programs to make the public aware of the importance of prevention and education.

Women Incested Needing Group Support (WINGS)
WINGS Foundation, Inc.
8725 W. 14th Street, Suite 150
Lakewood, CO 80215
Telephone: 303-238-8660; 800-373-8671
Fax: 303-238-8482
Website: http://www.wingsfound.org

Women Incested Needing Group Support is a nonprofit organization founded in 1982 by survivors of incest. The group is dedicated to helping women tackle the issue of sexual abuse and start the healing process. It is a peer support group whose goal is to foster a confidential and caring environment in which members can share experiences and learn from each other. WINGS offers a clearinghouse for information on psychotherapists specializing in treating sexual abuse, weekly support group meetings, a sexual abuse handbook, organized social and recreational activities, a speakers' bureau, and assistance in starting WINGS groups in local areas.

8

Selected Print and Nonprint Resources

This chapter contains descriptions of recently published books, handbooks, manuals, journal articles, and training guides on childhood sexual abuse. Because so many books and journal articles have been published recently, this chapter contains a representative sample on various topics within this field. By no means is it a comprehensive listing of the current literature. Also included here are nonprint resources including films, videocassettes, DVDs, and other sources of information.

Books

Ainscough, Carolyn, and Kay Toon. 2000. *Surviving Childhood Sexual Abuse: Practical Self-Help for Adults Who Were Sexually Abused as Children.* Rev. ed. Cambridge, MA: De Capo. ISBN 1–5556–1225–3.

Ainscough and Toon offer practical advice to adults who were sexually abused as children. They explain how understanding the past is key to surviving the experience. Chapters focus on the damage caused by abuse; anxiety, fears, and nightmares resulting from the abuse; emotional effects such as depression and low self-esteem; eating disorders and negative body image often experienced by victims of childhood sexual abuse; feelings the victim experienced against the abuser; how to overcome the problems created by the abuse; and suggestions for ways to prevent child sexual abuse.

Anderson, Orieda Horn, and Shirley Paceley. 2003. *Safe Beginnings: Protecting Our Children from Sexual Abuse.* Decatur, IL: Blue Tower Training Center. ISBN 1–9315–6820–0.

Anderson and Paceley, who were sexually abused as children, speak from personal experience as they describe strategies for protecting children from being sexually abused. Individual chapters cover attitudes about sexuality, key skills to help children develop a healthy self-concept and help protect them, the different messages that society sends boys and girls in which girls are seen as victims, ways in which to create a safe environment, strategies that managers and administrators can employ to create safe environments for children in group settings, and symptoms of child abuse. The importance of keeping children safe once they get into school, the importance of participating in child advocacy efforts, and ways in which parents can protect their children are also discussed.

Angelica, Jade Christine. 2002. *We Are Not Alone: A Guidebook for Helping Professionals and Parents Supporting Adolescent Victims of Sexual Abuse.* Binghamton, NY: Haworth [Haworth Maltreatment and Trauma Press]. ISBN 0–7890–0924–2.

In 1990, Angelica was asked by the Child Abuse Project of the Middlesex County, Massachusetts, district attorney's office to develop a court-oriented resource for children who had been sexually abused and were in the criminal justice system. This book grew out of that assignment. Angelica aims to help guide children who have been sexually abused through the social services and criminal justice systems. She describes the criminal justice system, reasons for becoming involved with the criminal justice system, cases accepted for prosecution, typical evidence, inherent barriers for child victims, courtroom modifications, and preparing the victims for trial. The importance of understanding the victims is explored. Part 2 explores social service and criminal justice policies and procedures, as well as the importance and use of multidisciplinary teams. In Part 3, adolescent victims share their experiences. Finally, Part 4 guides adolescent victims through the adjudication process.

Arnaldo, Carlos A., ed. 2001. *Child Abuse on the Internet: Ending the Silence.* New York: Berghahn. ISBN 1–57181–245–8.

Based on presentations made during the international conference on Sexual Abuse of Children, Child Pornography and Pedophilia on the Internet, sponsored by UNESCO in 1999, this book examines the impact that the Internet has made on the market for the sexual exploitation of children. Part 1 examines the sexual abuse of children; the sociological, psychological, and legal aspects of child pornography and pedophilia; and their presence on the Internet. Part 2 explores the strategies employed by governments, individuals, parents, NGOs, and other organizations to combat the problems faced by children on the Internet. Part 3 provides the Declaration and Plan of Action adopted by conference participants, as well as other useful information on follow-up activities.

Baker, Robert A., ed. 1998. *Child Sexual Abuse and False Memory Syndrome.* Amherst, NY: Prometheus. ISBN 1–5739–2182–3.

Psychologist Robert Baker has gathered contributors who examine the controversies surrounding false memories of child sexual abuse. Part 1 examines memory and its recovery, including children's memories of stressful events. Part 2 looks at repression and amnesia, including a review of the literature and whether memories of childhood sexual abuse can be repressed. Part 3 explores hypnosis, suggestion, and iatrogenesis, including the validity of repressed memories, a case study of an actual court case, and the process of retrieving memories. In Part 4, professional problems and ethical issues are examined, including the reliability of children's statements, avoiding false claims of child sexual abuse, and ethical issues for the family therapist. Part 5 focuses on research and legal implications, and the final part summarizes the information and discusses suggestions for future research and actions.

Bass, Ellen, and Laura Davis. 1994. *The Courage to Heal: A Guide for Women Survivors of Child Sexual Abuse.* 3d ed. New York: Harper-Perennial. ISBN 0–0609–5066–8.

When Ellen Bass and Laura Davis originally wrote this book, first published in 1988, little information was available about the sexual abuse of children, and no real support was available for adult survivors. Few therapists knew much about sexual abuse, and there were even fewer support groups available for adult survivors. This book was, and still is, an excellent resource for information related to sexual abuse. Topics covered include recognizing the damage that the sexual abuse has done, learning how to cope, deciding to heal, remembering the abuse, telling someone about the abuse, understanding that it was not the victim's fault, grieving, mourning, anger, disclosure, and forgiveness. The authors discuss how to change past patterns with regard to feelings, intimacy, sex, children, parenting, and counseling. Several stories of survivors are presented to help the reader understand that other women have been sexually abused, that they are not alone, and that they can heal.

Bolen, Rebecca M. 2001. *Child Sexual Abuse: Its Scope and Our Failure.* New York: Kluwer Academic/Plenum. ISBN 0–306–46576–0.

Bolen set out to provide a comprehensive review of the empirical literature on child sexual abuse. As her research evolved, however, she realized that the book would not be complete unless she examined the discrepancies between the current knowledge base and the professional response to child sexual abuse. Part 1 provides a historical overview of child sexual abuse and an examination of the prominent theories regarding its cause and treatment. Part 2 reviews the empirical knowledge base, including incidence and prevalence, extrafamilial and intrafamilial abuse, risk factors, and offending and nonoffending guardians. Part 3 examines the professional response to child sexual abuse. The book's intended audience includes professionals in the fields of law enforcement, government, medicine, and mental health.

Boston Globe Investigative Staff. 2003. *Betrayal: The Crisis in the Catholic Church.* New York: Back Bay. ISBN 0–3167–7675–0.

Reporters for the *Boston Globe* broke the sexual abuse scandal in the Boston archdiocese of the Catholic Church in January 2002. This book details the story of the abuse and the cover-up by Church officials. Beginning with the story of Father John Geoghan and his abuse of young boys in the Church, the book provides an intriguing, behind-the-scenes look at the Catholic Church, the investigations conducted by the Church, detailed descriptions of the priests and where they were sent following initial allegations of abuse were raised, and those in authority who knew about the abuse. The issues of whether a large number of priests are involved in sexually abusing young children and, if so, why they abuse children are explored.

Brohl, Kathryn, and Joyce Case Potter. 2004. *When Your Child Has Been Molested: A Parents' Guide to Healing and Recovery.* Rev. ed. New York: Jossey-Bass. ISBN 0–7879–7103–0.

As the title implies, Brohl wrote this book to provide a guide to help parents of children who have been sexually abused. She takes parents through the process from first learning that a child has been molested to professional treatment and support, the forensic interview, and the judicial process. Parents are provided with additional information concerning working with a counselor, understanding grief, helping the child to recover, the impact on family members, dealing with extended family members, and strengthening family communications.

Brown, Alyson, and David Barrett. 2002. *Knowledge of Evil: Child Prostitution and Child Sexual Abuse in Twentieth Century England.* Portland, OR: Willan. ISBN 1–9032–4063–8.

Brown and Barrett examine child prostitution in England between the 1880s and the 1980s. They view child prostitution as a form of child sexual abuse and pull together a variety of primary sources, including archival records and contemporary newspapers, to explore this topic. Topics include the socioeconomic contexts within which child prostitution occurs and the negative views and assumptions toward children who are involved in prostitution.

Butler, Edgar W., Hiroshi Fukurai, Jo-Ellan Dimitrius, and Richard Krooth. 2001. *Anatomy of the McMartin Child Molestation Case.* Lanham, MD: University Press of America. ISBN 0–7618–1983–5.

The authors provide a detailed analysis of the McMartin day-care sexual molestation case, examining the children's stories, the charges, the trial, the verdicts, and the aftermath. The book reveals how society and the criminal justice system dealt with the children, their parents, and the day-care providers, all in the search for justice. The authors raise critical questions about the criminal justice system, the behavior of the mass media, and the input and effectiveness of the therapists and other helping professionals. Individual chapters focus on the evolution of charges, the pretrial publicity, preliminary hearings, pretrial events prior to the first trial, impaneling the jury, the first trial, the jurors and their verdicts, the aftermath, the second McMartin trial, the constitutional rights of both the child abuse victims and the alleged perpetrators, and reform of the system.

Campbell, Terrence W. 1998. *Smoke and Mirrors: The Devastating Effect of False Sexual Abuse Claims.* New York: Insight. ISBN 0–3064–5984–1.

False allegations of child sexual abuse have consistently attracted a great deal of news media attention and have had a disastrous effect on the lives of all involved—from the families of those alleging the abuse to those accused of committing the abuse. Part 1 examines these false allegations, focusing on the origins of false allegations, interviewing or indoctrinating children, misinterpretations, and the persuasiveness of play therapy. Part 2 explores claims of repressed memories, whether they are science fiction or scientific fact, and the creation of repressed memories.

Ceci, Stephen J., and Helene Hembrooke. 2001. *Expert Witnesses in Child Abuse Cases: What Can and Should Be Said in Court.* Washington, DC: American Psychological Association. ISBN 1–55798–515–4.

The editors have gathered together lawyers, psychologists, and social workers to discuss various aspects of expert witness testimony and provide recommendations on the proper role of expert witnesses in cases of child abuse. Part 1 provides an overview of the use of expert witnesses, comparing the use of such witnesses and ethical standards for psychologists who serve as expert witnesses. Part 2 examines the actual experience of expert witnesses, including those used in child sexual abuse cases. Part 3 discusses the types of evidence offered in cases of alleged child abuse, its admissibility, and the effects of this testimony. Finally, Part 4 summarizes the usefulness of the expert witnesses and current thoughts in the field, including a discussion of the impact of Daubert on child sexual abuse prosecutions.

Cling, B. J., ed. 2004. *Sexualized Violence against Women and Children: A Psychology and Law Perspective.* New York: Guilford. ISBN 1–5938–5061–1.

Contributors to this volume provide information on the nature, prevalence, and psychological consequences of a variety of actions, including rape, stalking, sexual harassment, and child sexual abuse. Part 1 examines sexualized violence against women. Part 2 explores sexualized violence against children, and includes a discussion of recovered memories of sexual abuse. Part 3 focuses on the sexual offenders, and includes contributions on managing and treating the sexual offender, Megan's Law, and maternal violence.

Conte, Jon R., ed. 2002. *Critical Issues in Child Sexual Abuse: Historical, Legal, and Psychological Perspectives.* Thousand Oaks, CA: Sage. ISBN 0–7619–0911–7.

Written in part as a tribute to Roland Summit, this volume includes articles from six contributors who discuss the impact of Summit's ideas in the field of child sexual abuse. Chapter 1 provides an in-depth interview with Summit, who presents an overview of child sexual abuse as he sees it. The following chapters discuss prosecution of child sexual abusers, historical perspectives and views of child sexual abuse prior to the 1980s and 1990s, when Summit began examining this type of abuse, expert testimony, recovered memories of child sexual abuse, and approaches to treatment in dissociative identity disorder patients.

Cossins, Anne. 2000. *Masculinities, Sexualities, and Child Sexual Abuse.* Boston: Kluwer Law International. ISBN 90–411–1355–X.

Cossins examines the issue of why most child sexual abuse acts are committed by men and male adolescents against female and male children. She believes that existing theories don't adequately explain why men typically are the offenders. Cossins believes that an offender's relationship with other men, and whether he experiences powerlessness as a result, is the key to understanding why he chooses to abuse children sexually, since sexuality is a key social practice for alleviating feelings of powerlessness and for establishing relations of power with other men. Specifically, the theory argues that the extent to which a man believes in the relationship between sexuality and experiences of masculinity and power will be a key variable in determining whom he chooses as a sexual partner. Individual chapters focus on the male problem of child sexual offending, current explanations of child sexual abuse, a sociological theory, and a test of the power/powerlessness theory. Cossins concludes that "child sex offending needs to be tackled as a relatively widespread *social* problem, rather than a rare and aberrant type of sexual behavior committed by a handful of men" (p. 260).

Courtois, Christine A. 1996. *Healing the Incest Wound: Adult Survivors in Therapy.* New York: W. W. Norton. ISBN 0–393–31356–5.

Courtois offers specific knowledge and guidelines for clinicians and therapists to help adults recovering from incest. Part 1 provides a general overview of incest, by category, type, characteristics, and individual and family dynamics. Part 2 explores the symptoms exhibited by adults who experienced incest as children, as well as the long-term secondary effects, using four different theories: traumatic stress or victimization theory, developmental theory, feminist theory, and loss theory. Part 3 discusses the relevant issues and strategies employed in treating incest victims.

Davies, Graham M., and Tim Dalgleish, eds. 2001. *Recovered Memories: Seeking the Middle Ground.* New York: John Wiley and Sons. ISBN 0–471–49132–2.

Davies, Dalgleish, and the other contributors to this volume offer a well-balanced examination of the issues surrounding recovered memories. Part 1 explores the social aspects, including a sociohistorical perspective; effects of recovered memories on the individual, the family, and the community; and legal dilemmas. Part 2 examines the evidential aspects, including case-based analyses of authentic and fabricated discovered memories and an analysis of whether it is possible to distinguish between true and false memories. Part 3 looks at the clinical aspects, including therapeutic techniques, clinicians' beliefs and practices, practice-based guidelines, and functional memory loss. Part 4 offers concluding comments.

De Young, Mary. 2004. *The Day Care Ritual Abuse Moral Panic.* Jefferson, NC: McFarland. ISBN 0–7864–1830–3.

De Young, a university sociologist, offers the reader a sociological analysis of the day-care ritual abuse panic that began in the United States in the mid-1980s. She introduces the concept of "moral panic" and applies it to the ritual abuse scare. The ideological, political, and economic forces that led to the panic are explored, along with the importance of the McMartin day-care case as the precipitating incident that brought ritual abuse to the public's attention. The interest groups that played a role in the growth of the panic, the spread of the panic to foreign countries, and the outcome are also discussed.

Denov, Myriam S. 2004. *Perspectives on Female Sexual Offending: A Culture of Denial.* Aldershot, England: Ashgate. ISBN 0–7546–3565–1.

In her examination of female sexual offenders, Denov conducted in-depth interviews with fifteen survivors of sexual abuse, twelve police officers, and ten psychiatrists in two Canadian cities, and she was a participant observer for three months with a police sexual assault unit. This book explores the results of that research. Denov believes that sexual abuse by women is under-reported, and this under-reporting has negative consequences for the children victimized. She provides a framework for understanding the reasons why people find it difficult to believe that women can and do sexually abuse children. Police also may have a difficult time in proving the abuse: traditionally, evidence of sexual abuse includes sperm, DNA, penetration—all male-oriented pieces of evidence. Denov also discusses the view of many police officers as well as psychiatrists that female sexual offenders are often seen as harmless and not a threat to society. In her final chapter, Denov argues that sexual offenses committed by women are frequently overlooked or minimized, and must be examined in more depth.

Dokecki, Paul R. 2004. *The Clergy Sexual Abuse Crisis: Reform and Renewal in the Catholic Community.* Washington, DC: Georgetown University Press. ISBN 1–58901–006–X.

Dokecki analyzes the sexual abuse scandal plaguing the Catholic Church by examining clergy sexual abuse through the actions of the priest/abuser and the organizational process of the Church—specifically, the use and abuse of power. He uses the McKeown case as a starting point: McKeown was a priest who served in several parishes throughout Tennessee, admitted to sexually molesting approximately thirty boys, and was first sent to St. Luke's Institute and then to the Hartford Institute for Living for treatment. Dokecki examines McKeown's story and then explores clergy sexual abuse in a historical, cultural, and organizational context. He looks at the use and abuse of power exhibited by many Church officials, the various theories of human behavior, and ecclesiastical perspectives of the clergy sexual abuse system, and offers recommendations on ways in which to reform Church governance and policies to prevent child sexual abuse.

Dorais, Michel. 2002. *Don't Tell: The Sexual Abuse of Boys.* Translated from French by Isabel Denholm Meyer. Montreal: McGill-Queen's University Press. ISBN 0–7735–2261–1.

While many books have been written about the sexual abuse of girls, fewer focus on sexual abuse of boys. Written in part to help professionals become more aware of the characteristics and dynamics of the sexual abuse of boys, Dorais presents the detailed stories of twelve boys who experienced sexual abuse; each describes a different type of sexual abuse and the boy's reactions to it. Dorais offers a glimpse into the devastating impact of sexual abuse on its victims.

Durham, Andrew. 2003. *Young Men Surviving Child Sexual Abuse: Research Stories and Lessons for Therapeutic Practice.* New York: John Wiley and Sons. ISBN 0–4708–4459–0.

Durham focuses on the experiences of young boys who were sexually abused as children, using their stories to examine the impact of their experiences on their lives as well as on society as a whole. Part 1 examines the theoretical and social context of child sexual abuse, facts and myths regarding sexual abuse of boys, and the development of a sensitive approach to researching child sexual abuse. Part 2 offers the young men's stories, while Part 3 examines the implications for treatment.

Faller, K. C. 2003. *Understanding and Assessing Child Sexual Maltreatment.* 2d ed. Thousand Oaks, CA: Sage. ISBN 0–7619–1997–X.

Faller provides a comprehensive review of the multiple skills and knowledge that are needed by child protection workers and other professionals working with children, specifically children who have been sexually abused. Chapters focus on definitions and signs of abuse, the importance of collaboration with other professionals and services, assessment strategies, children's memory issues, and allegations of sexual abuse in day-care and foster-care settings, as well as in divorce situations.

Finkel, Martin A., and Angelo P. Giardino. 2001. *Medical Evaluation of Child Sexual Abuse: A Practical Guide.* 2d ed. Thousand Oaks, CA: Sage. ISBN 0–7619–2082–X.

A basic reference manual for the medical evaluation of children who are suspected of having been sexually abused, this book examines the physical examination and diagnosis of sexually abused children, interviewing children, collecting evidence for criminal investigations, and documenting examinations. Additional chapters focus on legal issues, collecting forensic evidence, issues specific to nurses, and the special needs of adolescents.

France, David. 2004. *Our Fathers: The Secret Life of the Catholic Church in an Age of Scandal.* New York: Broadway. ISBN 0–7679–1430–9. Bibliography, Index.

As a senior editor at *Newsweek,* France covered the emerging stories of the sexual abuse of children by priests in the Catholic Church. In this book, France provides a historical view of the Church, beginning in the 1950s, to answer the question of how widespread the abuse scandal was and how the Church could have let this abuse happen. He takes the reader through a chronological account of priest after priest who was charged with sexually abusing children and how individuals within the Church hierarchy reacted.

Hagood, Maralynn M. 2000. *Art Therapy Sex Abuse.* Philadelphia: Jessica Kingsley. ISBN 1–8530–2228–4.

Hagood offers a comprehensive examination of the use of art therapy in counseling children who have been sexually abused. She discusses the various models that have been proposed and tested in the field, and describes successful applications. The use of art in counseling for various audiences is discussed, including counseling sexually abused children, mothers of sexually abused children, adult survivors, and adolescent sex offenders. She describes the dangers of interpreting artwork in diagnosing issues of concern to sexually abused children.

Hammel-Zabin, Amy. 2003. *Conversations with a Pedophile: In the Interest of Our Children.* Fort Lee, NJ: Barricade. ISBN 1–56980–247–5.

Dr. Hammel-Zabin met Alan, a pedophile, while working as a music therapist in the maximum security prison where Alan was incarcerated, serving several life sentences for sexually abusing young boys. In a series of letters to Hammel-Zabin—letters that can help parents and the general public spot warning signs and prevent child sexual abuse—Alan describes the steps he took to locate a child. Abused by her father and grandfather as a young child, Hammel-Zabin reflects on his descriptions of what he has done, as well as on her own experiences of incest. She believes that the only way to prevent pedophilia is to understand it.

Jenkins, Philip. 2001. *Beyond Tolerance: Child Pornography Online.* New York: New York University Press. ISBN 0–8147–4262–9.

Jenkins examines the online subculture of child pornography from the view of the participants themselves, primarily using information posted on message boards that cater to individuals attempting to gather pornographic images of young children. Jenkins, focusing on men who are attracted to adolescent or prepubescent girls, examines efforts to regulate Internet content, explores the reasons why society generally does not believe that the online threats to children are serious, and explores the online child pornography subculture and theories of deviance. Individual chapters focus on the concept of child pornography; the organization of the online subculture, including newsgroups on Usenet, storyboards, interest groups, and bulletin boards; the structure of the online community; rationalizations that users create to justify their activities; responses of law enforcement and private organizations; the global reach of the online subculture; and ways to reduce online child pornography.

Johnston, Moira. 1998. *Spectral Evidence: The Ramona Case: Incest, Memory, and Truth in Napa Valley.* Boulder, CO: Westview. ISBN 0–8133–3587–6.

Johnston tells the story of how Holly Ramona, when she was nineteen years old, began to have flashbacks—memories of being raped by her father—and the ensuing accusations and lawsuits. Marche Isabella and Richard Rose, Holly Ramona's therapists, set up a meeting with Gary Ramona, Holly's father, in which Isabella and Gary's wife, Stephanie, confronted Gary about the abuse. Johnston takes the reader through the flashbacks, the confrontation, the lawsuit, and all of the repercussions from these recovered memories. She shows how the family was destroyed by the accusations, and describes the lawsuits that Holly filed against her father and the malpractice case that he filed against the therapists.

Kempe, Ruth S., and C. Henry Kempe. 1984. *The Common Secret: Sexual Abuse of Children and Adolescents.* New York: W. H. Freeman. ISBN 0–8147–4262–9. References, index.

Ruth and Henry Kempe, long known for their work with abused and neglected children, wrote this book to help readers—students, nurses, physicians, teachers, ministers, priests, lawyers, legislators, and the general public—understand the extent of child sexual abuse and the major issues surrounding it. Chapters provide information on definitions and incidence, extrafamilial sexual abuse, incest, legal aspects, comprehensive first aid after childhood sexual abuse, evaluation and treatment of extrafamilial sexual abuse, evaluation and treatment of incest, the effects of abuse on children and adolescents, and ways in which to prevent child sexual abuse. Appendices provide information on a model criminal diversion program, forms for evaluation and case records, and educational materials on child sexual abuse. The authors have included examples from case histories throughout the book.

Kitzinger, Jenny. 2004. *Framing Abuse: Media Influence and Public Understanding to Sexual Violence against Children.* London: Pluto. ISBN 0–7453–2331–6.

Many people believe that the mass media shape our perceptions of how we think about things, that certain stories attract our attention, that journalists use a variety of strategies to persuade us to respond in certain ways. Kitzinger has provided insight into the media influence through interviews with 500 journalists, campaigners, survivors of sexual abuse, and the public, using sexual abuse of children as a case study. Chapters examine the news media's role in contemporary society, feminist initiatives challenging sexual violence, the emergence of incest as a social problem, stereotypes of sexual abusers, the role of media in community notification laws, and the impact of disputed allegations of abuse.

Koenig, Linda J., Lynda S. Doll, Ann O'Leary, and Willo Pequeg-nat, eds. 2003. *From Child Sexual Abuse to Adult Sexual Risk: Trauma, Revictimization, and Intervention.* Washington, DC: American Psychological Association. ISBN 1–59147–030–7.

The editors have gathered a wide variety of experts and re-searchers in the field to examine the latest research into the effects of child sexual abuse on adult sexual health. They explore the the-ory that children who have been sexually abused are more likely to participate in risky sexual behavior as adults and, as a result, may experience negative reproductive and sexual health prob-lems, including sexually transmitted diseases, HIV infection, un-wanted pregnancy, and adult sexual violence. Individual authors explore the theory and research of the epidemiology and trauma of child sexual abuse, as well as resulting sexual health and risk behaviors as adults. The final chapter suggests areas for future re-search.

Krane, Julia. 2003. *What's Mother Got to Do with It? Protecting Children from Sexual Abuse.* Toronto: University of Toronto Press. ISBN 0–8020–0958–1.

This book examines the social relations that form the basis of child welfare practices that aim to protect children from child sex-ual abuse—specifically, the fact that women are held responsible for the welfare of their children and are often blamed when they are unable to protect them. Krane conducted in-depth interviews of seven female social workers and eight nonoffending mothers from a particular child welfare agency in Ontario, Canada. Four additional nonoffending women are discussed, even though they weren't interviewed. Offenders were related to the women in a variety of ways: as current or former husbands, a common-law partner or his brother or nephew, son, adoptive grandson, son's friend, and daughter-in-law's husband. Victims included sixteen female and one male child. Krane presents the results of her study, including a review of the child welfare literature, the statu-tory issues, and the processes of protecting children, including legal and therapeutic practices, that rely on mothers as protectors of their children.

La Fontaine, Jean. 1998. *Speak of the Devil: Tales of Satanic Abuse in Contemporary England.* New York: Cambridge Univer-sity Press. ISBN 0–521–62934–9.

In the early 1980s, allegations of satanic abuse in day-care settings began to appear in the United States. By the end of the 1980s, similar allegations surfaced in Great Britain. La Fontaine, an anthropologist, was asked by the Department of Health in Great Britain to examine the allegations of satanic abuse, and this book describes her research and findings. She reviews the geographic distribution of these allegations between 1987 and 1992. She reviews the lack of evidence available to support the allegations, the role of social workers and children in perpetuating the scare, and the role that the adults played in creating these alleged memories, either through selective interpretation of innocent remarks or suggestive interviewing.

Levesque, Roger J. R. 1999. *Sexual Abuse of Children: A Human Rights Perspective.* Bloomington: Indiana University Press. ISBN 0–253–33471–3.

Levesque, who is a lawyer and a psychologist, brings a unique perspective to an examination of child sexual abuse—specifically, how human rights law can provide an understanding of what can be done to protect children from child sexual abuse. Chapters explore child sexual maltreatment across world cultures, the global human rights revolution, deconstructing childhood and sexual maltreatment, and various forms of sexual maltreatment. Offenders, both adult and juvenile, are examined. Levesque looks at the ways in which different types of abuse across cultures can be linked with one another, and how differing social views of children may put them at risk for sexual abuse.

Lew, Mike. 2004. *Victims No Longer: The Classic Guide for Men Recovering from Sexual Child Abuse.* Rev. ed. New York: Harper-Collins. ISBN 0–06–053026–X.

Written as a handbook for men recovering from childhood incest and other types of sexual abuse, and for the people who care about these men, this book is intended to reach a wide audience. Lew also wanted to provide a framework in which healing can take place, show people that recovery is possible, start people thinking about and discussing childhood sexual abuse, and share some of the experiences of men in recovery to help others just beginning on that road. Chapters include a discussion of the myths and realities of incest, messages about masculinity that often make it difficult for men to admit that they were sexually abused as children, men and feelings, sexuality and homosexuality, strategies for survival, forgetting, denying, distancing, pretending, numbing, self-image, self-esteem, telling the secret, relationships and the importance of social support, individual and group counseling, forgiving and forgetting, and moving on. An expanded list of resources is provided in this revised edition.

Mather, Cynthia, and Kristina E. Debye. 2004. *How Long Does It Hurt? A Guide to Recovering from Incest and Sexual Abuse for Teenagers, Their Friends, and Their Families.* Rev. ed. San Francisco: Jossey-Bass. ISBN 0–7879–7569–9. Bibliography, index.

As a survivor of child sexual abuse, Mather speaks from first-hand experience of the wide range of feelings that a sexually abused child experiences, including the confusion, fear, sadness, and despair encountered by many children. In Part 1 she focuses on the abuse itself, if it was really abuse, and Internet sex crimes. Part 2 focuses on telling someone about the abuse, including chapters on telling someone, what people will say, what is happening to the child, living with the child's family after the story comes out, and going to court. Part 3 looks at healing, forgiveness, and sexuality. Finally, Part 4 provides information regarding offenders, what friends of victims need to know, and what some survivors would like everyone to know.

Miller, Alice. 1986. *Thou Shalt Not Be Aware: Society's Betrayal of the Child.* Translated by Hildegarde and Hunter Hannum. New York: Meridian. ISBN 0–253–33471–3. Bibliography.

Dr. Miller, in this groundbreaking book, presents her premise that sexually abused children have obeyed the dictum "Thou shalt not be aware," believing that they are to blame for what happened to them. Miller argues that therapists have harmed those they have treated by trying to make them fit neatly into popular psychological theories, instead of listening to and learning from them. She argues that therapists must start listening to the children, and must identify with them, in order to understand them. Therapists must become advocates for their clients instead of representing current societal theories and values. They must not spare the parents at any cost, but must understand the ways in which sexuality can be used to control or have power over those weaker in society.

Moffatt, Gregory K. 2003. *Wounded Innocents and Fallen Angels: Child Abuse and Child Aggression.* Westport, CT: Greenwood. ISBN 0–275–97848–6.

When children are abused, including when they are sexually abused, research has shown that they may become aggressive against adults, other children, or personal property belonging to themselves or others. Written for professionals, including counselors, teachers, and psychologists, as well as for the general public, this book explores crimes against children and the resulting aggressive behavior that those children may exhibit. Following a description of three child abuse cases that made headlines throughout the country, Part 1 explores the prevalence of child abuse, the prevalence and effects of Munchausen Syndrome by proxy, physical and emotional abuse and neglect, child sexual abuse, child abduction, and treating victimized children. Individual case studies are presented, describing the experiences of abuse and the short- and long-term effects of the abuse. Part 2 of the book focuses on the aggressive and violent actions of children who have been abused, discussing how these children become bullies, murderers, or sexual predators, or how they may destroy their own property or the property of others. Finally, Moffatt offers specific strategies for treating such children, as well as suggesting the role that parents, medical personnel, and religious communities can play in treating and preventing child abuse.

Murphy, Jenny. 2001. *Art Therapy with Young Survivors of Sexual Abuse: Lost for Words.* New York: Taylor and Francis. ISBN 0–415–20571–9. Index.

Murphy offers a practical guide to working with children who have been sexually abused, using art therapy as a valuable tool in helping them to heal. Part 1 focuses on the therapeutic relationship in context, including male therapist countertransference and how assessment using art and play therapy can help children disclose sexual abuse. In Part 2, Murphy explores working with individuals, including using the reflective image, use of sand and water, a developmental approach to art therapy, and a case study. Part 3 focuses on experiences with art therapy in groups.

Noblitt, James Randall, and Pamela Sue Perskin. 2000. *Cult and Ritual Abuse: Its History, Anthropology, and Recent Discovery in Contemporary America.* Rev. ed. Westport, CT: Praeger. ISBN 0–275–96664–X.

Allegations of child sexual abuse as part of ritual abuse were often headlines in the 1980s and 1990s. While allegations of abuse in these settings have dropped off, they still occasionally occur. This book grew out of one therapist's personal experiences in treating individuals who made allegations of having been sexually abused as children. The authors begin by examining the history of ritual abuse reported in various religions, cults, and other organizations. They explore the use of ritual abuse in various settings and offer several theories regarding possession, ritual abuse, and dissociation. They conclude that the diagnosis of dissociative identity disorder, or DID, is what was historically known, especially in non-Western societies, as possession.

Ogilvie, Beverly A. 2004. *Mother-Daughter Incest: A Guide for Helping Professionals.* Binghamton, NY: Haworth. ISBN 0–7890–0917–X.

Written to provide guidance for therapists who work with women who have been sexually abused by their mothers, this book examines the issues faced by these female victims. Sexual abuse by men is examined more frequently than abuse by women and, as a result, victims of female abusers tend to suffer silently, according to Ogilvie, silenced "by a society that continues to deny that mothers do sexually abuse their daughters" (p. 7). For this book, Ogilvie interviewed sixty-two adult women who were sexually abused by their mothers. Part 1 examines the enigma of mother-daughter incest. Part 2 focuses on common themes among daughters, including shame, feeling trapped with no place to go, betrayal and grief, identification with and differentiation from the mother, impaired sexual development, and difficulty in coping. Part 3 examines common themes among mothers, including being emotionally needy and unstable, and boundary violations. In Part 4, specific counseling interventions are offered. Finally, Part 5 explores special issues such as stepmothers versus biological mothers who abuse, the effect of the gender of the therapist, transference, countertransference, and theoretical frameworks and treatment approaches.

Parkinson, Patrick. 2003. *Child Sexual Abuse and the Churches: Understanding the Issues.* Binghamton, NY: Haworth. ISBN 0–3406–3015–9.

Parkinson explores the relationship between child sexual abuse and the role of the Church in responding to such abuse in Australia and elsewhere. He examines breaking the silence of abuse perpetrated by members of the clergy and the Church's responsibility in protecting children and dealing with perpetrators; the nature and prevalence of child sexual abuse; the perpetrators of sexual abuse; the process of victimization, including choosing and grooming the victim; controversies and issues concerning child sexual abuse, including sexual relations between children and adults, repressed memories, and ritual abuse; effects of abuse on children; issues specific to clergy abuse of children; forgiveness; issues in child protection for Christians; disclosure, investigation, and the legal process; procedures with clergy abuse of children; and ways to make churches safe for children.

Plante, Thomas G., ed. 2004. *Sin against the Innocents: Sexual Abuse by Priests and the Role of the Catholic Church.* Westport, CT: Praeger. ISBN 0–2759–8175–4.

Plante has gathered professionals in a wide variety of fields, including mental health professionals, theologians, canon lawyers, ethicists, journalists, and victim advocates, to examine the issues of sexual abuse committed by clergy in the Catholic Church. The view of the Vatican on the scandal in the United States, canon law as it applies to the priests who are abusing children, promises made by the Church hierarchy to end the abuse, and the role of oversight review boards are discussed. The issues of celibacy among priests and homosexuality are explored. Implications for future research, programs for survivors, insights from attachment theory, treatment issues and the Church hierarchy, barriers to responding to the crisis, and collaboration among the Church, mental health organizations, and the criminal justice system are examined.

Prendergast, William E. 2004. *Treating Sex Offenders: A Guide to Clinical Practice with Adults, Clerics, Children, and Adolescents.* Binghamton, NY: Haworth. ISBN 0–7890–0930–0.

The characteristics of adult, adolescent, and child sex offenders are described in this reference book, along with treatment options depending on the type of offense as well as the perpetrator's motivation for offending. The first part of the book explores obsessive-compulsive characteristics, personality characteristics, the need for control, and sexual performance problems that can lead to sexually abusive behavior. The second part describes treatment options for sexual offenders, including strategies for treatment, depending on whether the offender was sexually abused as a child or is a pedophile, a father sexually abusing a child, or a sexually assaultive or seductive offender.

Pryor, Douglas W. 1999. *Unspeakable Acts: Why Men Sexually Abuse Children.* New York: New York University Press. ISBN 0–8147–666–8.

While many books focus on men after they have sexually abused young children, this book examines what makes men make that decision to abuse, and how they become abusers in the first place. Pryor focuses on what makes them cross the line into criminal behavior, and how such information can help prevent the sexual abuse of children. Thirty men who abused their own children or other children were interviewed for this book. Pryor examines how their lives prior to the abusive acts contributed to the abuse, how the men became interested in the abuse of the child, how the abuse began, how it continued over time, how the abusers felt as they were abusing the child, and how they stopped abusing children.

Quinsey, Vernon L., and Martin Lalumiere. 2001. *Assessment of Sexual Offenders against Children.* 2d ed. Thousand Oaks, CA: Sage. ISBN 0–7619–2431–0.

In this updated edition, Quinsey and Lalumiere review relevant literature on the topic of assessing child molesters for mental health professionals. General characteristics of sex offenders and implications for research are discussed, and recommended assessment instruments are made.

Rabinowitz, Dorothy. 2003. *No Crueler Tyrannies: Accusations, False Witness, and Other Terrors of Our Times.* New York: Simon and Schuster. ISBN 0–7432–2834–0.

During the 1980s and 1990s many accusations were made, cases filed, and day-care workers sent to prison for child sexual abuse and ritual abuse acts that children allegedly experienced in their care. Rabinowitz explores many of these cases, focusing on the case against the Amiraults, a mother and her two adult children who operated a preschool in Malden, Massachusetts. All three of them were sent to prison on charges of child sexual abuse, even though no physical or scientific evidence was produced at the trial. They were convicted on the basis of the testimony of children who were highly coached and asked leading questions throughout the investigation. Other cases explored include the case against Kelly Michaels, a New Jersey nursery school worker; Patrick Griffin, a physician who was falsely accused of molestation; and Grant Snowden, a Miami, Florida, police officer who was sentenced to five consecutive life terms for sexual abuse of a three-year-old, a crime that he did not commit. Rabinowitz examines these and other cases and analyzes the evidence produced, exposing the results as social injustice based on public hysteria.

Reavey, Paul, and Sam Warner, eds. 2003. *New Feminist Stories of Child Sexual Abuse: Sexual Scripts and Dangerous Dialogues.* London: Routledge. ISBN 0–415–25943–6.

Reavey and Warner focus on female child sexual abuse and how this topic is discussed and examined. They demonstrate that "child sexual abuse is never transparent in terms of what it means: either as an event itself or in the memory of it. It is something that, as survivors, theoreticians or practitioners, we make sense of in the re-telling, and how we make sense of it shifts according to the contexts in which we speak, with whom we speak," and the person whom we speak about (p. 1). Part 1 explores the cultural and political landscape of child sexual abuse in both Western and non-Western environments. Contributors examine the various ways in which societies speak about child sexual abuse, including the ways that different cultures understand childhood, sex and gender issues, and child sexual abuse. Part 2 examines how we interpret theories and intervene in the lives of women who have been sexually abused.

Richardson, Sue, and Heather Bacon, eds. 2001. *Creative Responses to Child Sexual Abuse: Challenges and Dilemmas.* Philadelphia: Jessica Kingsley. ISBN 1–85302–884–3.

Beginning with the 1987 child sexual abuse allegations made in Cleveland and in the United Kingdom, and the public furor that followed, Richardson and Bacon examine treatment issues based on the theory of attachment. The book addresses the challenges that professionals face in treating victims of child sexual abuse. Chapters focus on an exploration of attachment and trauma theories of child sexual abuse, disclosure, the stories of victims as told by the mothers, pediatricians and recognition of child sexual abuse symptoms, advocacy issues, therapy, legal and trial issues, and surviving the impact of child sexual abuse and response to the abuse, including ways to manage fear and to promote healing.

Rosencrans, Bobbie. 2001. *The Last Secret: Daughters Sexually Abused by Mothers.* Brandon, VT: Safer Society Foundation. ISBN 1–884444–36–9.

Based on the results of a questionnaire Rosencrans sent to daughters who were sexually abused by their mothers, this book provides insight into the experiences of these women. She describes their experiences, the effects of the abuse, and the extent of the relationship that these women have with their mothers. Most of the women never discussed the abuse with anyone; even those who were in therapy often did not mention the abuse they experienced as young girls.

Rush, Florence. 1980. *The Best Kept Secret: Sexual Abuse of Children.* New York: McGraw-Hill. ISBN 0–1307–4781–5.

In this classic on child sexual abuse, Rush counters the common beliefs about the sexual abuse of children that were held prior to the 1980s, including the belief that children usually are not seriously harmed by sexual abuse and that they are often the instigators of the abuse. She provides a detailed historical analysis of child sexual abuse throughout history, including both Christian and Judaic traditions concerning children, as well as early Greek actions toward children, child marriage in India, and growing up in Victorian England. The ways in which law, religion, the news media, and psychological theories have contributed to the victimization of children are explored. Sexual abuse of boys, more common than many people once believed, is discussed. Child prostitution and child pornography also are examined.

Russell, Diana E. H., and Rebecca M. Bolen. 2000. *The Epidemic of Rape and Child Sexual Abuse in the United States.* Thousand Oaks, CA: Sage. ISBN 0–7619–0301–1.

Russell and Bolen analyze various incidence and prevalence surveys of rape and child sexual abuse conducted in the United States. The first part of the book focuses on rape and the second part on child sexual abuse. In Part 2 they examine the law and legal statutes relating to child sexual abuse, the incidence and prevalence of child sexual abuse, and comparisons of child sexual abuse prevalence rates and the epidemic of child rape. They explore the various definitions of child sexual abuse and the methodologies used by various researchers to collect data.

Sanderson, Christiane. 2004. *The Seduction of Children: Empowering Parents and Teachers to Protect Children from Child Sexual Abuse.* New York: Jessica Kingsley. ISBN 1–84310–748–X.

Sanderson's purpose in writing this book is to provide parents, teachers, and other adults with a basic knowledge and overview of child sexual abuse in order to protect children from abuse and eventually to prevent it from occurring. Chapter 1 focuses on a definition of child sexual abuse, historical evidence and cultural experiences in defining it. Chapter 2 examines the development of children's sexuality. Chapter 3 focuses on the child sex abuser, presenting profiles of different types of abusers and their motivations. Chapter 4 looks at the use of the Internet, child pornography, and the dangers of Internet grooming. In Chapter 5, Sanderson examines how abusers groom children offline, befriending parents or other adults in children's lives. Chapter 6 assesses the impact of child sexual abuse on the children. The signs and symptoms of child sexual abuse are examined in Chapter 7. Chapter 8 gives the reader an understanding of the various ways in which children respond to child sexual abuse. Chapter 9 explores the most effective ways of protecting children, and the final chapter examines ways to prevent child sexual abuse.

Schultz, Pamela D. 2005. *Not Monsters: Analyzing the Stories of Child Molesters.* Lanham, MD: Rowman and Littlefield. ISBN 0–74275–3057–4.

With her perspective as a survivor of child sexual abuse, Schultz examines the impact of child sexual abuse on the victims as well as on the perpetrators. She provides a narrative study of nine perpetrators that she interviewed, providing the reader with an in-depth look into the lives of these offenders, their motives for committing their crimes, their treatment while in prison, and their hopes for the future.

Silverman, Jon, and David Wilson. 2002. *Innocence Betrayed: Paedophilia, the Media and Society.* Malden, MA: Blackwell. ISBN 0–7456–2888–5.

The authors examine the issues surrounding community notification laws that attempt to "name and shame" pedophiles in the community in order to prevent them from reoffending, as well as other attempts to best protect children from sexual offenders. It examines Sarah's Law, enacted following the murder of eight-year-old Sarah Payne in July 2000 in the United Kingdom. The authors report on the results of their interviews with pedophiles, some of whom were still in prison at the time of their interview, and others who had been released; they were located in England, Wales, and North America. Silverman and Wilson also interviewed victims of sexual abuse.

Spanos, Nicholas P. 2001. *Multiple Identities and False Memories: A Sociocognitive Perspective.* Washington, DC: American Psychological Association. ISBN 0–1307–4781–5.

Spanos, a leading expert in the study of hypnosis, does not believe that multiple personality disorder (MPD) is a legitimate psychiatric disorder but rather a cultural construct, having a history in earlier beliefs about demonic possession: it is believed and encouraged today by misguided psychotherapists and their patients. He examines the myths and reality of hypnosis, high hypnotizability and dramatic behaviors, hypnotic amnesia, and distortions of memory. The seduction theory regarding child sexual abuse is explored, along with recovered memories of child sexual abuse. Complex false memories and UFO abductions, as an example of complex false memory, are explored. Spanos discusses cross-cultural studies of spirit and demonic possession, the social functions of possession, and dissociation and multiple personality disorders.

Spiegel, Josef. 2003. *Sexual Abuse of Males: The SAM Model of Theory and Practice.* London: Taylor and Francis. ISBN 1–5603–2403–1.

Spiegel examines the biological, psychological, interpersonal, familial, and social characteristics of victims of childhood sexual abuse, based on life histories of more than 1,000 sexually abused boys and adult men who were sexually abused as children. The first part presents an overview of the dynamics and effects on boys of being sexually abused, and describes the development of the SAM model. Spiegel provides excerpts from case histories to illustrate the dynamics of the cycle of abuse. Part 2 discusses the treatment of boys and men who have been sexually abused, and focuses on philosophical assumptions and principles, anticipating issues that may be raised during treatment as well as the objectives of treatment. Finally, strategies for intervention are discussed.

Taylor, Max, and Ethel Quayle. 2003. *Child Pornography: An Internet Crime.* London: Taylor and Francis. ISBN 1–58391–244–4.

The expanding scope of the Internet and its wide availability to children bring up concerns regarding the protection of children from harmful influences. Taylor and Quayle examine the ways in which child pornography is used on the Internet and the social context in which it appears. They offer a model of offending behavior and explain how it can help us to understand all aspects of sexual offending and treatment. In addition, the authors believe that a more comprehensive understanding of the connections between possession of child pornography and the actual commitment of sexual offenses is necessary in order to develop successful models for protecting children from sexual predators.

Van Dam, Carla. 2001. *Identifying Child Molesters: Preventing Child Sexual Abuse by Recognizing the Patterns of the Offenders.* Binghamton, NY: Haworth. ISBN 0–7890–0743–6.

Van Dam, a clinical and forensic psychologist, wrote this book to provide parents with tools to help protect their children from sexual predators. The hope is that these tools will help to identify individuals who might molest children and will help parents and children know what to do when faced with a potential molester.

Chapters focus on knowing that child sexual abuse is a problem; knowing why it is a problem, including psychological, moral, and cultural issues; prevalence; the characteristics of child molesters; the grooming process; social climates that help to foster child sexual abuse; visible grooming; and setting boundaries to help prevent child sexual abuse.

Wortley, Richard, and Stephen Smallbone, eds. 2006. *Situational Prevention of Child Sexual Abuse.* Monsey, NY: Criminal Justice. ISBN 1–881798–61–5.

Contributors to this volume include criminologists as well as researchers who focus on sexual offenders and their behavior, and ways of preventing the sexual abuse of children. Chapters include applying situational principles to sexual abuse of children, clinical perspectives on situational as well as dispositional factors in child sexual abuse, legislation enacted to prevent abuse, prevention and investigation of abuse, a situational prevention model for child sexual abuse, places where predators meet children, the use of the Internet, situational prevention of crimes perpetrated by intellectually challenged individuals, various approaches to the treatment of sex offenders, and strategies used by offenders to encourage the participation of children in sexual activity.

Journal Articles

Alaggia, Ramona, and Stacey Kirshenbaum. 2005. **"Speaking the Unspeakable: Exploring the Impact of Family Dynamics on Child Sexual Abuse Disclosures."** *Families in Society: The Journal of Contemporary Social Services* 86, no. 2: 227–234.

The authors report on a study of twenty male and female survivors of child sexual abuse to identify various family dynamics that could affect a child's willingness to disclose sexual abuse. They discuss four major themes which suggest that disclosure of child sexual abuse can be significantly compromised when various conditions exist, including rigidly defined gender roles based on a patriarchic family structure; the occurrence of family violence; closed or indirect communications patterns; and social isolation. They point out the necessity of identifying barriers to disclosure in order to ameliorate them effectively, because if children are not able to disclose to an adult the fact that they were sexually abused, the effects are potentially devastating. Implications for treatment of children and their families, including the relevance of established methods of family assessment, are examined.

Banyard, Victoria L., Linda M. Williams, and Jane A. Siegel. 2004. **"Childhood Sexual Abuse: A Gender Perspective on Context and Consequences."** *Child Maltreatment: Journal of the American Professional Society on the Abuse of Children* 9, no. 3: 223–238.

The authors conducted a gender analysis of 128 women and 69 men gathered from an examination of childhood hospital records, looking for patterns among survivors. Results indicated that men and women had similar consequences from the sexual abuse they experienced. The researchers also examined variances in the mental health of 106 male victims and nonvictims and found that the higher the number of incidents of abuse and other traumas, the higher the number of mental health symptoms.

Bascelli, Elizabeth, Daniela Paci, and Patrizia Romito. 2004. **"Adolescents Who Experienced Sexual Abuse: Fears, Needs and Impediments to Disclosure."** *Child Abuse and Neglect: The International Journal* 28, no. 10: 1035–1048.

Adolescents who have been sexually abused may be afraid to reveal the abuse to their parents or other persons in authority. This study examined the reasons for children's fear of disclosure. The researchers conducted in-depth interviews with thirty-six young people in Italy who had been sexually abused. Results indicated that the primary reasons that subjects gave for not revealing the abuse included fear of not being believed, shame, and fear of creating trouble for the family. When the subjects did reveal the abuse, they received limited support from the adults. The authors suggest that professionals need to be better trained to respond when abuse is disclosed.

Berliner, Lucy. 1998. **"Sex Offenders: Policy and Practice."** *Northwestern University Law Review* 92: 1203–1224.

Berliner studied sexual offenders, how they are viewed and treated, and how they are treated differently from other types of criminal offenders. The first part of the article examines sexual offenders as a special case, why they are treated differently, and the consequences of sexual abuse on women and children, which is generally associated with higher levels of psychological harm than other crime categories. The characteristics of sexual offenders are also examined. The next section looks at legislative responses to sex offenders, including treatment options, standards and penalties, and legislation enacted specifically to deal with sexual offenders.

Boakes, J. 1999. **"False Complaints of Sexual Assault: Recovered Memories of Childhood Sexual Abuse."** *Medicine, Science, and the Law* 39, no. 2: 112–120.

Recovered memories of childhood sexual abuse remains a controversial topic. This article discusses false memories recovered in therapy and the influence of the beliefs and practices of therapists in "recovering" these memories. The problems faced in diagnosis, issues of confidentiality, and the role that the expert witness plays in educating the court and the legal community are discussed.

Cinq-Mars, Caroline, John Wright, Mireille Cyr, and Pierre McDuff. 2003. **"Sexual At-Risk Behaviors of Sexually Abused Adolescent Girls."** *Journal of Child Sexual Abuse* 12, no. 2: 1–18.

Several researchers have found that girls who have been sexually abused may participate in sexually risky behaviors as adolescents. This study examined sexually at-risk behavior: researchers interviewed 125 sexually abused adolescent girls between the ages of twelve and seventeen, looking at variables such as participation in consensual sexual activity, age at first consensual intercourse, number of sexual partners, use of condoms, and resulting pregnancies. Results indicated that the more severe the abuse—that is, penetration, more than one perpetrator, physical coercion, and more than one incident of abuse—the more likely that the girls will indulge in risky behaviors. While family characteristics were strongly correlated with sexual activity, those characteristics were not significant with regression analysis.

Cott, Melissa A., and Steven N. Gold. 2004. **"Ethnicity and Sexual Orientation as PTSD Mitigators in Child Sexual Abuse Survivors."** *Journal of Family Violence* 19, no. 5: 319–325.

In this study, the researchers explored the relationship between certain demographic characteristics of survivors of child sexual abuse and scores on the Impact of Scale instrument. The study included 257 women who had been sexually abused as children and were experiencing psychological difficulties relating to that abuse. Demographic variables included marital/relationship status, religious affiliation, ethnicity, level of education, spouse's educational level, income, and sexual orientation. Subjects who indicated that they were asexual had fewer intrusive and total post-traumatic stress disorder (PTSD) symptoms than heterosexuals, lesbians, and bisexuals. Hispanics reported fewer intrusive PTSD symptoms than non-Hispanic Caucasians.

Gibbons, Michael, and Dana Campbell. 2003. **"Symposium: General Aspects of Recreation Law: Liability of Recreation and Competitive Sport Organizations for Sexual Assaults on Children by Administrators, Coaches and Volunteers."** *Journal of Legal Aspects of Sport* 13: 185–229.

This article is part of a symposium on recreation law and examines the growing number of sexual assaults on children by coaches and coaching staff. Child sexual abuse as a social problem is examined, and federal and state legislation designed to protect children from sex offenders is reviewed. A variety of national and state sports organizations for youth are explored to determine how they approach the issue of sexual abuse of participants. Potential legal claims against organizations, if they fail to protect participants from sexual assault, are discussed. Suggested elements for an organization's screening program are provided to help minimize the chances of hiring a potential sex offender.

Gibson, L. E., and H. Leitenberg. 2000. **"Child Sexual Abuse Prevention Programs: Do They Decrease the Occurrence of Child Sexual Abuse?"** *Child Abuse and Neglect: The International Journal* 24, no. 9: 1115–1125.

The authors conducted this study to determine if rates of sexual abuse were different among female college undergraduates that had participated in a sexual abuse prevention program during their childhood. The study included a survey of 825 undergraduates regarding sexual experiences: they were asked about their histories of sexual abuse, their participation in prevention programs when they were young, their current levels of sexual satisfaction, and their sexual behaviors. Almost two-thirds (62 percent) reported that they had participated in a prevention program while in school. Eight percent of those who attended a prevention program revealed that they had later been sexually abused, compared with 14 percent among those who had never participated in a prevention program.

Jensen, Tine K., Wenke Gulbrandsen, Svein Mossige, and Sissel Reichelt. 2005. **"Reporting Possible Sexual Abuse: A Qualitative Study on Children's Perspectives and the Context for Disclosure."** *Child Abuse and Neglect: The International Journal* 29, no. 12: 1395–1413.

Researchers gathered data from therapeutic sessions and follow-up interviews with twenty-two children and their families regarding the context in which children were able to disclose their sexual abuse. Children were asked to describe what made it difficult to talk about their abuse, and what helped to make it easier. Results indicate that children need a supportive structure in which to reveal their abuse, one in which they are presented with an opportunity to talk about what they have experienced. Children also appeared sensitive to the needs of their families and to the consequences to themselves, their family, and the abuser.

Johnson, Dawn M., Timothy C. Sheahan, and Kathleen M. Chard. 2003. **"Personality Disorders, Coping Strategies, and Posttraumatic Stress Disorder in Women with Histories of Childhood Sexual Abuse."** *Journal of Child Sexual Abuse* 12, no. 2: 19–39.

The authors examined relationships among coping strategies, personality disorders, and post-traumatic stress disorder in adult females who had been sexually abused as children. The women exhibited several personality disorders, with specifically avoidant, antisocial, dependent personality disorders occurring more often than borderline personality disorders. The researchers found a significant correlation between avoidant coping and post-traumatic stress severity. Women who experienced severe PTSD also were more likely to exhibit avoidant behaviors and dependent personality disorders.

Kogan, Steven M. 2005. **"The Role of Disclosing Child Sexual Abuse on Adolescent Adjustment and Revictimization."** *Journal of Child Sexual Abuse* 14, no. 2: 25–47.

Using a subsample of 111 adolescents from the National Survey of Adolescents who reported having been sexually abused, the author found that adolescents who promptly disclosed the abuse to an adult were less affected by the abuse than those who did not disclose the abuse or disclosed it long after it had occurred. These adolescents also were less likely to experience or report additional sexual abuse.

Kouyoumdjian, Haig, Andrea R. Perry, and David J. Hansen. 2005. **"The Role of Adult Expectations on the Recovery of Sexually Abused Children."** *Aggression and Violent Behavior* 10, no. 4: 475–489.

This article reports the results of a study to examine the role that adult expectations play in children's recovery from sexual abuse. Results indicate that parental support is a strong variable in predicting how well a child will recover from sexual abuse. Investigations of the role that the expectations of adults—including parents, teachers, and other professionals—play in how well children recover from such abuse should be conducted. Recommendations for future research are included.

Lowe, Walter, Thomas Pavkov, Gisele Casanova, and Joseph Wetchler. 2005. **"Do American Ethnic Cultures Differ in the Definitions of Child Sexual Abuse?"** *American Journal of Family Therapy* 33, no. 2: 147–166.

For this study, researchers examined how members of different ethnic groups—Caucasian Americans, African Americans, and Hispanic Americans—define child sexual abuse, and whether there are differences among those definitions. Results indicated that there were no significant differences among the different ethnic groups' definitions of child sexual abuse, or in their willingness to report child sexual abuse, except at the least severe levels of abuse, in which African Americans and Hispanic Americans were more likely to recognize child sexual abuse and report it than were Caucasian Americans.

Mangold, Susan Vivian. 2003. **"Reforming Child Protection in Response to the Catholic Church Child Sexual Abuse Scandal."** *University of Florida Journal of Law and Public Policy* 14: 155–178.

Mangold analyzes child protection policy reform in response to the child sexual abuse scandal within the Catholic Church. She begins with an analysis of the two previous reform periods in the development of child protection: the first in the 1960s and 1970s, when there was the first widespread recognition of abuse by the medical community; the second in the 1980s and 1990s, when there was a move away from family preservation following serious child abuse by parents. The second part of this article examines the Catholic Church and the sexual abuse scandal; this period represents another reform period that she believes will result in the expansion of mandatory reporting laws. The final two parts examine the collaborative ramifications of the mandatory reporting systems suggested in Part 2, including children's rights and parental rights in the child welfare system and ways of legislating intervention without harming parents and children.

Martin, Graham, Helen A. Bergen, Angela S. Richardson, Leigh Roeger, and Stephen Allison. 2004. **"Sexual Abuse and Suicidality: Gender Differences in a Large Community Sample of Adolescents."** *Child Abuse and Neglect: The International Journal* 28, no. 5: 491–503.

In this study, 2,485 students from twenty-seven schools in South Australia, average age of fourteen years, completed a questionnaire regarding sexual abuse and suicidality, measures of depression, hopelessness, and family functioning. Researchers found that boys who self-reported sexual abuse tended also to have suicidal thoughts, plans, threats, self-injury, and suicide attempts. Girls who experienced sexual abuse and reported high distress over the abuse had a threefold increase in risk of suicidal thoughts and plans, compared with girls who were not abused. Boys who were sexually abused and reported high distress over the abuse had a tenfold increase in risk of suicidal plans and threats compared with boys who were not abused.

Plummer, C. A. 2001. **"Prevention of Child Sexual Abuse: A Survey of 87 Programs."** *Violence and Victims* 16, no. 5: 575–588.

Prevention programs attempt to provide children with knowledge and skills that will help to prevent their sexual abuse. This study attempts to determine how prevention programs function within the context of their communities. Plummer reports the results of a study of eighty-seven prevention programs. Variables in the study included funding, types of materials used, types of approaches used, barriers encountered to successful prevention, length of time the program was in existence, demographics of the population served, and demographics of those leading the local prevention programs. Results indicated that program existence is dependent on a variety of factors, including adequate funding, level of community involvement and denial, and competing agendas.

Redlich, A. D. 2001. **"Community Notification: Perceptions of Its Effectiveness in Preventing Child Sexual Abuse."** *Child Sexual Abuse* 10, no. 3: 91–116.

Community notification laws were enacted in response to the sexual abuse and murder of Megan Kanka by a neighbor who was a convicted sex offender. These laws generally authorize local law enforcement agencies to notify communities when a convicted sexual offender moves into the neighborhood. The laws are popular with the general public, but few studies have been conducted to determine their effectiveness. The authors of this study interviewed 109 community members, 78 law enforcement officials, and 82 law students to determine their attitudes toward community notification laws, as well as other techniques used to prevent child sexual abuse. They found that law enforcement officials were more likely to support community notification than community members or law students, and that the law students were concerned that these laws violate an individual's constitutional rights. Women were more likely than men to support these laws.

Renk, K., L. Liljequist, A. Steinberg, G. Bosco, and V. Phares. 2002. **"Prevention of Child Sexual Abuse: Are We Doing Enough?"** *Trauma, Violence and Abuse: A Review Journal* 3, no. 1: 68–84.

Following a review of the literature on the prevention of child sexual abuse, the authors suggest that not enough is being done to prevent the sexual abuse of children. Even though prevention efforts focus primarily on educating children, the authors believe that additional efforts need to focus on adults who are in a position to help children avoid situations in which they may be abused. Efforts also must focus on adults who sexually abuse children. Prevention programs should be implemented at the community level, including at schools, neighborhood centers, churches, and other local agencies.

Richards, Lauren Metivier, and Bruce A. Thyer. 2005. **"Behavioral Interventions with Female Victims of Childhood Sexual Abuse: A Review."** *Journal of Evidence-Based Social Work* 1, no. 4: 1–14.

Because social workers are often the ones who work directly with the victims of child sexual abuse and their families, the authors saw the need to provide an overview of research findings on the effects of child sexual abuse on the victims. A discussion of the most effective treatment and intervention techniques is also presented. The authors conclude that the use of behavioral and cognitive behavioral interventions shows some limited success in reducing symptoms and behaviors associated with the experience of child sexual abuse. Finally, the authors offer suggestions for areas of future research.

Roberts, Ron, Tom O'Connor, Judy Dunn, and Jean Golding. 2004. **"The Effects of Child Sexual Abuse in Later Family Life: Mental Health, Parenting and Adjustment of Offspring."** *Child Abuse and Neglect: The International Journal* 28, no. 5: 525–545.

This study examined the relationship between being sexually abused as a child before the age of thirteen years and later mental health, family structure, parenting behaviors, and adjustment in children. The sample was composed of 8,292 families from Avon, England, who were part of the larger Avon Longitudinal Study of Parents and Children (an ongoing study of women and their children). Results indicated that an experience of child sexual abuse can have long-term effects for adult mental health, parenting relationships, and child adjustment in future generations.

Savell, Sheila. 2005. **"Child Sexual Abuse: Are Health Care Providers Looking the Other Way?"** *Journal of Forensic Nursing* 1, no. 2: 78–81, 85.

Based on statistics indicating that, in 2002, health care professionals made only 7.8 percent of the child abuse reports, Savell suggests that screening for child sexual abuse should be part of basic checkups and other common encounters with children. She also believes that valid screening techniques should be developed.

Scheutze, Pamela, and Rina Das Eiden. 2005. **"The Relationship between Sexual Abuse during Childhood and Parenting Outcomes: Modeling Direct and Indirect Pathways."** *Child Abuse and Neglect: The International Journal* 29, no. 6: 645–659.

The authors examined the relationship between childhood sexual abuse and parenting outcomes, including the parents' level of stress, their feelings of competence, and their identified means of disciplining their children. Participants in the study included 263 pregnant women, 107 of whom were sexually abused as children.

They were interviewed twice for the study: once when they were between the 28th and 32nd week of their pregnancy, and once again after giving birth, when their child was between two and four years of age. Results indicate that women who experienced sexual abuse as a child were more likely to be depressed and experienced more partner violence.

Ullman, Sarah E., and Henrietta H. Filipas. 2005. **"Gender Differences in Social Reactions to Abuse Disclosures, Post-Abuse Coping, and PTSD of Child Sexual Abuse Survivors."** *Child Abuse and Neglect: The International Journal* 7: 767–782.

This study examined the differences between the ways in which men and women disclose their abusive experiences, their social reactions to the abuse, ways they cope with their abuse, and post-traumatic stress disorder (PTSD) of adult survivors of child sexual abuse. The study used a sample of 733 college students who completed a questionnaire about their demographics, experiences with sexual abuse, means and timing of disclosure, coping strategies, and other people's reactions to their abuse. Results indicated that the female students were more likely than the men to experience greater occurrences of childhood sexual abuse, more severe abuse, more distress and need to blame themselves following the abuse, and relied more on various coping methods such as withdrawal and attempts to forget the experience. The longer the women delayed the disclosure, the greater the severity of their PTSD symptoms.

Training Materials, Manuals

American Prosecutors Research Institute. 2005. *Finding Words: Interviewing and Preparing Children for Court.* Alexandria, VA: American Prosecutors Research Institute.

This training manual provides information on interviewing children who have been sexually abused and preparing them for a trial. A five-day training curriculum is included that covers effective interviewing, how children experience sexual abuse, diversity issues and the interview process, processes of disclosure, the use of age-appropriate guidelines when questioning children, the interview process, use of anatomical dolls, problems in the interview process, child development, hearsay and the victim, corroboration, suggestibility, preparing the child as a witness, and testifying in court. Suggested readings are provided, and a selection of articles from the news media regarding court cases are included.

Cobble, James, Richard Hammar, and Steven Klipowicz. 2005. *Reducing the Risk of Child Sexual Abuse in Your Church Reference Manual.* Rev. ed. Carol Stream, IL: Christianity Today international.

This reference manual can be purchased separately or as part of the *Reducing the Risk Kit,* which also includes a reference book and a DVD set of six videos. The training manual provides the reader with detailed lesson plans to help train church officials, staff, and volunteers in ways to make the church safe for children. The six videos are (1) "Making Your Church Safe from Child Sexual Abuse," (2) "The Behavioral Profile of Molesters," (3) "Selecting and Screening Workers," (4) "Principles of Supervision," (5) "Responding to Allegations of Abuse," and (6) "Implementing a Risk Reduction Program in Your Church."

Durham, Duane, John Keating, Andrew Leggett, and Margaret Osmond. 1998. *Treating the Aftermath of Sexual Abuse: A Handbook for Working with Children in Care.* Washington, DC: Child Welfare League of America.

The focus of this handbook is on ways to treat children in care who have been sexually abused. The physical and emotional impact on a child of being sexually abused is examined, along with the effect of abuse on their basic life experiences.

Finkelhor, David, Kimberly J. Mitchell, and Janis Wolak. 2000. *Online Victimization: A Report on the Nation's Youth.* Arlington, VA: National Center for Missing and Exploited Children.

Funded by the U.S. Congress through a grant to the National Center for Missing and Exploited Children, this report examines the problem of the risks faced by children on the Internet in order to help policy-makers, law enforcement professionals, and parents better understand the risks that children face and what can be done to reduce those risks. The authors conducted a telephone survey of 1,501 youth, between the ages of ten and seventeen, who regularly use the Internet. Interview topics included sexual solicitations, exposure to unwanted sexual materials, their knowledge of Internet safety procedures, and the nature and types of friendships they may have made over the Internet.

McGlone, Gerard J., Mary Shrader, and Laurie Delgatto. 2003. *Creating Safe and Sacred Places: Identifying, Preventing, and Healing Sexual Abuse.* Winona, MN: Saint Mary's.

This manual was developed to assist churches, schools, and youth organizations in the creation of safe environments that will protect children from abuse. The first part of the manual offers an overview of child sexual abuse, types of abuse, offenders, warning signs, cyber sex and abuse, the long-term effects of child sexual abuse, and sexual abuse in the Catholic Church. The second part of the manual provides training sessions for young children, clergy, and parents. These sessions include training strategies, group activities, suggestions for getting discussions started, and quizzes. The third part offers additional resources, including a sample code of conduct, a sample parish statement, questions to ask when screening volunteers, recommended organizations, and a community prayer service.

Morgan, Nancy. March 2005. *Resource Guide for Parents, Caregivers, and Service Providers Working with Alaska Native Children: How to Help When Someone You Care about Has Been Sexually Abused.* Seattle: Providence Health System.

This resource guide provides helpful information on sexual abuse and community resources to help sexually abused children once they return to their rural communities. Divided into six sections, the guide offers basic information on investigation of sexual abuse, warning signs, what to do if sexual abuse is suspected, safety tips for children, self-care for survivors and caregivers, guidelines for survivor support groups, a suggested reading list, answers to frequently asked questions, and a list of national and Alaskan resources concerning child sexual abuse.

National Center for Missing and Exploited Children. 2002. *Female Juvenile Prostitution: Problem and Response,* 2d ed. Alexandria, VA: National Center for Missing and Exploited Children.

The purpose of this book is to provide organizations and individuals with an understanding of the problems of child prostitution in order to provide better services to this population. The Office of Juvenile Justice and Delinquency Prevention of the U.S. Department of Justice, which funded this project, estimates that in 1999 more than 1.5 million children left their homes, were thrown out, or were asked to leave by their parents or guardians. These children are often sexually exploited, either through prostitution or pornography or other exploitative activities. Chapters include case histories, steps to establishing a program to help victims, and a case study of a successful program.

National Center for Missing and Exploited Children. 2003. *A Model State Sex Offender Policy.* Arlington, VA: National Center for Missing and Exploited Children.

The National Center for Missing and Exploited Children, in response to the challenge facing lawmakers in developing effective sexual offender management policies, has developed this model policy. This document provides background information on sex offenders, the development of a triage approach to managing sex offenders, and the reasons for developing a comprehensive criminal justice response. The authors provide eight goals of their recommended sex-offender policy.

National Sexual Violence Resource Center. 2005. *Preventing Child Sexual Abuse: A National Resource Directory and Handbook.* Enola, PA: National Sexual Violence Resource Center.

In addition to providing information from more than 400 sexual abuse prevention programs throughout the country, this handbook offers effective strategies for reducing child sexual abuse. Various types of programs are reviewed to help readers establish or improve current child sexual abuse prevention efforts. Entries on individual programs provide target audiences, a brief summary of the program, and contact information.

Saunders, B. E., L. Berliner, and R. F. Hanson, eds. 2004. *Child Physical and Sexual Abuse: Guidelines for Treatment (Revised Report: April 26, 2004).* Charleston, SC: National Crime Victims Research and Treatment Center.

To provide the best services to child victims of physical and sexual abuse, therapists need to have the best, most reliable information regarding treatment of these children. The purpose of this publication is "to encourage the use of mental health treatment protocols and procedures that have a sound theoretical basis, a good clinical-anecdotal literature, high acceptance among practitioners in the child abuse field, a low chance for causing harm, and empirical support for their utility with victims of abuse" (p. 5). By providing direction to the mental health community in the treatment of child physical and sexual abuse, these guidelines encourage therapists to make informed treatment decisions.

Videos

Close to Home

Type:	Videotape
Length:	79 minutes
Date:	2001
Cost:	$95.00
Source:	http://www.directcinema.com

The purpose of this video is to raise awareness of child sexual abuse. Five personal accounts of being sexually abused as a child are presented by adults survivors of child sexual abuse, as are children who have more recently been sexually abused. Convicted offenders are also heard from; in group therapy sessions they describe the strategies they used in picking and grooming children.

Confronting Child Sexual Abuse: A Video Training Series

Type:	Videotape
Length:	unknown
Date:	1993
Cost:	$295.00
Source:	Child Welfare League of America
	440 First Street, NW, Third Floor
	Washington, DC 20001-2085
Telephone:	202-638-2952
	www.cwla.org

With an introduction by Oprah Winfrey, this two-part training series examines the daily realities of casework experiences with child sexual abuse. Dramatizations as well as real-life coverage of social workers investigating allegations of child sexual abuse, conducting home visits, and other activities demonstrate the joys and frustrations of working with this population.

Healing Years

Type:	Videotape
Length:	52 minutes
Date:	2001
Cost:	$90.00
Source:	The Safer Society Foundation, Inc.
	P.O. Box 340
	Brandon, VT 05733
	802-247-3132
	www.safersociety.org

Girls who are sexually abused by their fathers or other close relatives have a particularly difficult time dealing with all the emotions they experience throughout the ordeal, and even after the abuse has stopped. This documentary profiles three women who experienced incest as children: Marilyn Van Derbur, a former Miss America; Janice Mirikitani, president of the Glide Memorial Church in San Francisco; and seventy-eight-year-old Barbara Hamilton. The effects of the incest reach beyond the victims to their families and society as a whole.

Hiding in Plain Sight: Tales of an American Predator

Type:	DVD
Length:	93 minutes
Cost:	$17.95
Source:	Custom Flix
	140 Du Bois Street, Suite A
	Santa Cruz, CA 95060
	800-853-6077
	www.customflix.com

This documentary presents the story of Peter Martin Ebel, also known as Allan Scott, an imposter and child sexual abuser who terrorized his victims over a thirty-year period. At various times he pretended to be a priest, teacher, doctor, author, or pilot. His targets were young boys, usually around twelve years of age. He was finally caught and convicted for production of child pornography in 2001. Key players are interviewed, including parents, children, psychiatrists, the district attorney involved in the case, and the arresting officer. Viewers come away with a better understanding of how offenders convince children to play along with them.

I Am the Boss of My Body: Preventing Child Sexual Abuse

Type: Videotape
Length: 18 minutes
Date: 1999
Cost: $69.00
Source: The Health Connection
         55 W. Oak Ridge Drive
         Hagerstown, Maryland 21740
         800-548-8700
         www.healthconnection.org

In this entertaining video for children from five through eight years, information is presented that will help to protect them from being sexually abused by helping them to become aware of their own feelings, likes, and dislikes. Encouraging them to become "the boss" of their bodies, the video presents a variety of situations in which the children can learn to become "the boss" and avoid being sexually abused.

She's Just Growing Up, Dear

Type: Videotape
Length: 16 minutes
Date: 1996
Cost: $99 to purchase; $50 to rent
Source: New Day Films
         190 Route 17M
         P.O. Box 1084
         Harriman, NY 10926
         888-367-9154
         www.newday.com

In this video, an adult woman begins to confront her sexual abuse as a child and understand how it has affected her as an adult. Viewers have an opportunity to understand how to place child sexual abuse within a cultural context, showing how family members respond to accusations of sexual abuse.

Stories No One Wants to Hear

Type: Videotape
Length: 27 minutes
Date: 1993
Cost: $149

Source: Fanlight Productions
             800-937-4113
             www.fanlight.com

Retrieving memories of childhood sexual abuse that have been buried or repressed for many years is often difficult and traumatizing to the individuals involved. This video documents the process of retrieving such memories, telling the stories of four women who discover that they had been sexually abused as children—in three cases by their mothers, and in the fourth by a brother. This video is interesting not only because it discusses the controversial subject of retrieval of repressed memories but also because it talks about mother-daughter incest, a type of incest not often talked about.

View from the Shadows: Volume 1
    Type: Videotape
    Length: 18 minutes
    Date: 2000
    Cost: $189.00
    Source: Intermedia
               1165 Eastlake Avenue E., Suite 400
               Seattle, WA 98109
               800-553-8336
               www.intermedia-inc.com

This video presents interviews with sex offenders, parents, adults who were sexually abused as children, and experts in the field in order to prevent child sexual abuse. Offenders describe their motivations for abusing children and their rationalizations for their behavior. Parents are encouraged to talk with their children about sex and sexual abuse.

View from the Shadows: Volume 2
    Type: Videotape
    Length: 22 minutes
    Date: 2001
    Cost: $189.00
    Source: Intermedia
               1165 Eastlake Avenue E., Suite 400
               Seattle, WA 98109
               800-553-8336
               www.intermedia-inc.com

Children and families share their experiences in dealing with child sexual abuse. Topics include the signs of abuse, patterns of abuse, the process of disclosure, and factors influencing the decision to file charges against the perpetrator.

Why God, Why Me?

Type:	DVD
Length:	35 minutes
Date:	2002
Cost:	$29.95
Source:	Custom Flix
	140 Du Bois Street, Suite A
	Santa Cruz, CA 95060
	800-853-6077
	www.customflix.com

The effects of being sexually abused as a child are often devastating. This video focuses on adults who were sexually abused as children. Emotional and poignant, these personal stories help viewers to understand many of the feelings that sexual abuse victims have about themselves and their abuse, including the reasons why they may view traditional family life as threatening.

Internet Resources

In addition to many of the programs listed in Chapter 7 that have websites full of information, there are several websites that provide additional information relevant to the field of child sexual abuse.

http://www.kids.getnetwise.org

Organized and operated by a coalition of Internet industry corporations and public interest organizations, this website offers information to help parents and children make wise decisions concerning their children's use of the Internet. The site provides an online safety guide, tools for families to protect children, links to safe educational and entertaining websites for kids, and guidelines for identifying online trouble and reporting it to law enforcement agencies.

http://www.mapsexoffenders.com

This site provides information on sex offenders in forty-five states, with the goal of mapping all fifty states as soon as possible, in order to provide local communities with an easy-to-find resource for tracking the presence of sexual offenders in their neighborhoods. A link to click on for a map of sexual offenders in one's neighborhood is provided.

http://www.netsmartz.org

The Netsmartz Workshop and website is run by the National Center for Missing and Exploited Children and the Boys and Girls Clubs of America as a resource for children, parents, and other guardians, educators, and law enforcement agencies. It teaches children how they can remain safe when using the Internet. Their goals include enabling children to recognize dangers while using the Internet; helping children to understand that people they meet on the Internet should not be considered their friends; encouraging children to report dangerous incidents or victimization to a trusted adult; encouraging and enhancing community educational efforts; and increasing the ability of children and adults to communicate with each other concerning Internet safety issues.

Glossary

anorexia nervosa   a serious medical disorder characterized by a pathological fear of gaining weight. It generally occurs among young women while in their teens and early twenties. Symptoms may include troublesome eating patterns, malnutrition, and generally excessive weight loss.

bulimia   generally considered a serious medical/psychological disorder characterized by periods of binge eating followed by purging, which can include vomiting, use of enemas, and excessive use of laxatives and diuretics. May also include periods of compulsive exercise in an attempt to lose weight.

concubinage   the state of being a concubine—a woman who cohabits with a man but is considered to be of lower social status. In certain early societies, a young girl or woman could be contracted to a man as secondary to his wife, a position in which she would have few legal rights and in which she would be expected to provide sexual services to the man.

cunnilingus   oral stimulation of the clitoris or vulva.

defendant   a person or entity (such as an organization or school) charged with a civil or criminal action.

dissociative identity disorder   once known as multiple personality disorder, this condition is characterized by a person having more than one discrete identity. Generally considered to be a result of severe childhood trauma, including the experience of sexual abuse as a child.

exhibitionism   behavior that includes a psychological need to exhibit parts of one's body that are usually covered by clothes—specifically, genitalia or buttocks. Both males and females can be exhibitionists, but general patterns indicate that men are more likely to be exhibitionists than women, at least in instances of exhibiting genitalia to children.

expert witness   a witness, such as a medical expert, who has specific education, knowledge, training, or experience and is called on to provide testimony in a trial concerning relevant facts that are beyond the common knowledge of normal people. For example, persons with specific medical training and knowledge may be called on as expert witnesses to examine the child and provide testimony confirming a diagnosis of sexual abuse.

fellatio   oral stimulation of the penis.

guardian ad litem   a guardian for a child appointed by the court for the purpose of representing the child's best interests in a particular lawsuit.

incest   sexual intercourse between two or more persons who are closely related; marriage between these individuals is generally forbidden by law. Primary examples include sex between fathers and daughters, mothers and sons, or brothers and sisters.

incidence   studies that focus on determining the number of new cases of child sexual abuse arising during a given time period, usually one year.

plaintiff   the person or entity who institutes a legal claim or action.

plea bargain   a negotiated agreement between the prosecution and defense in which the defendant pleads guilty to a lesser offense or offenses in exchange for a more lenient sentence or dismissal of additional charges.

prevalence   studies concerning the prevalence of child sexual abuse focus on estimating the proportion of the population who will be sexually abused as children, generally expressed as a percentage of the population.

pseudomemory   in cases of child sexual abuse, false memories that are generally believed to be created during hypnosis or other types of therapeutic treatments. The existence and validity of pseudomemories or recovered memories are questioned by many researchers.

psychosomatic   a condition that generally has physical symptoms, but the symptoms are created from mental or emotional causes. The term also refers to the influence of the mind on the body, and is generally used when referring to medical conditions, diseases, or disorders.

recantation   an act of recanting, or withdrawing, an earlier statement or testimony. In cases of child sexual abuse, testimony provided by a child to prosecutors or other investigators may be withdrawn by the child when put in a stressful courtroom situation, possibly because of fear of facing the abuser in the courtroom.

recidivism   the tendency to relapse into a previous pattern of behavior. In the field of child sexual abuse, the term is usually applied to sexual offenders who may be unable to stop their offending behavior once out of prison.

sodomy   a sexual act between two people consisting of oral or anal contact or penetration. Generally, it is more commonly defined as oral or anal sex between two men.

syndrome   a grouping of signs or symptoms that are found together and that form an identifiable pattern.

voyeurism   a sexual disorder that is generally characterized by the act of watching unsuspecting individuals who are in the process of undressing or who are naked. The voyeur generally seeks sexual stimulation from the experience.

vulvovaginitis   inflammation of the vulva and vagina.

Index

329

About the Author

Karen L. Kinnear holds an M.A. in sociology and is a paralegal, as well as a professional researcher, editor, and writer with more than twenty years of experience in sociological, economic, statistical, and financial analysis. Among her previous publications are *Violent Children: A Reference Handbook; Gangs: A Reference Handbook; Women in the Third World: A Reference Handbook;* and *Single Parents: A Reference Handbook,* all part of ABC-CLIO's Contemporary World Issues series.